A GLIMPSE INTO THE INFERNO . . .

All senses for the time are dead but the one of sight. The roar of the discharges, over the yells of the enemy, all pass unheeded; but the impassionate soul is all eyes and sees all things that the smoke does not hide. How madly the battery men are driving home the double charges of canister in those broad-mouthed Napoleons! How rapidly these long blue-coated lines of infantry deliver their file fire down the slope.

Men are dropping dead or wounded on all sides by scores and by hundreds; and poor mutilated creatures—some with an arm dangling, some with a leg broke by a bullet—are limping and crawling toward the rear. They make no sound of complaint or pain, but are as silent as if dumb and mute. A sublime heroism seems to pervade all and the intuition that to lose that crest and all is lost . . .

—Lt. Frank A. Haskell

Robert E. Lee (from a photograph taken after the War)

GETTYSBURG

★ ★ ★

Colonel William C. Oates
and
Lieutenant Frank A. Haskell

★ ★ ★

Edited and with an Introduction
by Glenn LaFantasie
General Series Editor, Paul Andrew Hutton

BANTAM BOOKS
New York • Toronto • London • Sydney • Auckland

GETTYSBURG
A Bantam Domain Book

Publishing History
William C. Oates's "The Battle of Gettysburg" was originally published in The War Between the Union and the Confederacy and Its Lost Opportunities with a History of the 15th Alabama Regiment and the Forty-Eight Battles in which It was Engaged *by The Neale Company, 1905*
Frank A. Haskell's "The Battle of Gettysburg" is reprinted with the permission of the Pennsylvania State Archives, Pennsylvania Historical and Museum Commission, Harrisburg, Pennsylvania
Bantam edition / September 1992

General Series Editor, Paul Andrew Hutton

DOMAIN and the portrayal of a boxed "d" are trademarks of Bantam Books, a division of Bantam Doubleday Dell Publishing Group, Inc.

All rights reserved.
Introduction copyright © 1992 by Glenn LaFantasie.
Cover art copyright © 1992 by Lou Glanzman.
Designed by M 'N O Production Services, Inc.
No part of this book may be reproduced or transmitted in any form or by any means, electronic or mechanical, including photocopying, recording, or by any information storage and retrieval system, without permission in writing from the publisher. For information address: Bantam Books.

If you purchased this book without a cover you should be aware that this book is stolen property. It was reported as "unsold and destroyed" to the publisher and neither the author nor the publisher has received any payment for this "stripped book."

ISBN 0-553-29832-1

Published simultaneously in the United States and Canada

Bantam Books are published by Bantam Books, a division of Bantam Doubleday Dell Publishing Group, Inc. Its trademark, consisting of the words "Bantam Books" and the portrayal of a rooster, is Registered in U.S. Patent and Trademark Office and in other countries. Marca Registrada. Bantam Books, 666 Fifth Avenue, New York, New York 10103.

PRINTED IN THE UNITED STATES OF AMERICA

OPM 0 9 8 7

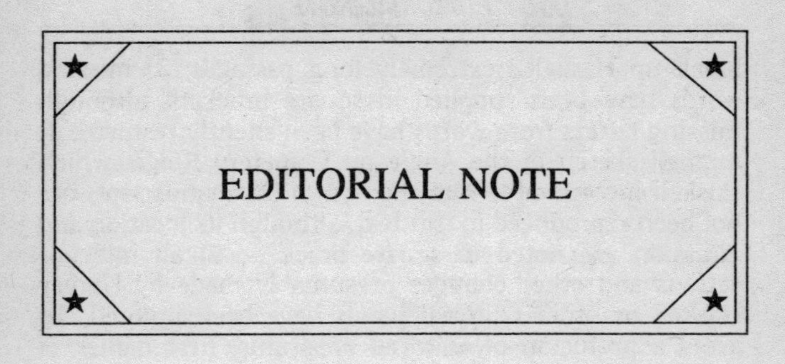

EDITORIAL NOTE

The text of William C. Oates's "The Battle of Gettysburg" has been reprinted from the three chapters dealing with Gettysburg found in his *The War Between the Union and the Confederacy and Its Lost Opportunities with a History of the 15th Alabama Regiment and the Forty-Eight Battles in which It was Engaged* (New York and Washington, D.C.: The Neale Company, 1905), pp. 189–249. Original spelling, punctuation, and paragraphing have been faithfully followed.

The text of Frank A. Haskell's "The Battle of Gettysburg" has been transcribed from the manuscript located in the collections of the Pennsylvania State Archives, Pennsylvania Historical and Museum Commission, Harrisburg, Pennsylvania; the text is reprinted with the permission of the commission. A few rules have been used to prepare the text for modern readers: 1) all spelling, punctuation, and capitalization have been regularized according to modern conventions; 2) paragraphing has been altered to break up Haskell's extremely long passages; 3) missing words have been supplied in square brackets, although missing letters from words have been silently restored; 4) a small sketch of the Angle on Cemetery Ridge, which Haskell incorporated into the text of his manuscript, has not been reproduced in this text, although its location and omission are noted in square brackets; 5) all interlineations and other changes presumably made by Harvey Haskell or other editorial hands have been ignored. To avoid a profusion of editorial apparatus, first names of individuals have not been supplied in square brackets in the text. For the full names of most officers mentioned by Oates and Haskell, see the Order of Battle for the Army of the Potomac and the Army of Northern Virginia, which follows the two accounts.

CONTENTS

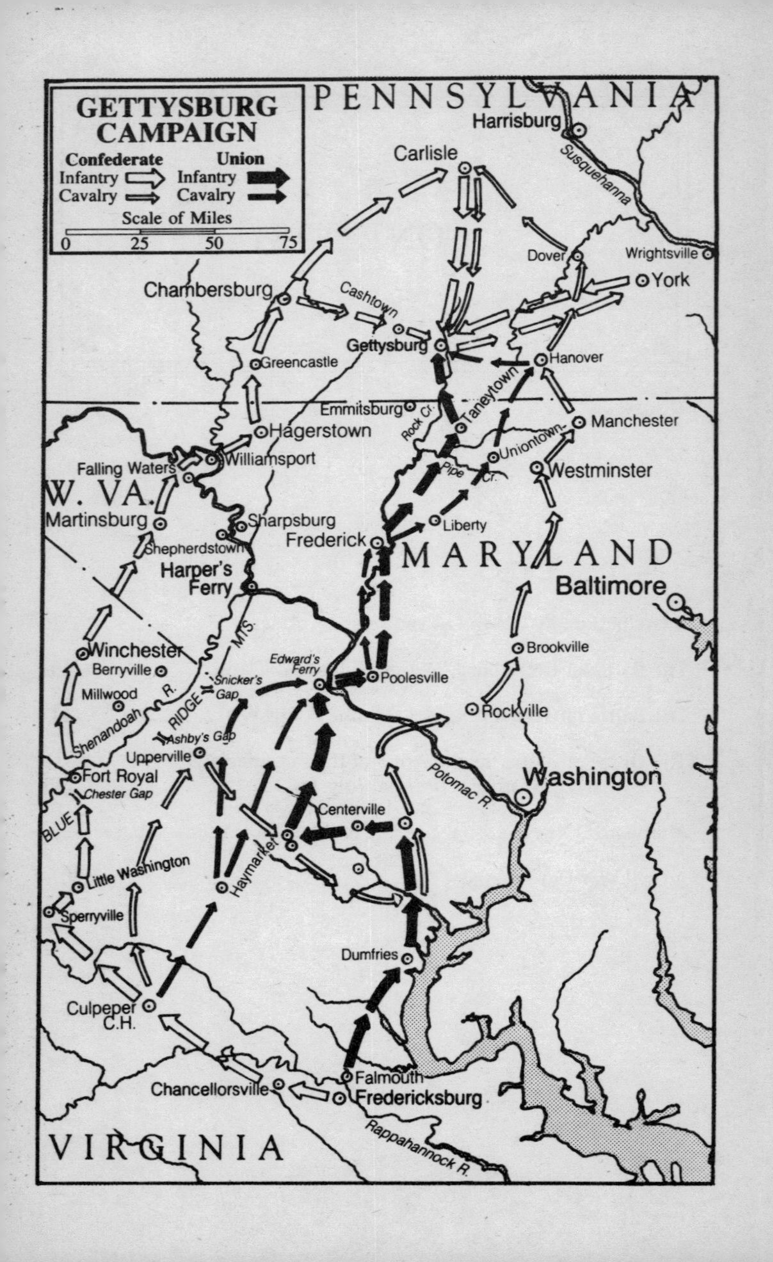
GETTYSBURG CAMPAIGN
Confederate
Union
Infantry
Cavalry
Infantry
Cavalry
Scale of Miles
0
25
50
75
PENNSYLVANIA
Harrisburg
Susquehanna
Carlisle
Dover
Wrightsville
York
Chambersburg
Cashtown
Gettysburg
Hanover
Greencastle
Emmitsburg
Taneytown
Rock Cr.
Manchester
Hagerstown
Uniontown
Williamsport
Falling Waters
Pipe Cr.
Westminster
W. VA.
Martinsburg
Sharpsburg
Liberty
Frederick
Shepherdstown
MARYLAND
Harper's Ferry
Baltimore
MTS.
Winchester
Brookville
Berryville
Edward's Ferry
Snicker's Gap
Poolesville
Millwood
RIDGE
R.
Shenandoah
Rockville
Ashby's Gap
Upperville
Fort Royal
Chester Gap
Potomac R.
Washington
BLUE
Centerville
Haymarket
Little Washington
Sperryville
Dumfries
Culpeper C.H.
Falmouth
Chancellorsville
Fredericksburg
Rappahannock R.
VIRGINIA

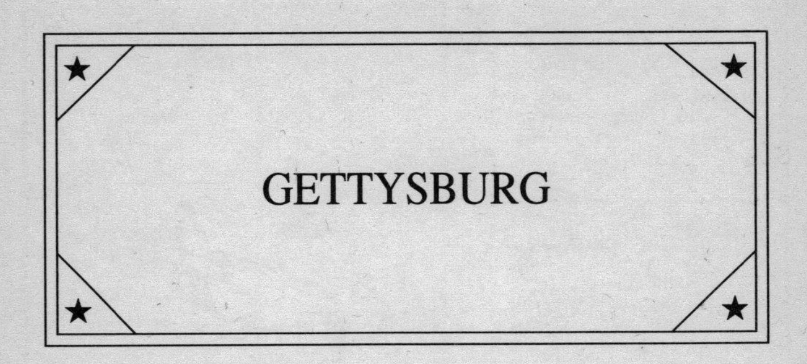

GETTYSBURG

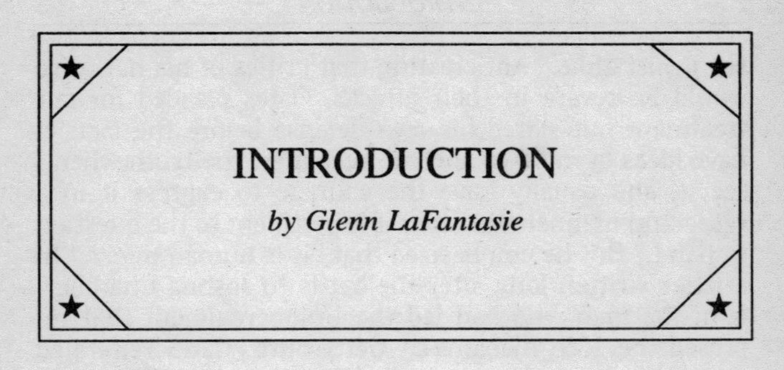

INTRODUCTION

by Glenn LaFantasie

NO ONE will ever write a complete history of the battle of Gettysburg. So predicted Frank A. Haskell, a resourceful and stouthearted Wisconsin lieutenant who participated in the battle as an aide to Union General John Gibbon and who wrote his own account of what he had seen. According to Haskell, the story of Gettysburg could not be adequately captured in words. "Who could sketch the changes, the constant shifting, of the bloody panorama?" he asked. Even those who had experienced the battle firsthand could not do it justice. Soldiers in the combat, Haskell said, would be limited by their own "literary infirmity" and by "their not seeing themselves . . . as others would have seen them."

Haskell's opinion was echoed by another veteran of the battle, Colonel William C. Oates, the tough and dauntless commander of the 15th Alabama Infantry at Gettysburg. "No two men," Oates wrote in the preface to his memoirs, which he composed late in life as a history of the War Between the States, "can participate in a great battle and see it just alike." Anticipating that critics of his narrative would be severe in their attacks, Oates pleaded for fair treatment but stated his own defense before the fact: "I have ideas of my own and can recognize the truth when I see it, and usually have the courage to express it in a respectful manner whenever it is pertinent to the question in hand." But he emphasized that "it is human to err." In a letter written long after the battle to Joshua Chamberlain, the man who had led the Union regiment that repulsed the 15th Alabama at Gettysburg, Oates reiterated that "No one man can see all that occurs in a fight, even between regiments."

Like so many other Americans of the Civil War generation, these two seasoned officers believed that no one could ever accurately describe the war or its battles in words. Walt Whitman, who saw the gruesome effects of the Civil War while working as a hospital attendant in Washington, agreed: "Future years will never know the seething hell and the black infernal background of countless minor scenes and interiors (not the official surface courteousness of the generals, not the few great battles) of the Secession War; and it is best they should not. The real war will never get in the books." Later generations, who were fairly inundated by the ocean of Civil War writings—memoirs, reminiscences, letters, histories, and novels—that continued to be published after most of the veterans had passed quietly away, reached the same gloomy conclusion. Trying to grasp the significance of the war and the experiences of the soldiers who fought it, Sherwood Anderson, the famous novelist, could not overcome his own frustration with the elusiveness of its reality and substance. "No real sense of it," he declared, "has yet crept into the pages of a printed book."

If we accept these statements at face value, including the ones made by Oates and Haskell, we must suppose that no account of Gettysburg, even those written by men who stood in the thick of the fighting, can adequately tell us what this battle was like or how the soldiers, Union and Confederate, who clashed in the July heat of 1863 must have felt as they stumbled up the steep and rocky slopes of Little Round Top or ran for cover as shells burst around them during the most furious cannonade ever to take place in North America. We must assume, from what Oates and Haskell assert so forcefully and from what many critics and writers have since pronounced as authoritatively, that the battle of Gettysburg will always remain unknown and unknowable.

But the narratives of Colonel Oates and Lieutenant Haskell, like hundreds of other firsthand accounts written by Gettysburg veterans after the battle was over, actually belie this supposition. It is from their accounts, from the rich and plentiful array of evocative eyewitness reports, that we may indeed gain a realistic sense of what this supreme battle of the Civil War, a battle that marked the turning point of the conflict between the North and the South, must have looked like and sounded like in all its fury, horror, and glory. It is from these accounts that we can, by using our historical imagination, transport ourselves back in time more than one hundred twenty-five years to stand shoulder-to-shoulder in the long gray lines of General Robert E. Lee atop the wooded crest of Seminary Ridge or to kneel with blue-clad comrades firmly clutching their muskets behind the low stone wall on Cemetery Ridge.

The power of words did not fail Oates and Haskell as much as they had assumed or feared. Ever since their narratives of Gettysburg were first published, they have been ranked by students of the battle as classic accounts. No historian would dare write about Longstreet's assault on the afternoon of July 2 without first consulting Oates's lively testimony; likewise, scholars and other writers have relied heavily on Haskell's extensive and dramatic account of the Federal repulse of Pickett's Charge on July 3. Of the two, Haskell's discourse is the more famous, and deservedly so; his felicitous (though sometimes florid) use of language, particularly his flair for metaphor, reveals his special talents as an alert observer and a skillful writer. Haskell's account of Gettysburg is regarded not only as a useful and informative historical source but also as a minor masterpiece in the literature of the Civil War. In comparison, Oates's workmanlike prose, especially when he writes about events he did not personally witness, often falls flat in its sparseness and straightforward simplicity. Differences aside, however, the fact remains that these two tellings of the Gettysburg story are remarkable first-person accounts that have long been valued and praised for their perspicuity and verisimilitude.

If we seek today to know something more about Gettysburg than the strategy and tactics employed by the generals, something beyond the impersonal engagement of armies that move on chessboard fields, something more closely connected to the men who faced the volleys of minié balls and grapeshot, we must first attempt to overcome the distance that separates our modern sensibilities from the lives of the soldiers who marched and fought and died at Gettysburg. The chronicles of Oates and Haskell help us to bridge the gap between the present and the past. Reading their accounts, we see events unfold before us through their eyes. We are taken back to the fields and hills of Gettysburg to see the action as it occurs, with Oates and Haskell as our trusted guides.

Obviously what we experience in reading these accounts cannot compare with the human ordeal that men like Oates and Haskell actually endured in the front lines at Gettysburg. We cannot pretend to ourselves that reading about a battle is anything at all like living through it. Nor do we, in reading these accounts, necessarily see the battle in all its terrible wholeness or complexity, for the eyewitness reports of Oates and Haskell are circumscribed, just as they suspected they would be, by the limits of their own position on the battlefield—a phenomenon called "the fog of war" that happens to every soldier in every battle. No one engaged in combat ever knows what is precisely going on beyond the smoke of battle that engulfs him. His range of understanding is necessarily narrowed to events that occur around him, within his immediate line of vision, or to his own personal experiences on the battlefield. Haskell, knowing full well how severely his own perspective was restricted and even obstructed, explained that his narrative was "not designed to be a history, but simply *my account.*"

But if our national fascination with Gettysburg—indeed, with the Civil War in general—is in fact motivated by a desire to know what it was all about and what the soldiers thought and felt and did as they were swept up into this colossal conflict of arms, these accounts are surely a good place to begin. Reading these personal annals, written by two accomplished officers who survived some of the worst and bloodiest fighting at Gettysburg, we come as close as we can get to touching their world and understanding what this battle meant to them.

Even before the Civil War, the world of William Calvin Oates was filled with hardship, turmoil, and violence. He was born on December 1, 1835, in Pike County, Alabama, the son of William and Sarah Oates. The family lived in extreme poverty. Education was considered a luxury, and young William had little opportunity to attend the local common school, though occasionally he did show up there for two or three months at a time. Raised on the untamed frontier, Oates learned most of his early lessons about life outside the classroom. Among the most important things he learned was that survival often meant standing up for himself and fighting his way out of tight corners. In fact, William Oates excelled at fighting.

His younger years were lived with gusto in an unbroken chain of brawling, hair-raising adventures. Oates frequently got into trouble because he could not control his temper; and whenever his temper flared, his fists began to fly. His biggest problem, however, was staying out of the clutches of the law. In March 1850, after a "great old bully" beat him up, Oates wanted to shoot him but could not find a gun. "I had it in me for years afterwards to kill him," he admitted in an autobiographical sketch written late in life, "but I never got a chance." In another fight that happened a few months later, this time with the father of a self-proclaimed spirit medium, whom Oates had exposed as a fraud, he fractured the man's skull and quickly fled for Florida, totally convinced he had murdered his opponent. Although the man recovered, a warrant issued for Oates's arrest kept him on the run—and out of Alabama—for several years.

During that time away from Alabama he found work in Florida as a housepainter's apprentice, joined the crew of a Gulf schooner, came down with yellow fever in Pensacola and was declared dead, and wandered along the coast admiring the beauty of mulatto women and laboring at odd jobs. He did not stay anywhere for very long, and mostly he managed to find trouble wherever he went. In Louisiana, where he successfully plied his trade as a painter, he accosted an employer who owed him money by choking him with his left hand and hitting him, as Oates bluntly told it, "in the face eight or nine times with my right fist." The next day, after a Louisiana warrant was issued for his arrest, Oates prudently and quietly moved on to Texas.

Texas was the perfect place for someone of his peculiar

talents. In the town of Marshall, which he described as a wild community "infested with gamblers," Oates worked as a painter, attended night school, and "became much addicted to gaming at cards." It did not take long for his temper to explode and his fists to do their damage. A drunkard's insulting remarks led to a street fight; Oates won the bout by nearly gouging the man's eyes out. The next morning the local authorities wrote out a warrant for his arrest, so Oates moved to Waco, Texas.

Life in Waco, one of the rowdiest towns in Texas, was not any better than it had been in Marshall. He found a job cutting shingles and succeeded for a while in minding his own business, but one day, by sheer happenstance (the kind of happenstance that seemed to be Oates's lot in life), he was in the wrong place at the wrong time and witnessed the cold-blooded murder of a Texas Ranger. As Oates pondered his plight he realized he had two choices. He could stay in town, where he would surely be questioned by the Rangers investigating the murder or discovered by the killer who was hiding out with the town's gamblers—all of whom, of course, knew Oates well—or he could get out of town. He decided to quit Waco, but he did not move fast enough. As he was making plans to leave he accidentally offended one of Waco's most notorious gunmen, a fellow known to be "very dangerous" and "half crazy all the time with whiskey and morphine." The gunman insulted Oates and challenged him to a showdown in the street, and Oates was about to buckle on his gunbelt when—for once in his impulsive life—he thought the whole situation over before reacting and concluded that the odds were overwhelmingly stacked in the gunman's favor. Oates satisfied himself by saying he would "pocket" the gunman's insult, and then slipped quietly and unobtrusively out of Waco.

Moving south and west, he settled for a while and worked on a plantation in Bastrop, where he won a good deal of money from his fellow workers in a card game. Before anyone had time to doubt Oates's honesty as a gambler, he packed his personal belongings together and moved to Port Lavaca. He worked again as a housepainter there and fell in love with his employer's daughter. He asked the young woman to marry him, and she accepted, but Oates changed his mind when he caught her one bright moonlit night embracing—much too fondly—a married man. He decided to move on. At his next destination, Henderson, Texas, he miraculously ran into his younger brother, John, who had been dispatched by the family in Alabama to search for Oates and, once he had been found, to bring him home. It appears that John Oates's timing was just about perfect, for William had had about all of Texas he could stand. The brothers agreed to return to Alabama together, but before they could get very far they somehow got involved in a high-stakes card game. When a fight broke out, as anyone who knew Oates could have predicted it would, he used his proven technique of trying to gouge out the eyes of his opponent, in this case a man named McGuire. "Both of his eyes," Oates later explained rather casually, "suffered badly."

Certainly William Oates was not a man to be trifled with. He was brave and reckless, to be sure, but he was also quite dangerous. His youthful appearance—he had a round, full face that made him look cherubic—was deceiving, yet there was no mistaking the stony glare of his dark eyes. Having tested his own strength and endurance so often on the frontier, Oates was self-confident, audacious, and unburdened by any pangs of conscience.

He was also handsome and a notorious womanizer. His adventures throughout the Southwest in his early years were punctuated by several lustful and romantic escapades. In Louisiana, he had become involved with "a pretty, rosy-cheeked, black-eyed country girl who had not been reared to closely observe the rules observed in the more cultured circles of society." In the back of her family's covered wagon, Oates had carried on "a little love affair" with her.

After returning to Alabama with his brother, Oates could not remain in Pike County, where he was still wanted by the law for assaulting the spirit medium's father. He moved to nearby Henry County and became a schoolteacher, despite his own lack of educational attainments. What he lacked in education, he made up for in ambition. He was determined to make something of himself, and he decided to obtain the kind of schooling that would help him achieve his goals. He attended and was graduated from the Lawrenceville Academy, where he worked hard on his studies. Next he read law with an established firm in Eufaula, and he passed the bar in October 1858. On his twenty-fifth birthday, he opened his own law office in Abbeville. Not content with just practicing law, he put together enough capital to purchase a weekly newspaper and make it a going concern. The newspaper became his own political mouthpiece, which meant that he and the paper regularly endorsed Democratic party politics, and it also gave him his first opportunity to write for publication. Both his law practice and the newspaper did very well, and Oates, though still a young man, was earning a decent living in Abbeville. In fact, he was pursuing success and respectability as vigorously as he had run from the clutches of the law in his youth.

The outbreak of the Civil War diverted his path, but it did not diminish his ambition. Although he was opposed to secession, and had stated his position publicly in the pages of his newspaper, he could not resist the fervor of Southern patriotism that accompanied the call to arms in the spring of 1861. He helped to raise a company of ornately dressed volunteers known as the "Henry Pioneers," which would later be mustered into the Confederate Army as Company G of the 15th Alabama Infantry. Oates was proclaimed captain by the members of the Pioneers, and though he knew nothing of military arts and conduct, he did his best to teach the men how to be good soldiers. By his own admission, he was "a strict disciplinarian when on duty, but otherwise allowed his men the largest liberty consistent with proper discipline and the good of the service." In August 1861 the 15th Alabama, under the command of Colonel James Canty, left Alabama to join the Confederate forces that had recently defeated General Irvin McDowell's Union Army at the first battle of Manassas.

About five miles north of Manassas Junction, the 15th Alabama made camp. "Drilling and performing the routine of camp duty was the regular order," Oates remembered, for there was very little for the regiment—or the Confederate Army—to do. During this time of inactivity the men were struck by what Oates called "the worst enemy of our army—the measles." Because the sick were kept in camp, the epidemic spread quickly and took lives by the hundreds. "Had the Confederate authorities made more persistent efforts than they did," Oates grumbled, "hospitals could have been established in sufficient numbers to have saved the lives of hundreds and thousands of good men, which were for the want of them unnecessarily sacrificed."

Wanting desperately to see action, Oates and his men instead were sent on marches and countermarches around the countryside. As winter approached, the regiment made camp about a mile from Manassas Junction and constructed huts to protect the men from the bitter cold. It was a long and disagreeable winter, Oates recalled, but the men had no cause for complaint: "They had plenty of rations, plenty of clothing, and even luxuries, which their relatives and friends at home sent them." Every two weeks the regiment was required to take its turn on picket duty for two days. "This was about all the service required during the winter," Oates wrote. When the spring of 1862 arrived, wet and miserable in northern Virginia, General Joseph Johnston evacuated the Manassas defense line and moved his army south to protect Richmond. The 15th Alabama marched to the Rappahannock River, where it barely survived several weeks of bad weather, short rations, and deadly disease.

The weather finally improved, and the regiment was assigned to join General T. J. "Stonewall" Jackson's army in the Shenandoah Valley. Oates was impressed by the fertile valley and the picturesque Blue Ridge Mountains, which he poetically compared to the Swiss Alps, but he was most favorably impressed by the pink-cheeked women and girls of the Shenandoah who stood by the roadsides cheering on Jackson's wily "Foot Cavalry" as it marched through the valley towns. The women, Oates admiringly wrote in his memoirs, "were the most perfect beauties my eyes ever beheld."

Although the 15th Alabama was present for several battles in Jackson's Valley Campaign that spring, including Front Royal, Winchester, and Cross Keys, it mostly stayed on the sidelines and was not engaged. It experienced some hot fighting at Gaines's Mill on June 27 during the Seven Days battles near Richmond, but most of the regiment's time was taken up waiting for orders that never came. At Cedar Mountain, where Jackson attacked General John Pope's Federal forces on August 9, 1862, the 15th again watched while their comrades did the fighting. As artillery shells screeched overhead, Oates came across a distraught young lady who had fainted on the battlefield when the thunder of the guns had taken her by surprise. She was, Oates said, "as perfect a beauty as was ever reared on the soil of the Old Dominion." He comforted her, led her to safety, and never saw her again, though he did later find out that her name was Crittenden.

Two weeks later, Jackson's army smashed into Pope's army on the old battlefield at Manassas, and the 15th Alabama was finally in the front ranks of the Confederate assault. On the evening of August 29 the regiment advanced against the enemy amid considerable confusion over whether the troops in front were actually friend or foe. Oates was sure, despite the darkness that enveloped the battlefield, that the musket fire from up ahead had to be coming from the enemy. "If they were friends," he reasoned, "they were firing in the wrong direction." As it turned out, they were not friends, and the regiment soon passed through a gully filled with Union dead and wounded. It was a bloody night. The 15th Alabama also suffered heavy losses as the battle lines swerved back and forth across the flashing landscape. "Everything around was lighted up by the blaze of musketry and explosion of balls like a continuous bright flash of lightning," Oates reported. "The carnage in our ranks," he said, "was appalling." He was particularly proud of his company for standing up to the enemy's "tornado of bullets." But Oates understood that courage was a relative attribute, for as he later confessed: "We were not all of us as brave as Caesar, nor were men with few exceptions, at all times alike brave. Much depends upon the state of the nervous system at the time." When a shell exploded near him the following morning, wounding two men beside him, he did not mind admitting that he was "very much frightened."

On September 1, as Lee attempted one last time to outmaneuver Pope's battered army, the 15th Alabama was with the Confederate force that hit the Federal flank at Chantilly during a cold, driving rainstorm. Under the weight of a fierce Union attack the 15th Alabama broke ranks and retreated on the run. Oates was wounded in the leg, but he was more concerned about "the disgraceful conduct of our men" than he was about his injury. The events at Chantilly, he said, put him in "a very unchristian state of mind." Eventually, the regiment re-formed with other Confederate units to its left, and it joined three brigades sent forward by General A. P. Hill that pushed the enemy back and regained the lost ground.

When Lee's army moved north in a few days to begin the invasion of Maryland, Oates and the 15th Alabama marched with it, but he took sick along the way to Sharpsburg and did not witness the bloody battle at Antietam on September 17. Laid up in a house near Shepherdstown, Oates could plainly hear the sounds of musketry across the river—certainly a safe place to be under the circumstances, he said, "but a more uneasy and annoying position than in the thickest of the fight." Propping himself up near a window, he watched the endless stream of dazed and wounded soldiers as they limped their way to the rear. Although Oates did not know it at the time, the 15th Alabama itself had suffered devastating—almost annihilating—casualties that day, including several of its officers. Four days after the battle, when he rejoined the regiment, he discovered he was the senior ranking officer, and he was immediately given temporary command. Confusion over Oates's rank for the remainder of the war dates from this moment.

Soon after Sharpsburg Oates gave up command of the regiment when Major Alexander A. Lowther returned to duty. Later that autumn Lowther left the regiment again, and it would appear that Oates and Captain Isaac B. Feagin alternated as acting commanders of the regiment. In May 1863 Oates was permanently promoted to colonel over Feagin, who technically was senior in rank; Oates's commission was retroactively dated to April 28. Although the commission was dutifully delivered to General Lee, the Confederate Congress—for reasons that are not apparent—neglected to confirm the promotion. From the spring of 1863 to the summer of 1864, Oates commanded the regiment using the title and rank of colonel.

But the mayhem over rank and command of the regiment had only barely begun. Major Lowther suddenly appeared on the scene again, this time after having used his political influence with Jefferson Davis to win back the command of the 15th Alabama. With signed orders and a commission promoting him to colonel in hand, Lowther resumed command in July 1864. His own orders contained a promotion for Oates as well—but only to the rank of major as of April 28, 1863, which would mean, of course, that Oates had never really been a colonel at all. It was an unhappy day when Oates turned over his command to Lowther, whom he despised with a vengeance. Knowing that he had been robbed of both rank and command by the insidious workings of politics, Oates went to General Lee and asked for his help in confirming his proper rank and getting his command back. Lee did not want to get involved and told Oates to take his case directly to President Davis.

Oates did just that, and succeeded in getting a private meeting with Davis in Richmond. Davis explained that there was nothing he could do to alter Lowther's command of the 15th Alabama and claimed that the entire matter was out of his hands. Nevertheless, Davis offered him the rank of lieutenant colonel and the command of another Alabama regiment, the 48th Alabama. Quite aware that he had little choice in the matter—that he could turn down Davis's offer and resume his duties as major in the 15th regiment, or that he could accept command of the 48th and settle for a promotion to a rank lower than the one he had previously held—Oates chose the latter and reluctantly agreed to Davis's proposal. "My regret," he recalled, "was to part with the men with whom I had served all through the war." On February 23, 1865, he was officially promoted to lieutenant colonel and given command of the 48th Alabama Infantry. For the next few months, as the fortunes of the Confederacy rapidly waned, Oates longed to be elevated to the rank of full colonel. He never made it. A commission was prepared in March 1865 to promote him to colonel of cavalry, but the war ended before the Confederate authorities could act on it.

Oates was an ambitious man, and this sordid affair over rank and command was, to him, an intolerable miscarriage of justice. Nevertheless, he did not let it stop him from calling himself "colonel" for the rest of his life. It is difficult not to sympathize with his plight; he does seem to have been badly treated and passed over. But it is also apparent that Oates's driving ambition, which caused him to focus so much of his attention on matters of rank and promotion, occasionally impeded his effectiveness as an officer. One soldier in the 15th Alabama, who remembered Oates as "a handsome and brave officer," pointed out that "he was regarded by many as too aggressive and ambitious but he usually was well to the front and did not require his men to charge where he was unwilling to go."

Oates was indeed intrepid on the field of battle. At Fredericksburg in December 1863 he led the 15th Alabama as it charged with the rest of the brigade into Burnside's left flank. "There we were," Oates wrote, "right under the muzzles of the guns, and the Federals replying with thirty-seven pieces, which made the position of the Fifteenth as perilous and disagreeable as well could be." He ordered the men to fix bayonets and advance, even though he would have personally preferred to stay in the trenches. During the frigid night the regiment occupied a railroad cut that was surrounded by piles of Union dead and wounded. "Several of our men were barefooted, the weather was cold, and

I ordered them to help themselves to dead men's shoes," he recalled—an honest confession from an officer who obviously cared less about the morality of pillaging shoes from enemy casualties than he did about the welfare of his suffering men. He was also concerned about his own welfare: during the night he expeditiously acquired a pair of Union boots for himself.

According to Oates's own tenets the state of his nervous system must have been in exceptionally good working condition throughout the remainder of the war, for he showed no lack of daring or courage in combat. At Gettysburg, as his account published here attests, he and his regiment fought valiantly and desperately to turn the Union left at Little Round Top on July 2; after several attempts to break the line of the 20th Maine, during which the struggle rolled back and forth along a narrow ridge that cut across the hillside, Oates and the 15th were finally driven back by a bayonet attack that surged down the jagged slopes into the hollow below. Casualties were high that day. Oates's brother John, the brother who had fetched him from Texas, lay mortally wounded among the boulders on Little Round Top. Caught in the swirl of confusion and exhausted nearly to the point of losing consciousness, Oates himself remained calm, clearheaded, and steady. In full command of the regiment for the first time in battle, he was at his finest at Gettysburg. He won no special laurels from his superiors for his resourcefulness and dogged determination during the hand-to-hand struggle with the 20th Maine on Little Round Top, but Joshua Chamberlain, his nemesis on the field that day, would later declare that there were "none braver or better in either army" than Oates and his 15th Alabama.

While Oates's valor cannot be denied, he did not always perform brilliantly on the battlefield. On September 20, 1863, at the battle of Chickamauga, he led his regiment forward in a spirited attack on the Union line, but his men became separated from the rest of the brigade. In the disorder that prevailed on the field, Oates decided—without orders—to go to the assistance of the 19th Alabama regiment, which was taking a beating from advancing Federal troops. When Oates's regiment formed its battle line and opened fire, it somehow caught the 19th Alabama in an enfilading volley. Oates later vehemently denied that the incident ever occurred, but it seems likely—whether he was fully aware of it or not—that the 15th Alabama had been responsible for the friendly fire that peppered the 19th's right rear.

It was not the only trouble Oates found that day. Later, as the 15th continued to advance, he saw from a hilltop three Union regiments threatening General Joseph Kershaw's South Carolina brigade. Without informing Kershaw, and with no other authority for his actions, Oates tried to persuade the South Carolinians to follow him in a charge against the approaching Federal ranks. Kershaw's officers, except for one captain, refused to move their troops on the orders of this interloping Alabamian; their advance would have countermanded Kershaw's placement of his own regiments. It was bad enough that Oates was wandering across the battlefield totally detached from his own brigade, but he certainly should have known better than to assert command over troops that were not his own. If Gettysburg was Oates's finest hour, Chickamauga was his worst.

To his credit he fully redeemed himself in later battles, especially at Brown's Ferry and Lookout Valley near Chattanooga in late October 1863, the Wilderness and Spotsylvania in May 1864, Cold Harbor in June 1864, and the siege of Petersburg. But Oates, ever the pragmatist, disdained heroic and romantic images of war and the fame some officers achieved on the battlefield. "All the newspaper talk during the war about 'gallant leaders,' " he declared, "was the veriest bosh." So-called gallant leaders, he said, "generally accomplished little else than to get themselves shot."

Oates never included himself among the gallant leaders of the Confederate Army, but he did get himself shot—several times, in fact. In all, he was wounded six times in combat, twice severely. Near Fussell's Mills in Virginia on August 16, 1864, as he led his new command—the 48th Alabama Infantry—into battle, he was struck in the right arm by a musket ball; under the surgeon's knife the arm was amputated. "One of those large minié-balls," Oates remarked, "strikes a hard blow." After recuperating in a Richmond hospital, he was sent home in October, and he never returned to field command. For William Oates the war was over.

Back in Alabama Oates resumed his law practice and became active in state politics. Although he had been opposed to secession before the war, he defended the constitutional right of states to leave the Union—a stand that surely helped him get elected to successively higher political offices in Alabama. He served in 1868 as a delegate to the National Democratic Convention. From 1870 to 1872 he won election to the Alabama House of Representatives. In 1880, at the age of forty-five, he was elected to the U.S. House of Representatives, where he served for fourteen years. Two years later he married Sarah Toney, a woman from Eufaula who was half his age. Their only child—William C. Oates, Jr.—was born in 1883. Always the ladies' man, Oates had at last found the right one with whom he could settle down.

He resigned from Congress in 1894 when he was elected governor of Alabama, after conducting what one historian has called "the most memorable campaign in the State's history." His war experience figured prominently in the campaign: Oates was known as "the one-arm hero of Henry County." Based on a campaign promise to serve only one two-year term, his governorship expired in 1896. The following year he ran for a seat in the U.S. Senate, but he failed to win his party's nomination.

Simply put, he was not always a popular fellow. After attending a reunion meeting of the Army of the Potomac and the Army of Northern Virginia in 1895, a Union veteran complained that "the joyful exercises were marred only by the discordant notes of . . . Governor Oates of Alabama." According to this offended Northerner, Oates declared from the speakers' platform that the Confederate cause had been just and that "had the Mississippi River run crosswise instead of lengthwise of the country, the peaceable separation of the North and the South would have been both wise and desirable." The Union man said that Oates also made "other remarks in equally bad taste and of all the Union officers on the platform, Howard alone shook hands with him after his address." What bothered this veteran and others like him was that Oates refused to renounce the cause for which he had fought so hard by using the rhetoric of reconciliation that many Southerners, like former Confederate General John B. Gordon, had elevated to a fine art.

After his unsuccessful bid for a Senate seat, Oates did not remain idle. In 1898, during the Spanish-American War, he was appointed a brigadier general of volunteers by President William McKinley. He spent the brief war at Camp Meade, Pennsylvania, where he commanded three different brigades. In the years before his death he practiced law in Montgomery and took an unpopular stand against the use of grandfather clauses to disenfranchise blacks.

His greatest disappointment during his final years came when he failed to persuade the commissioners of the

Gettysburg Battlefield Memorial Association to erect a monument on Little Round Top to pay tribute to the fallen soldiers of the 15th Alabama. Frustrated by the endless spools of red tape the commissioners deliberately had spun to block the monument, Oates somehow succeeded in putting his bitterness aside. When he published his Civil War memoirs in 1905, he echoed Lincoln's words by offering his book "without malice or ill-will to any, and in a spirit of charity toward all." He had come a long way since those early days when malice and violence had kept him on the run, always one step ahead of the law. He died on September 9, 1910. Today there is still no marker on Little Round Top to honor the deeds or the dead of the 15th Alabama Infantry.

Frank Haskell's world was very different from the rough-and-tumble Southern frontier where William Oates was raised. Yet despite their dissimilar backgrounds, Haskell and Oates had much in common—more, in fact, than the two men probably could have seen or admitted had their paths ever crossed during their lifetimes. As it happened, the two men never met, not even across the opposing Union and Confederate lines at Gettysburg, though it is entirely possible they faced each other from afar during the numerous collisions that occurred between the Army of the Potomac and the Army of Northern Virginia in the Eastern Theater of the Civil War.

Franklin Aretas Haskell was born on July 13, 1828, in Tunbridge, Vermont. His father, Aretas, and his mother, Anna Folsom, were both descended from long, solid lines of New England Yankee stock. Living in the lush shadows of the Green Mountains, young Frank Haskell did his part to help with the chores at East Hill, the family farm—planting in the spring, tilling in the summer, and harvesting in the fall. Until he was seventeen he attended a district school in winter and a "select" school in autumn. In 1845 he became the local schoolmaster, which Harrison Haskell, his older brother, said was "the almost inevitable fate of all New England boys of any promise." After teaching for three years, Frank Haskell left East Hill and moved to Columbus, Wisconsin, where, under the tutelage of his brother, he prepared himself for college.

He was an excellent student, well read in history and English literature. The townspeople of Columbus were impressed with his abilities and his enthusiastic desire to advance himself. Though he was still practically a newcomer to the community, he was appointed town clerk in October 1849, became superintendent of common schools the following month, and won election to the clerkship in the spring of 1850. His success in Columbus was meteoric but not miraculous: his brother, Harrison, was an attorney and a prominent member of the Congregational church. The influence of Haskell's brother boosted his opportunities, but Frank Haskell earned his own laurels. He was, in his brother's words, "better posted than most boys his age and station, for he always had had an eager thirst for knowledge and access to good books, which he read and remembered."

In the fall of 1850 Haskell entered Dartmouth College in Hanover, New Hampshire. Despite his arduous preparation he had trouble with his course work during the first year. To remedy the situation he simply studied harder. According to his brother, Haskell's "indomitable will and industry" enabled him to improve his grades and "take a respectable position in his class." Eventually Haskell succeeded in his studies and earned the respect of his fellow classmates, who admired him "for his excellent literary and poetic tastes, for his general intelligence, [and for his] good judgment and common sense."

But at least one other person at Dartmouth noticed a

different side to Frank Haskell's character. One of his professors, who praised his abilities as a scholar, remarked somewhat scornfully that Haskell was as "ambitious as Lucifer and possibly mischievous and irregular." Ambitious he most certainly was: Haskell ardently strived to improve himself by joining a debating society, teaching district school again in the winters, serving on class committees, and discharging the duties of class president. Like other students then and now he participated in harmless pranks and frolics, though his college records reveal nothing that might be construed as truly devilish. What his professor probably detected, however, was an imperious manner that could be interpreted as a pronounced air of superiority over others. Haskell, in other words, was occasionally a bit too full of himself.

After delivering two orations during commencement week in July 1854, Haskell was graduated from Dartmouth with "distinguished honors." With plans to become an attorney he returned to Wisconsin, established himself in Madison, and studied law in the offices of a prominent firm. He was admitted to the bar in 1856, and within a short time he became the junior partner in a law practice established by another former Vermonter, Julius P. Atwood. Success was coming easily for Haskell. While his law practice thrived and he gained a reputation as a competent attorney, he also made a name for himself in the community as a leading member of the Madison Institute (a lyceum created for the diffusion of knowledge), an unsuccessful candidate for mayor on the Republican ticket (he was badly beaten by the incumbent Democrat), and a founding member of the Governor's Guard (a volunteer company of the Wisconsin militia).

Although organized as a military unit, which prided itself on its fine uniforms and weekly drills, the Governor's Guard was mostly a social and political group that brought together many of Madison's most ambitious young men—several of whom were stalwart Republicans. Typically, Haskell rose quickly through the ranks. By 1860, having served for only two years in the Guard, Haskell was elected first lieutenant.

As an officer he was a stern and strict disciplinarian—a spit-and-polish sort who believed that soldiers should obey without question or complaint. Some of the guardsmen came to resent his overbearing and inflexible manner, and one member later accused Haskell of having "little sympathy for a raw soldier, no matter how much he was suffering from heat dust and thirst when on duty or on the march." Haskell ignored the protests and led his soldiers through drill after drill along the mud-soaked roads and around the dusty lots of Madison. For him this was serious business, which, in the perception of his men, was precisely the problem: Haskell took his part-time soldiering far too seriously for their liking.

Yet there was no denying that Haskell cut a fine figure as an officer. Tall and trim, he looked almost dashing in his uniform—almost, that is, because he appeared stiff and stuffy, less a knight errant than a zealous squire. He could not be called handsome, though he was by no means homely: he had a slender face, broad forehead (made broader by a receding hairline), hazel eyes, full mustache and a tuft beneath his lower lip (like George B. McClellan), and wispy sideburns down to his jaw. There was a look of determination about him—a serious, no-nonsense demeanor that probably worked well with judges and juries in the courtroom, but not so well with drilling guardsmen.

Despite his military bearing he did not rush to enlist when the first volunteer troops were called after the fall of Fort Sumter in April 1861. The Governor's Guard marched off to war without Haskell leading its pivots and wheels. Not that he lacked patriotic sentiment or devotion to the cause; his Republican principles made him a true believer in the crusade to save the Union. But all things considered, he did not want to rush off to war unless he could go as an officer of high enough rank to suit his ambitions. So he bided his time by joining another militia unit, the Hickory Guards, and watched for the right opportunity to present itself. It came the following June when he was commissioned a first lieutenant and adjutant of the 6th Wisconsin Infantry Regiment.

As the regiment's adjutant, Haskell's experience as a drillmaster was put to good use. At Camp Randall, outside Madison's city limits, he instructed novice officers and their doe-eyed volunteers in the fundamentals of marching and military conduct. Rufus R. Dawes, who would later command the regiment, recalled Haskell's efforts at Camp Randall: "He took great interest and pride in the instruction of the regiment, and so elevated his office, that some men then thought the Adjutant must at least be next to the Colonel in authority and rank." Haskell was a stickler for detail and military deportment. One of his important goals, Dawes reported, "was to exact cleanliness and neatness of personal appearance, an essential condition of true soldierly bearing." Haskell's emphasis on prim and proper appearance, however, sometimes went to extremes. He required the recruits to wear cotton gloves that were to be kept "snow white" at all times, an impractical nicety that could not have lasted very long. As Dawes ruefully observed, "Fancy uniforms are useless sleeping in the mud." But most of the new troops overlooked Haskell's affectations and admired his penchant for precision and his skillful methods of instruction.

In late July 1861, following the Union defeat at the first battle of Bull Run, the 6th Wisconsin was ordered to the defense of Washington. Although the regiment's location was changed, its daily activities remained pretty much the same. The troops guarding the city were put through nearly constant drilling. Haskell must have been in his glory. There was little for the regiment to do except march and then march some more. As summer turned to fall, and as boredom began to sink the regiment's spirits, the 6th Wisconsin still had not seen action on the battlefield. Nevertheless, the morale of the regiment was heightened that autumn when it was placed in a brigade that included the 2nd and 7th Wisconsin and the 19th Indiana regiments. It was the only brigade in the Army of the Potomac made up exclusively of regiments from the western states, which certainly was distinction enough for any of its proud ranks, but this brigade would soon embark on a remarkable journey of triumph and valor, of death and loss, that would earn for itself the celebrated name of the Iron Brigade.

While Haskell waited impatiently for General George B. McClellan, the commander of the Army of the Potomac, to make a decisive move against the Confederate Army in Virginia, he filled his time by trying to obtain higher rank. He used his influential friends in Madison to put pressure on the newly installed Republican governor of Wisconsin, Louis P. Harvey, but his hopes for advancement faded when Harvey died suddenly in the spring of 1862. A month after Harvey's death, Haskell was appointed aide-de-camp to General John Gibbon, who had been placed in permanent command of the brigade. Being an aide to Gibbon was a definite improvement over his job as regimental adjutant, but Haskell's rank of lieutenant did not change.

Still hoping to get a field-grade commission in the 6th Wisconsin, or in any Wisconsin regiment for that matter, Haskell instructed his political friends to bring his name to the attention of the new governor, Edward Saloman. Unfortunately, they seem to have done the job too well. Saloman, a Milwaukee Democrat who despised the Republican power brokers who infested the state capital, openly complained that Haskell's advocates had harassed him "beyond my patience." He gave the only available commission to Rufus Dawes, making him a major in the 6th Wisconsin. Haskell was angry and bitter over the outcome. "If I could win myself some great battle alone," he wrote to his family, "and then could blow in the papers, and pay newspapers to blow for me, and then was besides a d——d politician, I suppose I could be promoted."

Yet his situation was not as dismal as it appeared. As General Gibbon's aide he at least held a position that suited his abilities and talents, if not his driving ambition. The two men worked well together. Gibbon, a feisty Pennsylvanian who had been raised in the South and had seen service in the Mexican War, grew extremely fond of Haskell and relied on his keen attention to details. Haskell, in turn, learned about professional soldiering from Gibbon and trusted him as a superior officer and as a friend. "He is a most excellent officer," Haskell wrote home about Gibbon, "and is beloved and respected by his whole command."

By the end of the summer of 1862 Gibbon's brigade finally got a chance to prove itself. At the battles of Gainesville and Second Bull Run in late August, the brigade passed its first brutal tests under fire. Observing the action near the front lines, Haskell learned his own hard lessons about the reality of war. Hardest of all, he admitted, was to "look upon our thinned ranks—so full the night before, now so shattered—without tears." The lessons, however, were only beginning. At South Mountain on September 14 the brigade slogged its way up the heights of Turner's Gap, muskets and artillery flashing in the night, and dislodged the enemy from the crest. It was a night to remember, for this was the battle in which the Iron Brigade won its name. Three days later, in the bloodiest day of the entire war, Gibbon's ranks faced a maelstrom of fire and lead as they advanced toward the Confederate lines near Antietam Creek. While delivering a message to General Joseph Hooker, Haskell had his horse shot from under him. Over the rolling hills and the broad fields of Antietam, the day's slaughter was horrendous. The Iron Brigade left 47.5 percent of its men among the dead and wounded who fell that day.

War changes every life it touches, and this war, this cataclysm of flames and tears, was changing Frank Haskell's life in ways he could not have anticipated or understood. The world looked different to him now: gone were the pretensions of white gloves and orderly drills. The soldiers who fought this war, who risked their lives battle after battle, took on a different appearance to him: "The dust and blackness of battle were upon their clothes, and in their hair, and on their skin, but you saw none of these; you saw only their eyes, and the shadows of the 'light of battle,' and the furrows plowed upon cheeks that were smooth the day before, and now not half filled up."

And something else was happening to Haskell, a change that only war could bring about. While he still maintained his demure military posturing and his condescending attitudes toward anyone he regarded as inferior (including Abraham Lincoln, most politicians, and most general officers except for George B. McClellan), he was becoming something more than just an opinionated and haughty officer. He was, in fact, becoming a true warrior. At Antietam, during the peak of the fighting, Haskell rallied a New York regiment by seizing its battle flag and leading the troops into the fray, an uncommon act of valor—to say the least—for a staff officer who had always stayed a safe enough distance behind the front lines. He was lucky to have survived the carnage of Antietam, but he seems not to have realized it. "I have not been afraid of anything in battle," he wrote to his family. "One does not mind the bullets and shells much," he added matter-of-factly, "but

[one] only looks to the men and the enemy to see that all is right." The thrill—and the danger—of combat excited him, and during times of inactivity he yearned for the next battle to occur. In one letter he confessed: "I want something more—a great, terrible, thundering battle, not for the fight but for victory, and victory not for fame but for peace."

In December, at the terrible and thundering battle of Fredericksburg, Gibbon was wounded but Haskell got through unharmed. While his general recuperated Haskell obtained a furlough and spent the winter in Wisconsin visiting with his family and telling them tales of his adventures. He returned to the army, encamped at Falmouth, Virginia, in March 1863. Within a month Gibbon, having recovered from his wound, was given command of the 2nd division of the Second Corps, and he asked Haskell to stay on as his aide. Reporting his new assignment to his brothers, Harrison and Harvey, and his sister, Alma, Haskell proudly informed them that the 2nd division had "the reputation of being one of the best in the service."

The reputation was well deserved. On May 3, while the bulk of the Army of the Potomac was reeling from the devastating blow Lee and Jackson had brilliantly executed at Chancellorsville, Gibbon's division was part of a Union column that attacked Lee's right at Fredericksburg and successfully swept the Confederates off Marye's Heights overlooking the town. After taking and holding the heights, the division withdrew back across the Rappahannock River and the Confederates reoccupied their abandoned rifle pits. With the opposing lines uneasily facing each other across the Rappahannock, Haskell expected that "we shall be up to something soon." He was right. In June Lee moved his army into Maryland and Pennsylvania, and Gibbon's division with the rest of the Army of the Potomac marched north to check the Confederate invasion.

At Gettysburg on the first three days of July, the two armies met in the great and terrible battle that Haskell had been longing for. During Pickett's Charge on the third day of the battle, Haskell was no mere spectator. He plunged himself into the fighting and ignored the bursting shells and the blazing volleys as he helped to shore up the Union line at the vulnerable wedge of the Angle. It was his moment of glory. He was wounded slightly in the leg, although he did not notice it until the fighting was over. After the battle several field officers mentioned Haskell in their dispatches, commending him for his bravery and for the heroic part he played in stemming the Confederate assault. General Winfield Scott Hancock, who commanded the Second Corps on Cemetery Ridge, singled Haskell out for praise, noting that this courageous lieutenant, "who, at a critical period of the battle, when the contending forces were but 50 or 60 yards apart, believing that an example was necessary, and ready to sacrifice his life, rode between the contending lines with the view of giving encouragement to ours and leading it forward, he being at the moment the only mounted officer in a similar position."

Gibbon was seriously wounded in the battle, but Haskell remained with the 2nd division as an aide to General William Hays, whom he disliked intensely, and later to General Gouverneur K. Warren, whom he called a "man of the right sort." In November Haskell rejoined General Gibbon, who was back on his feet, in Cleveland, Ohio, where Gibbon had been ordered to take charge of conscripts. But Haskell and his general discovered there was little for them to do in Ohio, so they journeyed together to see the battlefield at Gettysburg and attend the dedication ceremonies of the Soldiers' National Cemetery there on November 19. Haskell thought the cemetery was an abomination, "a badly arranged graveyard" located where no real fighting had occurred. Writing home, he made no mention of Lincoln's Gettysburg Address, although he and Gibbon most certainly heard the president deliver it.

Gibbon was reassigned to Philadelphia, and naturally Haskell accompanied him there, which is where he remained until February 1864. During the early winter Haskell's thoughts returned to the prospects of promotion. "I desire promotion—am ambitious," he acknowledged to his brother Harrison, but he refused to return to Wisconsin to lobby personally for his own advancement, as his brother had urged him to do, for his place, he said, was at his assigned post. Nevertheless, he declared that he would accept no promotion, if one should come to him, below that of a regimental colonel.

His ambition was fulfilled that February when he was commissioned colonel of the newly created (but not yet organized) 36th Wisconsin Infantry. While it was true that Haskell received glowing recommendations from generals and field commanders, two additional factors served him well in winning the promotion; first, a new governor replaced Saloman, and second, Haskell's brother Harrison hammered away at the new administration with petitions and political influence until the governor finally relented. By the end of February Haskell was in Wisconsin working to fill the ranks of his regiment with recruits and training his men to be soldiers. The training, even under Haskell's expert guidance, did not last long enough at all. In May 1864 the regiment was ordered to join General Ulysses S. Grant's army in its spring campaign against Lee's Army of Northern Virginia. The campaign, in fact, was already under way, and Grant had been victorious in pushing Lee to the south at the battle of the Wilderness. Haskell and his regiment arrived in Virginia just in time to be placed in reserve during the next battle, at Spotsylvania Court House, but his men did not experience their first real fighting until two weeks later, on May 31, at Bethesda Church.

On June 3, less than four months after Haskell's regiment was created, the 36th Wisconsin was chosen for extremely hazardous duty; it was assigned to be among the forward ranks that would strike Lee's defenses in a direct frontal assault at Cold Harbor. For Haskell, the man who had come to understand the grisly horrors of war but who missed the whistle of bullets whenever the army was not engaged in combat, this would be his last battle. Early in the morning he moved his men forward in a grand assault that turned out to be a senseless slaughter, a pointless sacrifice of lives. It was like Pickett's Charge, only this time Haskell was with the long unwavering lines that marched toward the entrenched enemy; this time Haskell and his men were learning what it was like to advance against a steady hail of shot and shell. When his brigadier went down, Haskell assumed command, but the fire from the Confederate guns was ripping the ranks of the 36th Wisconsin to shreds. He ordered his men to lie down, and they quickly obeyed. To set a good example for his regiment, Haskell remained standing, leaning on his sword, oblivious to the danger all around him. He did not stand there long. An instant later he was hit in the temple by a musket ball, and his body slumped to the ground. Mortally wounded, he was carried from the field by his orderly, who himself was wounded twice. Three hours later Frank A. Haskell was dead.

His body was transported home to Portage, Wisconsin, where he was buried on June 12. Haskell's family, friends, and fellow soldiers could not contain their grief over his death. General Gibbon, receiving the news of Haskell's death, exclaimed: "My God! I have lost my best friend, and one of the best soldiers in the Army of the Potomac has fallen!" General Hancock mournfully declared in a field order: "At Cold Harbor the Colonel of the Thirty-sixth Wisconsin, as gallant a soldier as ever lived, fell dead on the field." Haskell's eulogist, the Reverend A.J.M. Hudson, spoke of his bravery in battle and of the heroism he had particularly shown in rallying troops to the defense of Cemetery Ridge at Gettysburg. "That one act," the Reverend Hudson proclaimed, "is fame enough for any man."

Fame is always fleeting, however, and Haskell's name has never become widely known, except to the relatively small number of people who have heard about his deeds at Gettysburg or who have, in fact, read his own words describing the battle and the climactic repulse of Pickett's Charge. Of the millions of tourists who have visited the battlefield and have stood at the stone wall where Pickett's men crashed into the Union line, few have ever heard of Haskell or of what he did there. No marker at Gettysburg tells Haskell's story, no monument bears his name. Perhaps it does not matter. Haskell left his own monument to posterity: a remarkable account of what he experienced on the field of this nation's greatest, and most tragic, battle. For that one act, rather than for any other individual deed he accomplished in his lifetime, Frank Haskell is remembered.

Frank Haskell began to write his account of Gettysburg soon after the battle ended. Composed in the form of a letter, and presumably addressed to his brother Harvey, the manuscript is dated July 16, 1863, but Haskell was still working on it as late as the following November. The manuscript contains telltale signs of careful preparation (there are only a few deletions and interlineations throughout the entire document of one hundred thirty-eight pages), which suggests that Haskell probably recopied the narrative from an earlier draft or from a set of notes. Based on these clues, some historians have concluded that he wrote his account fully intending to arrange for its publication, probably in a Wisconsin newspaper, where his brother Harrison had been successful in getting some of Haskell's earlier letters into print.

But other evidence—mostly found in the narrative itself—indicates that he wrote his long chronicle to inform his family of what he had experienced at Gettysburg—the greatest battle he had witnessed so far in his tour of duty with the Army of the Potomac—and to create for himself a precise record of what had happened there, a record he could later consult to refresh his fading memory. Actually, the contextual evidence is fairly obvious. For one thing Haskell's account contains candid criticisms of several prominent Union leaders—including generals Joseph Hooker, Daniel Sickles, Abner Doubleday, and President Abraham Lincoln—and a damning description of the Philadelphia Brigade's rout at the height of Pickett's Charge. To have paraded these scathing opinions in print would have been impolitic at best, foolhardy at worst, for any of his criticisms might easily have backfired and prevented him from achieving his utmost desire—namely, a promotion to field-grade command. Haskell was no fool, and he certainly knew better than to undermine his ambition by airing trivial complaints in public. For another thing the narrative's tone is mostly personal and intimate, except in a few passages where Haskell waxes eloquent about the inability of future historians to reconstruct the battle's many facets and complexities; otherwise, what Haskell relates are his personal experiences on the battlefield, not a report of the engagement resembling the ones written by his superior officers and submitted to the War Department. His touching asides about the fate of his horses, for instance, reveal his goal of imparting news that he cared deeply about, and that he knew his family would be interested in, rather than limiting himself to an objective delineation of the battle.

When Haskell emphasized that his narrative was "my account," he meant precisely what he said. It was as much his own saga that he was writing as it was a record of the battle, and he probably wrote it for his own satisfaction—to tell the story all in one place and to include everything he could remember—as well as to inform his family of what this terrible conflagration between the Army of the Potomac and the Army of Northern Virginia had been like. In May 1863 Haskell had asked his family to save all his letters: "Someday," he said, "I may wish to see them." He never got a chance to look at his correspondence again before his death, but his family dutifully kept each letter he sent, including the long Gettysburg essay. Had Haskell wanted his Gettysburg account to be published, he probably would have instructed one of his brothers to manage its publication for him; he never did, and he never mentioned the possibility of publication to any of his family.

The essay, in fact, was not printed until after Haskell's death. Not long after his burial, his brothers sent the Gettysburg account to a Portage newspaper, but the editor turned it down as being too lengthy. In 1881 Harvey Haskell edited the essay and published it as a pamphlet for private circulation. Seventeen years later Frank Haskell's account was edited by Daniel Hall (who took out some of Haskell's opinionated barbs) and published in a volume devoted to the history of Dartmouth's Class of 1854. In 1908 the Massachusetts Commandery of the Military Order of the Loyal Legion of the United States issued a reprint of the Dartmouth edition. That same year the Wisconsin History Commission published a new edition of Harvey Haskell's pamphlet; demand for the edition was so great that the commission published a second edition in 1910 and authorized Charles W. Eliot to reprint Haskell's account in the *Harvard Classics* series.

Other reprints of the Wisconsin History Commission's edition appeared in 1937, when the *Titusville Herald* in Pennsylvania published one; 1957, when Houghton Mifflin published another one (with an introduction and notes by Bruce Catton); and in 1964, when the Lakeside Press of Chicago issued a small volume, edited by Richard Harwell, entitled *Two Views of Gettysburg,* which paired Haskell's account with a description of Gettysburg written by Sir Arthur J. L. Fremantle, a British officer traveling with Lee's army. In 1963 James B. Stevenson, editor of the *Titusville Herald,* discovered that Haskell's original manuscript was located in the collections of the Pennsylvania Museum Commission in Harrisburg, and that year he published a new edition of Haskell's account, this time taken directly from the manuscript itself. But it was not until 1989 that a complete scholarly edition of Haskell's Gettysburg essay—along with nearly all of his extant wartime letters—was edited by Frank L. Byrne and Andrew T. Weaver and published by the Kent State University Press. This Bantam version is the eleventh edition of Haskell's account since its first publication as a pamphlet in 1881.

Unlike Haskell's narrative, which was probably completed within four or five months after the battle took place, William C. Oates's account of Gettysburg was not written until many long years after the fact. Oates had written an earlier article on Gettysburg, an essay called "Gettysburg—The Battle on the Right," published in the *Southern Historical Society Papers* in 1878. The article became the basis for the Gettysburg chapters (and especially for the chapter that treats the second day's fighting on Little Round Top) in Oates's massive chronicle and memoir, *The War Between the Union and the Confederacy and Its Lost Opportunities with a History of the 15th Alabama Regiment and the Forty-Eight Battles in which It was Engaged*, which was published by the Neale Company of New York and Washington in 1905.

Oates began working on his magnum opus in the autumn of 1902, after he returned from an extended trip to Paris with his wife and son. For the next two years he worked steadily on the manuscript and finished it before the fall of 1904, a prodigious feat given the fact that the manuscript must have been more than fifteen hundred pages long. The writing went quickly, but not quickly enough for Oates's liking. He hoped to be done with the entire project, including the preparation of accurate maps, by the spring of 1904 and to have books in hand by the following summer. It took him six months longer to complete the book than he had planned. And the maps, which he had apparently taken great pains to research, either were never drawn or were discarded at the last moment, for none at all was included in the volume. In any case he finally got the manuscript off to the publisher, and the book was released in mid–January 1905. It was probably not a huge seller, although it likely had respectable sales for its time. It was not reissued until 1974, when the Press of the Morningside Bookshop in Dayton, Ohio, reprinted it along with a superb introduction written by Robert K. Krick, one of the foremost experts on Lee's Army of Northern Virginia.

Given how quickly after the battle Haskell wrote his account and how long afterward Oates wrote his, both narratives are remarkably accurate and reliable. Haskell's narrative is not necessarily more trustworthy because he wrote it within weeks and months of the battle. To be sure his account is enlivened by the immediacy of his writing, but proximity in time alone probably had little to do with the reliability of his account. What made the difference was

Haskell's uncanny power of observation—his eye for detail—and the care with which he expressed himself. Frank Haskell chose his words carefully. He was the kind of man who liked to get things right.

Oates, in contrast, was a less careful writer than Haskell, and his words tended to tumble rather than flow across the page. He was, nevertheless, deeply earnest about the facts. Toward the conclusion of his Gettysburg account he wrote: "The truth of history and a sense of duty to the heroic conduct and sacrifices of the noble men I had the honor to command, and all Confederates who participated in the battle, demand that the whole truth be told, and hence I will contribute all that I know to that end." Despite the intervening years Oates's memory of Gettysburg remained relatively unclouded—a result, he said, of the importance he placed on the battle as the turning point in the war. In reconstructing what happened on the battlefield, he also had an advantage Frank Haskell did not have: Oates was able to check his facts—and, in a sense, refresh his own memory—by consulting the massive literature that had already begun to be published on the battle, including the memoirs of other participants and all the official correspondence and reports of the Union and Confederate armies at Gettysburg.

Yet both Haskell and Oates made their share of mistakes. Many of their errors were small and insignificant. Both men had trouble with numbers—the size of the armies, the number of men on the field or in a given unit, and the casualty counts after the fighting was over. In most instances Haskell and Oates are just plain wrong whenever they report or estimate numbers. Haskell, as he often admits in his account, usually had to guess at force strengths and numbers of casualties. Oates's fact checking through published sources did him little good as far as numbers were concerned: historians are still arguing over the size of the Union and Confederate armies that met at Gettysburg, and casualty rates, especially for the Confederates, will always be subject to speculation. At the very least, whenever Haskell and Oates each try to convey that huge numbers of soldiers were involved—either in ranks marching across fields or in rows of dead lined up for burial—the authors are generally close to the mark and not wildly exaggerating, even though their precise numbers are wrong.

Reporting the time of day was also a problem for Haskell and Oates. In most cases Haskell got his times right (or nearly right). Oates, however, relied on other accounts of the battle to fix the time of day, except in his narration of his own activities on July 2, where he seems to have worked from memory. Even so, the times he variously assigned to events were approximate at best. For instance, Longstreet did not launch his attack against the Union left on July 2 until about a half hour after Oates says he did. And the cannonade prior to Pickett's Charge began closer to when Haskell said it did—1:00 P.M.—rather than at noon, the time Oates thought was correct. Considering the chaos on the battlefield, it is a wonder that anyone knew what time of day it was—or what day of the week it was, for that matter. As one Union veteran explained when asked what time Pickett's column struck the stone wall on July 3: "We do not take note of time very often in things of that kind—at least the private soldier don't." Another veteran agreed, pointing out that he really was not paying attention to the time of day. "I had a good deal to do," he said.

Some of the mistakes in these two narratives are perplexing and, in fact, inexplicable. For no apparent reason, Haskell did not include four generals—David B. Birney, Daniel Butterfield, Gouverneur K. Warren, and Alpheus S. Williams—among the others he described as attending the council of war in Meade's headquarters on the night of July

2. Haskell, of course, was a witness to the event. It would have been quite difficult to have missed four generals in the tiny room where Meade gathered his officers together. But somehow he did. Perhaps he simply forgot they were there. Oates, in one passage, reported that the wounded Colonel Michael J. Bulger of the 47th Alabama surrendered his sword to Colonel James C. Rice of New York, noting that Bulger had informed him of this fact after the war. Colonel Joshua Chamberlain of the 20th Maine, however, claimed that *he,* not Rice as Oates had erroneously maintained, had accepted Bulger's sword. The difference in the two accounts became known only after Bulger and Rice had died, so it was impossible for these two men to confirm or deny the different versions. Indeed, there is no way the conflicting stories can be reconciled. There is also no accounting for another of Oates's errors. In describing the death of Union General Elon J. Farnsworth during a doomed cavalry assault on the Confederate left late in the day on July 3, Oates insisted that Farnsworth had committed suicide to avoid being captured—a story that was without foundation but that many Confederates believed to be true for years after the battle.

But a fair share of the blunders made by Oates and Haskell in their narratives can be blamed on a particular culprit—the fog of war. Oates, for example, swore that a troop of dismounted cavalry moved up behind the 15th Alabama as it was locked in a death struggle with the 20th Maine to its front. The reference to cavalry is puzzling. It is possible that a vedette of cavalry, which had been on duty as a provost guard near the Wheatfield, might have withdrawn to the vicinity of the saddle between the Round Tops, but it is only a very remote possibility. Otherwise, there does not seem to have been any other cavalry—mounted or dismounted—in the area, yet Oates insisted that as his men withdrew from Little Round Top they ran through a line of dismounted troopers and dragged a few of them along to the rear as prisoners. Oates did not imagine these Union soldiers, but probably it was the pandemonium of the moment that made him think (and declare emphatically for the rest of his life) that these soldiers were troopers on foot. Oates, however, was well aware of the distorting effects of the fog of war. In disputing how many of his men had been taken prisoner that day (Chamberlain put the figure at about double the number Oates thought was accurate), Oates insightfully observed: "All of us, on both sides, who were in such hot places as that were made to see double and are disposed to exaggerate in favor of our respective sides, and do it honestly in most cases."

Likewise, Haskell knew it was the fog of war that prevented him from seeing—and understanding—everything that was going on around him. He did his best, for instance, to recount the fighting that took place on Culp's Hill during the morning of July 3, but he realized that his report lacked crucial details, and he ultimately confessed that while he could hear the guns in the distance, all he could see for himself from where he stood "was the smoke." Later he filled in some of the details from information supplied to him by his fellow officers.

But it was bravado and conceit—and not the fog of war—that got Oates and Haskell into real trouble after their narratives were published. Each of them had cast himself in his own account as the savior of the day, the indispensable hero who stood between success and calamity and whose quick wits had staved off disaster. There was nothing wrong, of course, with painting oneself heroically: soldiers from the dawn of time have recounted their exploits by giving themselves the hero's role. Two factors, however, set the heroic pretensions of Oates and Haskell apart from the typically harmless histrionics of reminiscing soldiers. In the first place Oates and Haskell, by a quirky coincidence, separately described their heroic acts in passages that were plainly contrived; while they tooted their own horns, listeners could hear only the shrill notes of false heroism. In the second place both authors made the unfortunate mistake of advancing their own cause at the expense of others.

Haskell would never know that his account of Gettysburg caused a storm of controversy after it was published. In a passage that has since become well-known to historians, Haskell described his johnny-on-the-spot reactions when the Union line near the clump of trees began to crumble as Pickett's Virginia division plunged over the stone wall. According to Haskell, the Philadelphia Brigade (the 69th, 71st, and 72nd Pennsylvania regiments), under the command of General Alexander Webb, broke and fell back, "a fear-stricken flock of confusion." While he watched the "rabbits" running to the rear Haskell claimed that he was the only officer present who could halt the panic among Webb's men. "The fate of Gettysburg," as Haskell dramatically put it, "hung upon a spider's single thread!" To get the fleeing men back in line, he used his sword on several "unpatriotic" backsides, and "at its touch their love of country returned." Finally, he said, General Webb appeared and "did all that one could do to repair the breach." Having almost single-handedly restored the Union defenses, Haskell rode off to direct reinforcements toward the "melting line" near the Angle. At the end of his narrative he admitted that an unusual circumstance—the wounding of Gibbon so early in the battle—had resulted in his own extraordinary actions that otherwise "would not have fallen to my rank or place." All in all, his description of the Philadelphia Brigade's conduct was extremely derogatory.

Nor was it entirely accurate. Although the Philadelphia Brigade wavered when Pickett's division swept up to the stone wall, its lines did not disintegrate in hysteria and fear, as Haskell had maintained. The available evidence suggests that the brigade did falter, that Haskell was there to rally the men and put the lines back in order, and that the brigade actually performed exceptionally well, given the fact that it absorbed nearly the full brunt of the shock wave caused by the onslaught of Pickett's Virginia regiments. Significantly enough, other accounts of the crisis at the Angle credit Webb with rallying his own men as he waved his sword above his head. Webb, in fact, did not mention Haskell at all in his official report—certainly a strange oversight if Haskell had been as instrumental in saving the Union Army from destruction as he had claimed.

General Webb was the one who first took issue with Haskell's description of the Philadelphia Brigade. Although Webb had read Haskell's Gettysburg account in the pamphlet edition that Harvey Haskell had printed in 1881, it was not until the Massachusetts Commandery of the Loyal Legion published its version in 1908 that Webb discovered how denigrating the references to the brigade really were. Urging the Philadelphia Brigade Association to answer Haskell's account in print, Webb stated sharply that "what Haskell wrote he wrote in ignorance." Webb was sure that Haskell "thought he was leading a division" when actually he was in the rear of the brigade and was confused by the swirling mobs of "stragglers and prisoners" around him. The association obliged Webb by publishing a pamphlet of forty-two pages that called Haskell's account "foolish and absurd," ridiculed Haskell personally and attacked his credibility, and demanded that the narrative never be reprinted again. Yet the association did not directly refute the veracity of Haskell's description of the Philadelphia Brigade's conduct on the field, which suggests that even though Haskell may have exaggerated somewhat, there must have been a kernel of truth in what he had written.

Not everyone agreed with William Oates's account, either. The most controversial element of his Gettysburg story was his contention that the 20th Maine did not push the 15th Alabama off Little Round Top in a fierce bayonet attack that saved the Union left; instead, Oates said, he had ordered the 15th to withdraw just before the 20th Maine hit the Alabamians in its last assault. Oates admitted that the withdrawal of his men was not orderly at all; in fact, he wrote, the regiment "ran like a herd of wild cattle" down the slope of Little Round Top and back up the steep grade of Big Round Top. Emphatically pointing out that the historian of the 20th Maine was wrong in asserting that the bayonet charge had driven the 15th from the field, Oates declared: "This is not true; *I ordered the retreat*."

It is possible that Oates did instruct his regiment to withdraw just as Colonel Chamberlain was getting ready to send his men crashing through the underbrush in a desperate attack against the tenacious Confederates whom he thought were about to overrun his line. But even if Oates did give his order, it is unlikely that every man in the regiment heard it at once, or understood it, or knew what was happening before Chamberlain's 20th Maine came crashing down the hill, bringing the fire of hell with it. There seems to be little doubt that the 20th Maine acted quickly and courageously under chaotic conditions, and that Chamberlain absolutely deserved the Congressional Medal of Honor he won that day at Gettysburg for his decisive action in saving the Union left from the threat made by Oates and his battle-seasoned Alabama volunteers. Oates may have ordered the retreat as he claimed, but it was Chamberlain's order to charge and his quick execution of the order that rolled the 15th Alabama off the hillside of Little Round Top. In later life Chamberlain denied Oates's statements by pointing out that the 15th Alabama could never have accomplished all that Oates had claimed for it on Little Round Top's rocky ledges. But Oates, in the years before his death, also seems to have mellowed. Privately he wrote: "I concede the gallantry of Chamberlain and the 20th Maine and acknowledged my repulse. He [i.e., Chamberlain] was duly honored and promoted." Nevertheless, he and Chamberlain never saw eye to eye on this matter, and they never could reach agreement on several other points of contention as well, such as the precise location on Little Round Top where the fight between the two regiments took place and the number of men captured by the 20th Maine.

Oates was not content to fight one argument at a time; his Gettysburg account is also filled with grumbles about General James Longstreet's conduct during the battle. The controversy over Longstreet's role at Gettysburg had been raging in numerous Southern publications ever since the 1870s, when Longstreet published several of his own accounts in which he criticized Lee for not fighting a defensive battle in Pennsylvania. Lee's defenders immediately counterattacked and blamed Longstreet for the defeat at Gettysburg, pointing out that he had moved indecisively and too slowly on July 2 and 3. Oates joined the chorus of Longstreet bashers. In his Gettysburg account Oates laid the blame for the Confederate failure at Gettysburg squarely on Longstreet, proclaiming that the general should have been "arrested and dismissed from the service" as a penalty for his tardiness and his halfhearted response to Lee's orders.

But the tone of Oates's criticisms of Longstreet differed considerably from those put forth by the cadre of former Confederates who saw Longstreet as nothing less than the devil incarnate. Despite his strong pronouncements and unfavorable opinions Oates was actually ambivalent toward

Longstreet and his conduct at Gettysburg—or more sympathetic, at least, than most of Longstreet's other critics. Oates pointed out, for instance, that Longstreet might have been right in criticizing Lee for failing to fight defensively after crossing the Mason-Dixon line. "It may have been best," Oates admitted, "for Lee to have flanked Meade out of his strong position and have forced him to attack and thus to have acted on the defensive." Oates, unlike most Longstreet detractors, did not spare his criticism of Lee. In fact, though he complained about Longstreet's "mulishness," he implied that Longstreet's reluctance to obey Lee's orders on July 3 might have been well grounded. Concerning Pickett's assault upon the Union center, Oates wrote: "Lee, with all his robust daring and adventurous spirit, should not have ordered the impossible, as was apparent to the skilled observer." Longstreet, in other words, disapproved with good reason of Lee's plan for a frontal assault. When Oates considered the multitude of lost opportunities at Gettysburg, much of the blame—despite all his noisy denunciations of Longstreet—seemed to rest entirely on Lee's broad shoulders.

Unlike Oates, Haskell expressed only praise and support for his own commanding general, George G. Meade. But Haskell did have very harsh things to say about General Daniel Sickles, whom he considered the worst kind of general—a "political" general who had obtained his stars by influence with the right people rather than by demonstrated skill on the battlefield. But while Oates and Haskell separately complained about generals who blundered, they both agreed on at least one proposition: the men who fought this cruel war in the front ranks deserved every word of praise and honor they could get—and more. "Greater heroes never shouldered muskets than those Alabamians," said Oates of the men in his 15th Alabama Infantry. "The Army of the Potomac," said Haskell with pride, "was no band of schoolgirls."

It was the common soldier—the Johnny Reb and the Billy Yank—who determined the outcome at Gettysburg, not the generals who watched the struggle from afar. Oates and Haskell both knew that generals could make a difference—and that they definitely had done so at Gettysburg. But they also knew that the soldiers who marched straight into the flaming barrels of the guns were the ones who, in the end, controlled the fate of these two armies and the destiny of the nation that had declared war against itself. Haskell said it was the hand of God that had brought victory to the Army of the Potomac at Gettysburg. Oates said the defeat of Lee's army had nothing to do with God's providence. Either way, both seemed to know and accept that it was not God alone, or presidents, or generals who had won and lost the battle of Gettysburg; after all was said and done, they knew precisely who it was. It was the warriors, the men just like themselves. No doubt this was an unsettling revelation: what they ultimately came to understand was that the brutality of this horrific war was their very own brutality, that the gore and carnage belonged as much to themselves as they did to any soldier in the Union and Confederate armies. So both Oates and Haskell, seeking to distance themselves as much as possible from the death and destruction they and their fellow warriors had brought to pass, claimed that no words could ever describe what they had witnessed on those green fields and craggy knolls. But both left behind accounts to tell us in great detail what they saw and experienced.

Here, then, is the real war, the real Gettysburg. In these narratives we hear the voices of the past. These men, Colonel William C. Oates and Lieutenant Frank A. Haskell, wrote it all down, believing while they did so that their words could never really tell us what they had seen and heard, yet hoping, at the same time, that their words would never die. They wrote it down anyway. Beneath everything else, they shared an utter faith in the power of words to say something important, something that needed to be said. Listen to their voices. They are speaking to us now, talking to us through the thick fog, these iron men who felt the fire and knew what it was like.

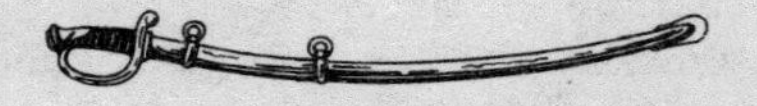

Col. William C. Oates, C.S.A., March 1864.
(Reproduced from the collections of the Library of Congress)

THE BATTLE OF GETTYSBURG

★ ★ ★

by

Colonel William C. Oates

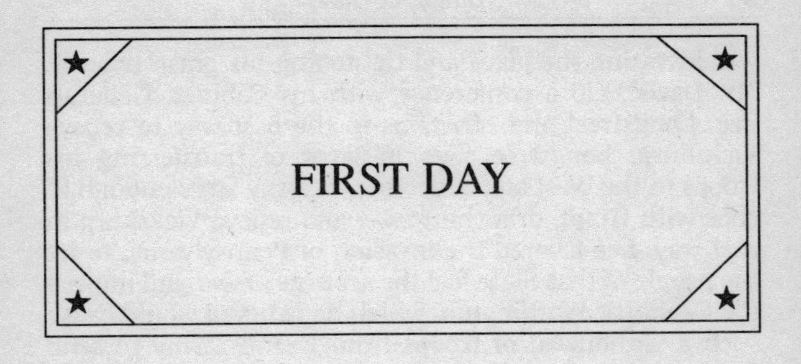

FIRST DAY

The Invasion of Pennsylvania and Its Objects—Preparations for the Invasion—Summary of Commands in the Confederate Army of Invasion—Why Stuart and His Cavalry Were Not With Lee—General Longstreet's Views—Incidents of the March Into Pennsylvania—Lee's Plans—The Advantage With the Confederates at the Close of the First Day—Two Supposed Dead Men Hold a Joyous Reunion—A Young Hero's Death.

THE MILITARY SITUATION after the battle of Chancellorsville, Va., early in May, 1863, was that while Richmond was in no immediate danger, the Confederacy was in danger of bisection. At this time the Confederates held the Mississippi River at Vicksburg and Port Hudson and between these points, but the Union troops and gunboats had complete possession above and below. Grant soon had Pemberton, with 30,000 Confederate soldiers, cooped up in Vicksburg, was investing the place and tightening his grasp upon it. Mr. Davis held a conference with his Cabinet, Generals Lee, Longstreet and others as to the best way to relieve Vicksburg. Longstreet was in favor of transferring his troops to the West and collecting an army large enough to cope with Grant, draw him away and relieve Vicksburg in that way. Lee favored the invasion of Pennsylvania, to let the people of that State feel the scourge of war and imperil the Capital at Washington, which he believed would cause such a withdrawal of troops from Grant's army to send against his and protect Washington as to raise the siege and relieve Vicksburg. Mr. Davis adopted it and ordered the campaign.

Subsequently General Longstreet says in his book that Lee told him that his campaign would be an offensive-defensive one; that he then assured Lee of his hearty co-operation and belief in his success.

Preparations for the invasion proceeded rapidly. General Lee reviewed Stuart's cavalry corps on John Minor Botts's plantation, near Culpeper Court House. It was a beautiful sight. General Stuart, a very handsome man, elegantly attired and mounted on one of the fleetest and most beautiful animals I ever saw, led several charges of his troops past General Lee in the temporary grandstand. Some of President Davis's Cabinet, a large number of ladies and Hood's division of infantry were present as spectators. In the afternoon there was a sham battle, in which the horse artillery, commanded by the gallant young Major Pelham, of Alabama, took part. The firing attracted the attention of the Yankees on the other side of the river. Their speculation as to the cause gave rise to the report that a part of the Confederates had mutinied and were fighting among themselves. Their anxiety to know, in part, caused them to cross the river that night, while General

Stuart and his principal officers were at a ball in the village of Culpeper Court House dancing with the pretty women and having a good time. The Yankees ruthlessly disturbed the Confederates and caused them to rush to the front as the officers of Wellington's allied army did from the grand ball in Brussels, in 1815, at the sound of Napoleon's cannon, the night before the battle of Waterloo. The next morning the Yankee cavalry, under General Pleasanton, had crossed the river in great numbers and a hard cavalry battle ensued. Hood's division was ordered out, formed line of battle and stood ready to support our cavalry, but our enemies discovered the infantry and retired across the river. If there be anything thoroughly dreaded by cavalry it is infantry. In the battle, General Butler, of South Carolina, lost one of his feet and was brought out on a litter through our line. Stuart reported a loss of 485 officers and men; Pleasanton of 907 and three pieces of artillery.

When forming to see the review the day before, the late Governor Watts, of Alabama, then Attorney-General of the Confederate States, was looking at the troops going into line. He held in his hand a fine pocket-knife, with which he had been whittling, and a private in the Fifteenth Alabama said: "Mr. Attorney-General, I wish that you would give me that knife." Upon the word the big-hearted Alabamian stepped forward and handed it to him, which brought forth a hearty cheer from the men.

When General Lee began the march for Pennsylvania he went through the Shenandoah Valley in rear of the Blue Ridge Mountains to shield his movement from Hooker, who was then in command of the Union army, and to keep him in ignorance, as far as practicable, of the object or purpose of the movement. General Longstreet, who was next in rank to Lee of any of the generals in that army, and therefore as to its organization and effective strength should be regarded as very competent authority, says there were three corps of infantry of three divisions each and four brigades in each division, except those of R. H. Anderson, Pickett and Rodes, in each of which there were five brigades.

The First Corps, commanded by General Longstreet, was composed of the divisions of McLaws, Pickett and Hood.

McLaws's division was composed of Kershaw's brigade—Second, Third, Seventh, Eighth and Fifteenth South Carolina regiments and Third South Carolina battalion; Barksdale's brigade—Thirteenth, Seventeenth, Eighteenth and Twenty-first Mississippi regiments; Semmes's brigade—Tenth, Fiftieth, Fifty-first and Fifty-third Georgia regiments; Wofford's brigade—Sixteenth, Eighteenth and Twenty-fourth Georgia regiments and Cobb's and Phillips's Georgia legions. Total, eighteen regiments and one battalion in this division.

Pickett's division was composed of Garnett's brigade—Eighth, Eighteenth, Nineteenth, Twenty-eighth and Thirty-sixth Virginia regiments; Kemper's brigade—First, Third, Seventh, Eleventh and Twenty-fourth Virginia regiments; Armistead's brigade—Ninth, Fourteenth, Thirty-eighth, Fifty-third and Fifty-seventh Virginia regiments. Total, fifteen Virginia regiments in this division. Jenkins's and Corse's brigades belonged to this division, but did not go to Pennsylvania.

Hood's division was composed of Law's brigade—Fourth, Fifteenth, Forty-fourth, Forty-seventh and Forty-eighth Alabama regiments; Robertson's brigade—Third Arkansas, First, Fourth and Fifth Texas regiments; Anderson's brigade—Seventh, Eighth, Ninth, Eleventh and Fifty-ninth Georgia regiments; Benning's brigade—

Second, Fifteenth, Seventeenth and Twentieth Georgia regiments. Total, eighteen regiments in this division.

The Second Corps, commanded by General Ewell, contained the divisions of Early, Johnson and Rodes.

Early's division was composed of Hays's brigade—Fifth, Sixth, Seventh, Eighth and Ninth Louisiana regiments; Smith's brigade—Thirty-first, Forty-ninth and Fifty-second Virginia regiments; Hoke's brigade—Sixth, Twenty-first and Fifty-seventh North Carolina regiments; Gordon's brigade—Thirteenth, Twentieth, Thirty-first, Thirty-eighth, Sixtieth and Sixty-first Georgia regiments. Total, seventeen regiments in this division.

Johnson's division was composed of Stuart's brigade—First and Third North Carolina, Tenth, Twenty-third and Thirty-seventh Virginia regiments and First Maryland battalion; Stonewall brigade—Second, Fourth, Fifth, Twenty-seventh and Thirty-third Virginia regiments; Nicholls's brigade—First, Second, Tenth, Fourteenth and Fifteenth Louisiana regiments; Jones's brigade—Twenty-first, Twenty-fifth, Forty-second, Forty-fourth, Forty-eighth and Fiftieth Virginia regiments. Total, twenty-one regiments and one battalion in this division.

Rodes's division was composed of Daniel's brigade—Thirty-second, Forty-third, Forty-fifth and Fifty-third North Carolina regiments and one North Carolina battalion; Dole's brigade—Fourth, Twelfth, Twenty-first and Forty-fourth Georgia regiments; Iverson's brigade—Fifth, Twelfth, Twentieth and Twenty-third North Carolina regiments; Ramseur's brigade—Second, Fourth, Fourteenth and Thirtieth North Carolina regiments; O'Neal's brigade—Third, Fifth, Sixth, Twelfth and Twenty-sixth Alabama regiments. Total, twenty-one regiments and one battalion in this division.

* * *

The Third Corps, commanded by Gen. A. P. Hill, was composed of Anderson's, Heath's and Pender's divisions.

Anderson's division was composed of Wilcox's brigade—Eighth, Ninth, Tenth, Eleventh and Fourteenth Alabama regiments; Mahone's brigade—Sixth, Twelfth, Sixteenth, Forty-first and Sixty-first Virginia regiments; Wright's brigade—Third, Twenty-second and Forty-eighth Georgia regiments and Second Georgia battalion; Perry's brigade—Second, Fifth and Eighth Florida regiments; Posey's brigade—Twelfth, Sixteenth, Nineteenth and Forty-eighth Mississippi regiments. Total, twenty regiments and one battalion in this division.

Heth's division was composed of Pettigrew's brigade—Eleventh, Twenty-sixth, Forty-seventh and Fifty-fifth Virginia regiments and Twenty-second Virginia battalion; Archer's brigade—First, Seventh and Fourteenth Tennessee regiments, Thirteenth Alabama regiment and Fifth Alabama battalion; Davis' brigade—Second, Eleventh and Forty-second Mississippi regiments and Fifty-fifth North Carolina regiment. Total, fifteen regiments and two battalions in this division.

Pender's division was composed of Perrin's brigade—First South Carolina regulars, First volunteers and Twelfth, Thirteenth and Fourteenth South Carolina regiments; Lane's brigade—Seventh, Eighteenth, Twenty-eighth, Thirty-third and Thirty-seventh North Carolina regiments; Thomas's brigade—Fourteenth, Thirty-fifth, Forty-fifth and Forty-ninth Georgia regiments; Scales's brigade—Thirteenth, Sixteenth, Twenty-second, Thirty-fourth and Thirty-eighth North Carolina regiments. Total, nineteen regiments in this division.

* * *

It will be seen from the foregoing enumeration of commands that the Confederate army when Lee began his march to invade Pennsylvania consisted of 39 brigades of infantry, composed of 164 regiments and 6 battalions; 7 brigades of cavalry and 287 guns of artillery, aggregating, as estimated by General Longstreet, 75,000 men.

The wagon-train of reserve supplies alone was 17 miles long.

General Longstreet says in his book (pp. 335, 336):

> J. E. B. Stuart's cavalry consisted of the brigades of Wade Hampton, Fitzhugh Lee, W. H. F. Lee, Beverly Robertson, and W. E. Jones. The cavalry of Jenkins and Imboden, operating in the Valley and West Virginia near our route, was to move, the former with Ewell, the latter on his left. Six batteries of horse artillery under Maj. R. F. Beckham were of Stuart's command, and to each army corps were attached 5 battalions of artillery of 4 guns to a battery, and 4 batteries to a battalion, making of the whole artillery organization, including batteries of reserve and the 30 guns of horse artillery, 287 guns.
>
> In the Union Army of the Potomac were 51 brigades of infantry, 8 brigades of cavalry, and 370 guns of artillery. The artillery appointments were so superior that our officers sometimes felt humiliated when posted to unequal combat with their better metal and ammunition. In small arms also the Union troops had the most improved styles. . . .
>
> The plan of defensive tactics gave hope of success, and, in fact, I assured General Lee that the First Corps would receive and defend the battle, if he would guard its flanks, leaving his other corps to gather the fruits of success. The First Corps was as solid as a rock—a great rock. It was not to be broken of good position by direct assault, and was steady enough to work and wait for its chosen battle. . . .

When the Third Corps had passed behind the First, the latter and the cavalry were to withdraw and follow the general march. Stuart, whose movements were to correspond to those of the First Corps, was to follow its withdrawal and cross the Potomac on our right flank at Shepherdstown. The brigades of Gens. M. Jenkins and M. C. Corse, of Pickett's division, left in Virginia near Petersburg and Hanover Junction, were to follow and join their division.

General Beauregard was to be called from his post, in the South, with such brigades as could be pulled away temporarily from their Southern service, and thrown forward, with the two brigades of Pickett's division (Jenkins's and Corse's) and such others as could be got together, along the Orange and Alexandra Railroad in threatening attitude toward Washington City, and he was to suddenly forward Pickett's brigades through the Valley to the division, and at his pleasure march on, or back toward Richmond. . . .

General Lee thought that Beauregard's appearance in northern Virginia would increase the known anxiety of the Washington authorities and cause them to draw troops from the South, when in the progress of events other similar movements might follow on both sides until important results could be developed north of the Potomac.

Lee's early experience with the Richmond authorities [meaning President Davis] taught him to deal cautiously with them in disclosing his views, and to leave for them the privilege and credit of approving, step by step, his apparently hesitant policy, so that his plans were disclosed little at a time; and, finding them slow in approving them, still slower in advancing the brigades of Pickett's division, and utterly oblivious of the effect of a grand swing north on our interior lines, he did not mention the part left open for Beauregard until he had their approval of the march of the part of his command as he held it in hand. . . .

> The authorities, not comprehending the vast strength to be gathered by utilizing our interior lines, failed to bring about their execution, and the great possibility was not fully tested.

Beauregard was not ordered and the brigades of Corse and Jenkins were not sent forward. Had they been present they would have added to Lee's strength from four to five thousand men and might have caused him to have won the victory at Gettysburg. Lee's plan for Beauregard, with a few thousand men, to threaten Washington would have created consternation in that city and doubtless have held there many thousands of the troops which he encountered at Gettysburg. It was a wise conception and President Davis should have ordered it. By his failing to do so a great opportunity of making Lee's campaign a grand success was lost.*

On the 10th of June Ewell, with the Second Corps, began the march and entered the Valley via Chester Gap. General Milroy had 9,000 men at Winchester and a brigade at Berryville. There were one or two regiments at Martinsburg and at Harper's Ferry there were about 10,000 men under General Kelley. Ewell stormed Milroy's fortifications at Winchester and soon drove all of the Union troops out of the Valley. They fled to Maryland in the direction of Washington.

Ewell took 4,000 prisoners, an equal number of small arms, 11 stands of colors, 25 cannon, 250 wagons, 400

---

*Mr. Davis wrote General Lee, after the latter entered Pennsylvania, that he declined to send Beauregard with such force as he could gather to threaten Washington and then send the two brigades of Pickett's division to Lee, as it would so uncover Richmond as to leave it subject to capture. This letter never reached General Lee, but was captured *en route*, and hence the Washington authorities knew that it was safe to reenforce General Meade with nearly all the troops which had been left to guard and protect the place. This revelation was, therefore, greatly to Lee's disadvantage, by not getting the brigades, and by the knowledge that Washington was not in danger.

horses and a large amount of subsistence and quartermasters' stores. He lost but 270 men of all arms. He crossed the Potomac on the 15th at Shepherdstown, or Sharpsburg, and occupied Hagerstown, Md., the same day without opposition. He continued his advance with a part of his command via Chambersburg and a part via Gettysburg to Carlisle, where he destroyed the United States barracks. On his march to that point he had sent back for the corps in his rear, 3,000 head of beef cattle and 5,000 barrels of flour. Gordon's brigade, sent in advance, passed Gettysburg and York, and reached Wrightsville on the Susquehanna, taking a few hundred of State militia prisoners. Ewell was at Carlisle on the 28th of June.

Longstreet, with the First Corps, on the 19th held the Blue Ridge at Ashby's and Snicker's Gaps, while Hill, with the Third Corps, was passing down the Valley in his rear. Hill crossed the Potomac on June 23 at Shepherdstown. On the 20th Longstreet crossed the Shenandoah, his men wading the stream. He halted on the opposite side to support Stuart, if necessary, as he was heavily engaged with Pleasanton's cavalry at Upperville, Va. Stuart was driven back into Ashby's Gap, but the brigade of infantry (Wofford's), ordered back to his support, caused the Federal cavalry to retire. The First Corps then proceeded and crossed the Potomac at Williamsport, the men wading the river, on June 23.

Longstreet claims that he understood that as his corps was to guard the rear that the cavalry was to operate with it and follow its withdrawal to the west of the Blue Ridge, cross the Potomac at Shepherdstown, make his ride toward Baltimore, and that Stuart was really under his orders. But Stuart afterwards claimed that General Lee had given him authority to cross east of the Blue Ridge if he saw proper to do so. Longstreet complains in his book (p. 343) that Stuart disobeyed his orders and induced General Lee to consent to his going on a raid, which took three of the best brigades of the cavalry out of touch with the army when so much needed, and then adds: "So our plans, adopted after deep study, were suddenly given over to gratify the youthful cavalryman's wish for a nomadic ride."

This implies a severe censure of General Lee, whose friendship Longstreet claims to have enjoyed to the close of his life. It was written after Lee's death.

To show the injustice of Longstreet to the memory of Generals Lee and Stuart, we copy Longstreet's reports to Lee dated June 22, the day before he crossed the Potomac, showing in the last one, written at 7.30 o'clock P.M., that he had suggested to Stuart that he cross the river in the enemy's rear.

After they are both dead, he publishes in his book that Stuart refused to obey him and that Lee gave him permission to go on "a nomadic ride" merely to gratify his ambition, and implies that thereby the campaign was a failure and the battle of Gettysburg was lost.

Millwood, June 22, 1863, 7 P.M.

Maj.-Gen. J. E. B. Stuart, Comdg. Cavalry.

General: General Lee has enclosed to me this letter for you, to be forwarded to you, provided you can be *spared from my front*, and provided I think that you can move across the Potomac without disclosing our plans. *He speaks of your leaving via Hopewell Gap and passing by the rear of the enemy*. If you can get through by that route I think you will be less likely to indicate what our plans are than if you should cross by *passing to our rear*. I forward the letter of instructions with these suggestions. Please advise me of the condition of affairs before you leave, and order General Hampton, whom I suppose you will leave here in command, to report to me at Millwood, either by letter or in person, as may be the most agreeable to him.

Most respectfully,

JAMES LONGSTREET,

Lieutenant-General.

June 22, 1863, 7.30 P.M.

Gen. R. E. Lee, Comdg., etc.

General: Yours of 4 o'clock this afternoon is received. I have forwarded your letter to General Stuart, *with the suggestion that he pass by the enemy's rear* if he thinks he may get through. We have nothing of the enemy today.

Most respectfully,
JAMES LONGSTREET,
Lieutenant-General Commanding.

Stuart, leaving two of his brigades to protect Lee's communications, cut loose three of his best ones from the Confederate army, passed across the rear of the Union army, crossed the Potomac south of it, approached within a few miles north of Washington and Baltimore, destroying the railroad between, in the neighborhood of the old Relay House, destroyed the telegraph and railroad communication on the Baltimore and Ohio east of Frederick City, caused great alarm in Baltimore and Washington, kept French's division from reenforcing Meade, captured within a few miles of Washington one hundred and twenty-five wagons and well-equipped teams—the wagons full of choice army supplies, destroyed much public property and took over 1,000 prisoners.

Let us not, because he is dead and cannot speak for himself, allow the memory of this wizard of the saddle, "Jeb" Stuart, to be aspersed. His judgment perhaps on that occasion may have been erroneous and its consequence serious, but as a patriot he sealed his devotion to the Confederacy with his life at Yellow Tavern, Va., in 1864. He had Longstreet's permission and approval of the "nomadic ride" before he made it.

Had Lee been promptly informed of Hooker's army crossing the Potomac on the 25th and 26th of June, as he would have been but for Stuart's absence, he would doubt-

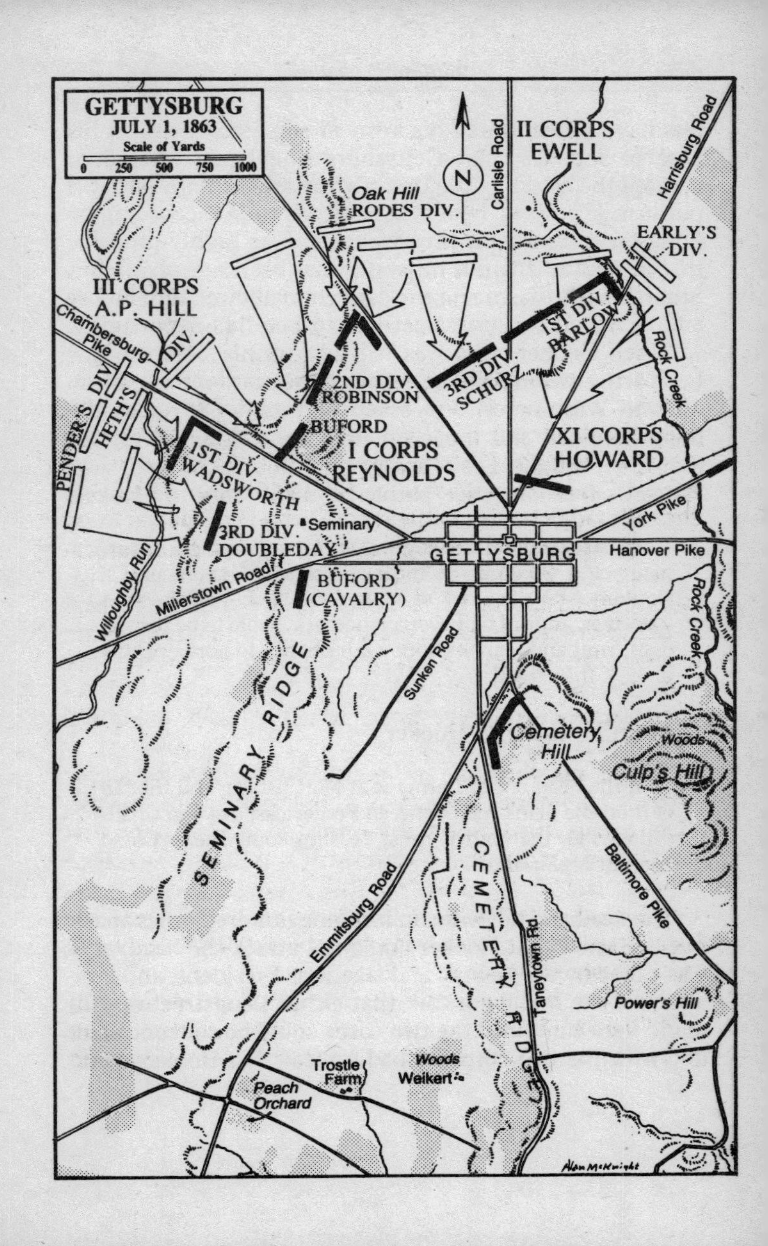
GETTYSBURG
JULY 1, 1863
Scale of Yards
0 250 500 750 1000
N
Carlisle Road
II CORPS
EWELL
Harrisburg Road
Oak Hill
RODES DIV.
EARLY'S
DIV.
III CORPS
A.P. HILL
Chambersburg
Pike
DIV.
PENDER'S DIV
HETH'S
1ST DIV.
BARLOW
Rock Creek
2ND DIV.
ROBINSON
3RD DIV.
SCHURZ
BUFORD
I CORPS
REYNOLDS
XI CORPS
HOWARD
1ST DIV.
WADSWORTH
Seminary
3RD DIV.
DOUBLEDAY
York Pike
GETTYSBURG
Hanover Pike
Millerstown Road
BUFORD
(CAVALRY)
Willoughby Run
Rock Creek
Sunken Road
SEMINARY RIDGE
Cemetery
Hill
Woods
Culp's Hill
CEMETERY RIDGE
Emmitsburg Road
Baltimore Pike
Taneytown Rd.
Power's Hill
Trostle
Farm
Woods
Weikert
Peach
Orchard
Alan McKnight

less have concentrated his army at some point nearer his base of supplies than Gettysburg and have received or awaited the attack of the Union army, in harmony with his purpose expressed before leaving Virginia, according to Longstreet, to act on the defensive. It is highly probable that in such an attitude he would have been successful. But Stuart's enthusiasm and the discretion allowed him by Lee and approved by Longstreet lost to Lee this opportunity.

When Hooker, who was still in Virginia, learned how Lee's army was moving he reported the scattered condition of it to Washington and asked permission to cross the Rappahannock and move on Richmond. Lincoln replied that he thought Lee's army, and not Richmond, was Hooker's true objective point. He also wrote to Hooker:

> In case you find Lee coming to the north of the Rappahannock, I would by no means cross to the south of it. I would not take any risk of being entangled upon the river like an ox jumped half over a fence, and liable to be torn by dogs front and rear, without a fair chance to gore one way or kick the other.

Again he wrote to Hooker:

> If the head of Lee's army is at Martinsburg and the tail of it on the plank road between Fredericksburg and Chancellorsville, the animal must be slim somewhere. Could you not break him?

The head and tail were, in fact, one hundred miles apart; but Lee knew that Hooker could not attack the head, as it was called by the laconic and facetious President, and if he attacked the middle or tail, that either Longstreet or Hill could fight him until the two corps could be concentrated, and with the two corps he had no fear that Hooker could break the animal. With but two corps Lee worsted Hooker at Chancellorsville.

The army passed through Hagerstown, Md., and Chambersburg, Pa., at which last-named place the corps of Longstreet and Hill were halted for two days, while Ewell pushed on as far as Carlisle.

The weather was very warm when we marched from Culpeper, and so continued until the day we crossed the river, when there was a very heavy cold rain, which drenched us to the skin. A good many of the men fainted or had sunstroke on the march, yet the morale of the army was never better. The Fifteenth Alabama had 600 men in ranks and 42 officers when we started on that march, and during its progress lost four men by desertion and over fifty by heat and sickness.

After crossing the river and marching through Hagerstown, Hood had issued to his division several barrels of captured whiskey, and the consequence was that there were quite a number of drunken officers and men. This, as I well remember, was the case in the Fifteenth Alabama Regiment. We marched into Pennsylvania that afternoon and went into camp before night near Greencastle. I, with Adjutant Waddell, rode out into the country and found some of the soldiers committing depredations upon the Dutch farmers, which I promptly rebuked, and ordered the men to camps wherever we found them. This was done in obedience to General Lee's order, forbidding interference with private property because it was wrong and should never be done, even in an enemy's country, except when absolutely necessary. But as far as I saw these depredations extended only to taking something to eat and burning fence rails for fuel. Some men would do this when they had plenty of rations in camp. At one house we found some of our regiment milking the cows and catching the milk in canteens, which seemed to be very expert work of that kind. The people, as far as I could learn, seemed a good deal alarmed, but behaved well. Waddell and myself took supper that night with some very loyal people to the Union. I sent them a guard and protected them and their property from trespass and spoliation.

There were two young ladies in the family and they, in common with the men of the household, conversed very freely after I assured them of their perfect right to speak their real sentiments. One of the ladies said she wished that the two armies would hang the two Presidents, Jeff Davis and Lincoln, and stop the war. These people, although educated in books of some kind, and apparently well informed on nearly everything else, were remarkably ignorant of the causes of the war and the real character of the Government. They looked upon the war as a personal contention between two ambitious men for the supremacy and they were particularly spiteful toward Davis because they seemed to think that he wanted to dissolve the Union merely to be President of the Southern Confederacy. The same measure of ignorance existed in the minds of two-thirds of the people in the Northern States. There was not one in ten of the very men who fought us could give anything like a true or intelligent account of the causes which led to the war or the issues involved. They were taught like parrots to say that they were fighting for the Union, when they could speak English at all. About one-third of the rank and file were foreigners, recruited in Europe for the bounty merely. Many of them, when captured, could give no other account of the command they belonged to or what they were fighting for, than "Me fights mit Zegel," and we staked the best and most chivalric blood that ever flowed in the veins of the young men of any land or country against such trash as this—the hireling paupers of Europe—just such as flock to our shores, frequently through the assistance of their home government in Europe, because it is cheaper to send them to America than to support and govern them at home, and the United States unwisely admits too many of those who come. More than half a million of foreigners come to our shores every year.

Twelve months after they arrive, in nearly all of the States they are invested with the elective franchise and given a homestead of 160 acres of land. Two or three decades hence the folly of thus receiving them by the wholesale will be condemned. A dense population expels loneliness and presents scenes of active business, but it contributes nothing to longevity, virtue and happiness and makes the battle of life much harder for the poor. I have never been able to perceive the wisdom of those legislators who, not satisfied with the immense immigration we are receiving, like Oliver Twist was with the soup, "want more," and cry, "let them come."

There were in the Fifteenth Alabama about thirty foreigners, all Irish except one, who was a Frenchman. They fought well while they remained with us. But they generally belonged to the floating population of the country, and hence after three or four of them were killed and the excitement began to grow cold, all except four or five deserted. All honor to O'Connor, Brannon, McArdle, McGuire, McEntyre and others who stayed and fought to the last.

On the 27th Hooker wanted to withdraw the garrison from Harper's Ferry and with this force and the Twelfth Corps to cut Lee's communications, but General Halleck would not allow it and Hooker resigned. Meade was put in command. He was the sixth commander of the Army of the Potomac and probably the best. That army then consisted of the First, Second, Third, Fifth, Sixth, Eleventh and Twelfth Corps of infantry, eight brigades of cavalry, and mustered on the 30th of June 105,000 men.

All the houses were closed when the Confederates marched through Chambersburg. The people stood in crowds on the sidewalks and at the upper story windows to see the "rebels pass." Guards were stationed to prevent depredations by our troops. We encamped beyond the town.

Stuart having gone to the eastward, had to keep to the east of the Union army and perform an extensive circuit by Carlisle Barracks, and was not in communication with Lee until the battle which ensued was more than half over, as stated by Longstreet and in official reports. On the 28th, 29th and 30th of June, Lee knew nothing of the whereabouts either of Stuart or the Union army, except the report of a scout on the morning of the 29th or night of the 28th. He had not with him a sufficient force of cavalry to keep him accurately advised of the movements of his enemy. He did not know that Hooker had been superseded by Meade until the scout reported it. Major-General Trimble was serving on Lee's staff as chief of engineers. He told the writer after the war that Lee told him on the 28th that his plan of operations was to fall upon the advance of the Union army, when and wherever he found it, crush and hurl it back on the main body, press forward and beat that before its commander could have time to concentrate his whole force; that in the event of his success he intended to march on Philadelphia. But he was greatly perplexed that he could not hear from Stuart, who had with him three of the best brigades of cavalry. Lee was, therefore, uninformed of the exact movements of the Union army. He despatched Trimble with orders to Ewell for a detachment to move on and capture Harrisburg, the capital of Pennsylvania. On the 30th of June Trimble was moving with a brigade and a battery of artillery against that town when an order from Lee to Ewell recalled him and put the whole corps in motion for Cashtown, but Hill becoming engaged without orders, Ewell had to go to his support at

Confederate Skirmishers at the foot of Culp's Hill

Gettysburg. On the first day of July a division of Hill's corps was approaching that place by the Cashtown Road, which enters it on the western side, to collect supplies. When about three miles out the pickets of Buford's cavalry were encountered. Meade had selected a position on Pipe Creek, nine miles southeast from Gettysburg, on the Baltimore Pike, to concentrate and receive Lee's assault if he moved in that direction, but sent forward the corps of Reynolds and Howard, preceded by Buford's cavalry, as an army of observation. Lee did not intend to fight at Gettysburg, but at Cashtown, and ordered Ewell there at first, where Lee could, with his back to the mountains, have protected his communications and acted on the defensive; but General Hill inconsiderately blundered into the fight and hence Ewell had to leave the Cashtown Road and go to his assistance, and after that day's terrible battle Lee thought it inexpedient to withdraw to Cashtown.

They gave ground before Hill's vanguard, General Archer's brigade, for about one mile, when, after considerable delay in crossing Willoughby Run, it was, with its commander, surrounded and captured. Hill then ordered the remainder of that division forward, and the brigades of Scales, Brockenbrough and Davis drove everything before them and halted only when they had carried the crest or top of the hill. In this fight W. W. Dudley, well known in political circles as "Blocks-of-five" Dudley, on account of his method of controlling Republican voters in Indiana, then a colonel in the Iron Brigade, lost one of his feet. Hill brought into action another division. His third was in the rear and did not arrive in time to participate in that action. In a little skirt of woods on the top of the hill, east of the mill on the Run, is where General Reynolds was killed. A splendid bronze statue of him stands on the spot and another in front of the entrance to the Soldiers' Cemetery.

General Doubleday succeeded to the command and interposed a stubborn resistance.

In an open space to the east of where Reynolds fell the color bearer of a New York regiment, when all had fled, turned, and holding his colors in one hand, shook his fist at the North Carolinians advancing on him, and in that attitude was killed. A marble statue on the spot represents him at the moment he received the fatal shot. It is a fine piece of art.

Howard's corps formed line of battle on the north side of the town, out about one mile, to confront Ewell, who was just then arriving from Carlisle. Ewell despatched Early's and Rhodes's divisions to attack, holding Johnson's in reserve, and they swept forward, hurling Howard's corps, broken and bleeding, back on the town. Rodes's right wing united with Hill's left at right angles and the four divisions, then forming one continuous line, drove the two Federal corps from the field and through the town. Gordon's large brigade struck the Federal right in flank and was driving everything and capturing prisoners by the hundreds, when he was ordered to halt, which he did not obey until twice repeated. A great opportunity lost to the Confederates.

Most unfortunately, General Ewell failed to follow up the victory and dislodge those broken corps from Cemetery Ridge and Culp's Hill that evening. He hesitated and awaited the arrival of Lee. Therein was Ewell's deficiency as a general. He had a splendid tactical eye, capable of grand military conceptions, and once resolved quick as lightning to act, yet he was never quite confident of his judgment and sought the approval of others before he would execute. And why did General Early halt Gordon's brigade in its splendid achievements? Ramseur pushed his brigade up Culp's Hill that evening, but was ordered back to the line of his division. That night Culp's was occupied and fortified by the Twelfth Corps of the Union army, commanded by the intrepid H. W. Slocum. Another lost opportunity of the Confederates.

In addition to the loss of Archer's brigade of Hill's corps, Iverson's brigade of Ewell's corps was also captured, but both were small and did not aggregate more than 2,000 men. Near 5,000 Federals were taken prisoners that day and the killed and wounded on both sides were large, the advantage being decidedly with the Confederates. They held the town of Gettysburg and the entire field of that day's fighting.

General Hancock had been sent forward with written authority from General Meade to take command of all the troops at the front and to exercise his judgment as to whether the battle should be fought there or on Pipe Creek. With the perception of a great general he saw the strength of the position, seized upon it, reformed the broken corps and reported to his chief that he had a favorable position. Had Ewell only occupied Culp's Hill that night, which he could easily have done, the genius of Hancock would have been foiled and the Union army could not have made a further stand at Gettysburg; but Ewell delayed and the opportunity was lost. Had Stonewall Jackson been alive and in Ewell's stead, as he would have been, Hancock would not have been able to rally on Cemetery Ridge the broken and demoralized corps of Howard and Doubleday. They would have been pursued and driven from their strong position and the history of this country, in all probability, made to read very differently from what it does. The school geographies of today would probably—yes, most likely—have shown the existence of a nation now extinct forever. Ah! so much depends on celerity of action in military maneuvers. Just at this time occurred the great riots in New York in resistance to the draft. Lee's success would have so strengthened the peace party that negotiations would have followed. The credit of the United States at that time was badly shattered and at a comparatively low ebb. Their bonds were worth but fifty cents on the dollar. The National Bank Act had not then fairly got in its work. It afterwards appreciated the bonds to par, restored the credit of the United States and conquered the Confederacy. It did more to that end than did the Army of the Potomac. To O. D. Potter, of New York, as the originator of the scheme, and Salmon P. Chase, the then Secretary of the Treasury, for putting it into execution, was the Union indebted.

Hill's corps lay that night in line of battle along Seminary Ridge, nearly parallel with and about one mile distant from Cemetery Ridge, along which Hancock was forming in line the remains of Howard's and Reynolds's corps. Sickles's and Hancock's corps arrived after dark and during the night and were placed on the left and extended the line next morning only to the northern foot of Little Round Top. General Lee arrived on Ewell's part of the field about the close of the battle, a little before sunset, and with Trimble went up in the observatory of the college building, which stands in the northern suburbs of the town, and surveyed the surroundings. He then ordered Trimble to find a practicable road to carry the artillery around to the right, to which he proposed transferring Ewell's corps during the night, but from some cause, known to me only by hearsay, it was not done. General Trimble told me after the war that it was so late at night before a practicable way was found that General Lee deemed it impracticable; and thus ended the first day's fight at Gettysburg, with the advantage decidedly on the side of the Confederates, except that Ewell's failure to press on and gain the heights that night left them at a decided disadvantage as to position the next day.

During the fighting General Gordon, of Georgia, found upon the field General Barlow, of the Union army, mortally wounded, as he and Gordon believed. He told the latter that his wife was with the army and gave him a message to be conveyed to the wife after he was dead. Gordon had him removed to a house and that night obtained permission for Mrs. Barlow to come into the Confederate lines to her husband, but heard no more of him and supposed that he died. Long after the war, when Gordon was serving in the United States Senate, he met at a dinner one evening a General Barlow and inquired if he was related to the General Barlow who was killed at Gettysburg? He replied yes, that he was the same Barlow. He then inquired if Gordon was related to the General Gordon who aided him when he lay helpless upon the field and was afterwards killed in 1864, as he had seen reported. Gordon replied that the General Gordon who was killed in 1864 was from North Carolina, and that he was the General Gordon who aided him (Barlow) at Gettysburg. Each had believed the other among the angels for more than twenty years when they, to the utter surprise of each other, met in the flesh and had a joyous reunion.

At an angle on a hill in the Union line there was a battery well served, where a lieutenant, after his captain was killed and his men but few, stood by the guns until one of his thighs was broken, nearly torn off. His guns were taken by some of Early's division, which swept right on, paying no attention to the wounded. The lieutenant was but twenty years old. He lay bleeding where he fell. He took out his pocket knife and amputated his own limb, then crawled over a hundred yards to a house in the hope of finding some relief, and especially a drink of water, but there was no one at the house but wounded men, who could not help him. One of his wounded men lay near him and his cries and those of others for water caused a straggling Confederate who had a canteen to go to them; seeing the mangled condition of the lieutenant he gave him the canteen of water. The wounded man cried most piteously, imploring his lieutenant to give it to him. The young officer handed it to him, and as the soldier emptied the canteen and enjoyed it so much, the young hero smiled and soon breathed his last. Heroism is admired even in an enemy. A monument should be erected to that lieutenant on that spot. His name was Wilkinson.

Lieutenant Bayard Wilkinson directing fire

SECOND DAY

The Fifteenth Arrives Upon the Field—General Hood's Report—On Great Round Top—Ordered to Capture Little Round Top, if Possible—Vincent's Federal Brigade There Ahead of Me—The Fight—Some Federal Misstatements of Fact—Our Retreat—General Longstreet Not Loyal to General Lee—A Gallant Attempt to Recover Our Wounded—Devil's Den.

LAW'S BRIGADE WAS on picket some several miles from Chambersburg, near New Guilford Court House, on the first day of July, when in the afternoon the cannonading of the engagement between portions of Ewell's and Hill's corps, and the Federals, under Reynolds, Howard and Doubleday, near Gettysburg, was distinctly heard by us. About dark we received an order to be ready to move at any moment. Subsequently we were ordered to cook rations and to be ready to move at three o'clock A.M. It was near 4 o'clock when the brigade was put in motion, and after a rapid and fatiguing march, passing the smoking ruins of Thad. Stevens's property, it arrived on the field within sight of Gettysburg at about 2 o'clock P.M., having marched twenty-five miles. For two or three miles before we arrived we saw many field hospitals—wounded men and thousands of prisoners, evidencing the bloody engagement of the previous evening.

When we arrived Generals Lee and Longstreet were together on an eminence in our front—on Seminary Ridge—and appeared to be inspecting with field glasses the position of the Federals. We were allowed but a few minutes' rest, when the divisions of McLaws and Hood were moved in line by the right flank around to the south of the Federal position. There was a good deal of delay on the march, which was quite circuitous, for the purpose of covering the movement from the enemy. Finally Hood marched across the rear of McLaws and went into line on the crest of the little ridge across the Emmitsburg Road, with Benning's brigade in rear of his center, constituting a second line—his battalion of artillery, sixteen pieces, in position on his left. McLaws then formed his division of four brigades in two lines of battle on Hood's left, with sixteen pieces of artillery in position on McLaws's left.

This line crossed the Emmitsburg Road and was partially parallel with it. The extreme right of Hood's line was considerably in advance and north of that road, and its right directly opposite to the center of the Great Round Top Mountain. Law's brigade constituted the right of Hood's line and was formed at first in single line, as follows:

My regiment, the Fifteenth Alabama, in the center, the Forty-fourth and Forty-eighth Alabama regiments to my right and the Forty-seventh and Fourth Alabama regiments to my left. Thus formed, about 3.30 o'clock P.M., both battalions of artillery opened fire. The Federals replied from their guns on and near Little Round Top, and within a few minutes our line advanced in quick time under the fire of our guns, through an open field about three or four hundred yards and then down a gentle slope for a quarter of a mile, through the open valley of Plum Run, a small, muddy, meandering stream running through it near the base of the mountains.* Law's brigade was the first to move, but the two regiments to my right were dropped back a short distance, and as we entered the valley the Forty-fourth Alabama was directed to the left to attack the Devil's Den, and the Forty-eighth continued as a reserve or second line, which made the Fifteenth a little in advance and on the extreme right of Longstreet's column of attack. Benning's, the Texas, and Anderson's brigades moved in echelon into the action so that our division was spread out like the outer edge of a half-open fan, and as the right drove the enemy from the base of the mountain, each brigade in succession would strike the enemy's line on the flank or quartering, so that as we drove them our line would shorten and hence strengthen, but General Sickles had changed his line after the first formation, so that Birney's division with Ward's brigade on its left at the Devil's Den and extending along a ridge to the Emmitsburg Road, was facing us, instead of the other way, as General Lee thought. Sickles thus gave us an unexpected and very

*The advance was not skilfully made in all respects. Five companies from two of the regiments of the brigade covered its front as skirmishers. The two from the Forty-eighth on the right were under the command of a captain, the three from the Forty-seventh likewise commanded by a captain, and in the advance were soon disconnected from each other, but all moved directly toward the center, and bore to the right of the southern front of Great Round Top, and passed around it to the right on the eastern side. Capt. A. O. Dickson, then first lieutenant of Company A, one of the skirmish companies of the Forty-eighth regiment, now lives in Brooksville, Blount County, Alabama, and is an intelligent, reliable man. He says that these

warm reception. He constantly received reenforcements, which made his line hard to drive. Sickles's apprehension of another flank movement on Lee's part as at Chancellorsville was well founded, but the same man was not there to conduct it as at that place two months before. To guard against a similar surprise, Sickles changed his first formation and placed Birney's fine division, well supported, on his flank and facing to the rear, which thwarted Lee's plan of attack made two hours before, which was a masterly piece of strategy when made. Rapid change of conditions in all human affairs bring unexpected results. As the most authentic account of Longstreet's attack and the spirit in which he made it, I quote from Major-General Hood's report to him long after the battle as follows:

> *General Lee was, seemingly, anxious you should attack that morning*. He remarked to me, "The enemy is here, and if we do not whip him, he will whip us." You thought it better to await the arrival of Pickett's division—at that time still in the rear—in order to make the attack; and you said to me, subsequently, whilst we were seated together near the trunk of a tree: "The General is a little nervous this morning; he wishes me to attack; I do not wish to do so without Pickett. I never like to go into battle with one boot off."

---

companies passed entirely around to the northern side of the mountain without encountering any Union troops, and in this way these companies were not in the battle of July 2d. Capt. J. Q. Burton, of the Forty-seventh, who lives at Opelika, and is a reliable gentleman, says that three companies from that regiment went the same way, never encountered the enemy, and were not in the battle. Had these five companies gone farther and joined my column on the north side of Great Round Top, I could have captured the ordnance train, and it would have enabled me, in all probability, to have captured Little Round Top. The Forty-eighth Regiment was ordered across the rear to the left early in the advance. The attack, instead of being straight forward, as the skirmishers doubtless believed it would be, was a left half wheel, but of which the skirmishers were not informed, so they

Thus passed the forenoon of that eventful day, when in the afternoon—about 3 o'clock—it was decided to await no longer Pickett's division, but to proceed to our extreme right and attack up the Emmitsburg Road. McLaws moved off, and I followed with my division. In a short time I was ordered to quicken the march of my troops and to pass to the front of McLaws.

This movement was accomplished by throwing out an advanced force to tear down fences and clear the way. The instructions I received were to place my division across the Emmitsburg Road, form line of battle, and attack. Before reaching this road, however, I had sent forward some of my picked Texas scouts to ascertain the position of the enemy's extreme left flank. They soon reported to me that it rested upon Round Top Mountain [meaning Little Round Top]; that the country was open, and that I could march through an open woodland pasture around Round Top [meaning Great Round Top], and assault the enemy in flank and rear; that their wagon trains were parked in rear of their lines and were badly exposed to our attack in that direction. As soon as I arrived upon the Emmitsburg Road I placed one or two batteries in position and opened fire. A reply from the enemy's guns soon developed his lines. His left rested on, or near, Round Top [meaning Little Round Top], with line bending back and again forward, forming, as it were, a concave line, as approached by the Emmitsburg Road. A considerable body of troops was posted in

---

went to the right and the line of battle to the left. On such an occasion a competent field officer should have been in command of the skirmish line of the brigade and before he began the advance have received definite instructions from the brigade commander. There was no such arrangement on this occasion, and as a consequence five companies of the brigade were not in the battle.

No communication as to what was intended to be done was made to the regimental commanders, until after the advance began. This was a common practice in those days, but it was wrong. The colonels of the regiments about to engage in battle should always be informed of what is to be done before the advance begins, and it is the duty of the staff officers to see the orders carried out.

front of their main line, between the Emmitsburg Road and Round Top Mountain. This force was in line of battle upon an eminence near a peach orchard. [This was Birney's division of Sickles's corps.]

I found that in making the attack according to orders, viz.: up the Emmitsburg road, I should have first to encounter and drive off this advanced line of battle; secondly, at the base and along the slope of the mountain, to confront immense boulders of stone, so massed together as to form narrow openings, which would break our ranks and cause the men to scatter whilst climbing up the rocky precipice. I found, moreover, that my division would be exposed to a heavy fire from the main line of the enemy in position on the crest of the high range, of which Round Top was the extreme left, and, by reason of the concavity of the enemy's line, that we would be subject to a destructive fire in flank and rear, as well as in front; and deemed it almost an impossibility to clamber along the boulders up this steep and rugged mountain, and, under this number of cross fires, put the enemy to flight. I knew that if the feat was accomplished, it must be at a most fearful sacrifice of as brave and gallant soldiers as ever engaged in battle.

The reconnaissance of my Texas scouts and the development of the Federal lines were effected in a very short space of time; in truth, shorter than I have taken to recall and jot down these facts, although the scenes and events of that day are as clear to my mind as if the great battle had been fought yesterday. I was in possession of these important facts so shortly after reaching the Emmitsburg Road, as ordered, and to urge that you allow me to turn Round Top, and attack the enemy in flank and rear. Accordingly I despatched a staff officer, bearing to you my request to be allowed to make the proposed movement on account of the above-stated reasons. Your reply was quickly received; "General Lee's orders are to attack up the Emmitsburg Road." I sent another officer saying I feared nothing could be accomplished by such an attack, and renewed my request to turn Round Top. Again your answer was, "General

Lee's orders are to attack up the Emmitsburg Road." During this interim I had continued the use of the batteries upon the enemy, and had become more and more convinced that the Federal line extended to Round Top, and that I could not reasonably hope to accomplish much by the attack as ordered. In fact, it seemed to me that the enemy occupied a position by nature so strong—I may say impregnable—that, independently of their flank fire, they could easily repel our attack by merely throwing and rolling stones down the mountain side as we approached.

A third time I despatched one of my staff to explain fully in regard to the situation and suggest that you had better come and look for yourself. I selected, in this instance, my adjutant-general, Col. Harry Sellers, whom you know to be not only an officer of great courage, but also of marked ability. Colonel Sellers returned with the same message: "General Lee's orders are to attack up the Emmitsburg Road." Almost simultaneously, Colonel Fairfax, of your staff, rode up and repeated the above orders.

After this urgent protest against entering the battle at Gettysburg, according to instructions—which protest is the first and only one I ever made during my entire military career—I ordered my line to advance and make the assault.

As my troops were moving forward, you rode up in person; a brief conversation passed between us, during which I again expressed the fears above mentioned, and regret at not being allowed to attack in flank around Round Top. You answered to this effect: "We must obey the orders of General Lee." I then rode forward with my line under a heavy fire. In about twenty minutes, after reaching the peach orchard, I was severely wounded in the arm, and borne from the field.

With this wound terminated my participation in this great battle. As I was borne off on a litter to the rear, I could but experience deep distress of mind and heart at the thought of the inevitable fate of my brave fellow-soldiers, who formed one of the grandest divisions of that world-renowned army; and I shall ever believe had I been permitted to turn Round Top Mountain, we would not only have

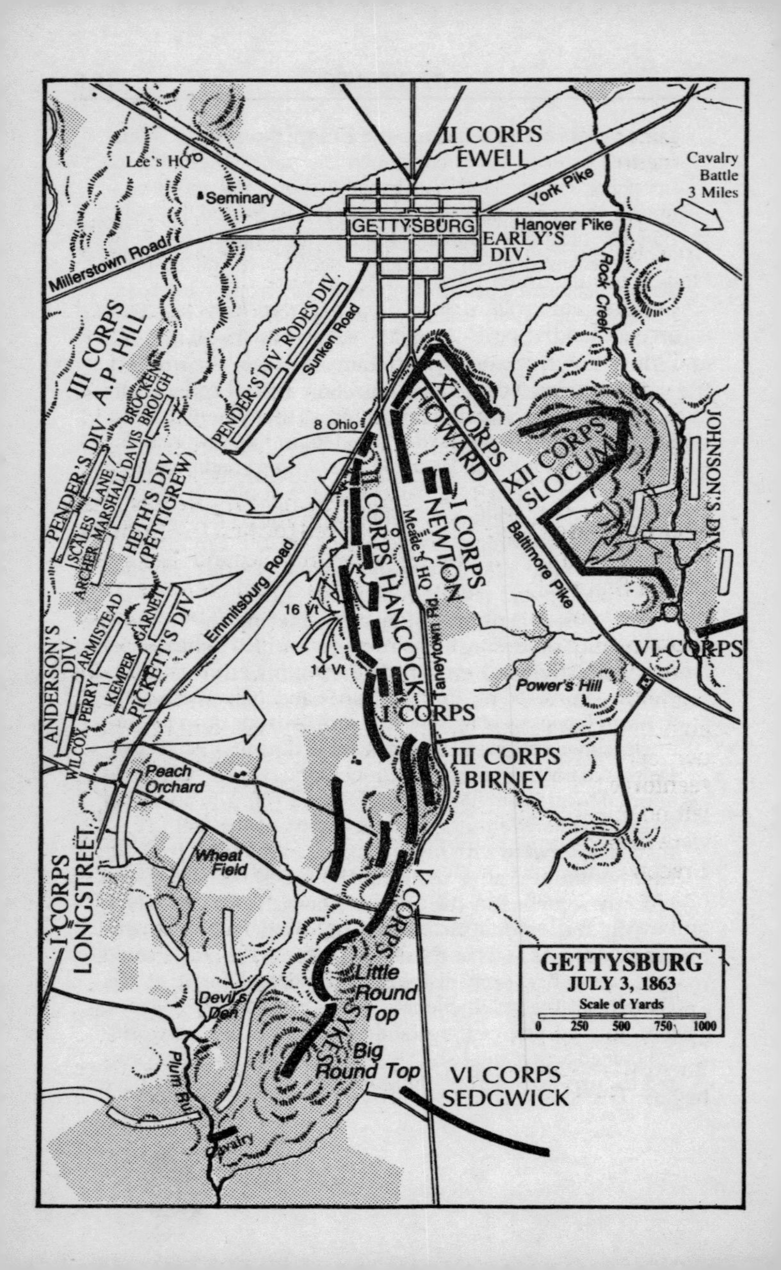

II CORPS
EWELL
Lee's HQ
Seminary
York Pike
Cavalry
Battle
3 Miles
GETTYSBURG
Hanover Pike
Millerstown Road
EARLY'S
DIV.
Rock Creek
RODES DIV.
PENDER'S DIV.
Sunken Road
III CORPS
A.P. HILL
BROCKENBROUGH
DAVIS
XI CORPS
HOWARD
8 Ohio
PENDER'S DIV.
LANE
SCALES
MARSHALL
ARCHER
HETH'S DIV.
(PETTIGREW)
XII CORPS
SLOCUM
JOHNSON'S DIV.
II CORPS
HANCOCK
I CORPS
NEWTON
Meade's HQ
Baltimore Pike
Emmitsburg Road
16 Vt
14 Vt
ARMISTEAD
GARNETT
KEMPER
PICKETT'S DIV
ANDERSON'S DIV.
PERRY
WILCOX
Taneytown Rd.
VI CORPS
Power's Hill
I CORPS
III CORPS
BIRNEY
Peach
Orchard
I CORPS
LONGSTREET
Wheat
Field
V CORPS
SYKES
Little
Round
Top
Devil's
Den
Big
Round Top
Plum Run
Cavalry
VI CORPS
SEDGWICK
GETTYSBURG
JULY 3, 1863
Scale of Yards
0
250
500
750
1000

gained that position, but have been able finally to rout the enemy.

Skirmishers from Law's brigade, who passed around Great Round Top on its east side, confirm the statement of Hood's scouts that no Union troops were there.

General Law rode up to me as we were advancing, and informed me that I was then on the extreme right of our line and for me to hug the base of Great Round Top and go up the valley between the two mountains, until I found the left of the Union line, to turn it and do all the damage I could, and that Lieutenant-Colonel Bulger would be instructed to keep the Forty-seventh closed to my regiment, and if separated from the brigade he would act under my orders. Just after we crossed Plum Run we received the first fire from the enemy's infantry. It was Stoughton's Second Regiment United States sharp-shooters, posted behind a fence at or near the southern foot of Great Round Top. They reached that position as we advanced through the old field. No other troops were there nor on that mountain at that time. I did not halt at the first fire, but looked to the rear for the Forty-eighth Alabama, and saw it going, under General Law's order, across the rear of our line to the left, it was said, to reenforce the Texas brigade, which was hotly engaged. That left no one in my rear or on my right to meet this foe. They were in the woods and I did not know the number of them. I received the second fire. Lieutenant-Colonel Feagin and one or two of the men fell. I knew it would not do to go on and leave that force, I knew not how strong, in our rear with no troops of ours to take care of them; so I gave the command to change direction to the right. The seven companies of the Forty-seventh swung around with the Fifteenth and kept in line with it. The other three companies of that regiment were sent forward as skirmishers before the advance began. The sharp-shooters retreated up the south front of the mountain, pursued by my command. In places the men had to climb up, catching to the rocks and bushes and crawling over the boulders in the face of the fire of the enemy, who kept retreating, taking shelter and firing down on us from behind the rocks and crags which covered the side of the mountain thicker than grave-stones in a city cemetery. Fortunately they usually over-shot us. We could see our foe only as they dodged back from one boulder to another, hence our fire was scattering. As we advanced up the mountain they ceased firing about half way up, divided, and a battalion went around the mountain on each side. Those who went up to the right fired a few shots at my flank. To meet this I deployed Company A, and moved it by the left flank to protect my right, and continued my rugged ascent until we reached the top. Some of my men fainted from heat, exhaustion, and thirst. I halted and let them lie down and rest a few minutes. My right lay exactly where the observatory now stands, and the line extended down the slope westward. I saw Gettysburg through the foliage of the trees. Saw the smoke and heard the roar of battle which was then raging at the Devil's Den, in the peach orchard, up the Emmitsburg road, and on the west and south of the Little Round Top. I saw from the highest point of rocks that we were then on the most commanding elevation in that neighborhood. I knew that my men were too much exhausted to make a good fight without a few minutes' rest.

To show their condition, I quote from General Longstreet, who says in his book (page 365):

> Law completed his march of twenty-eight miles in eleven hours, the best marching in either army, to reach the field of Gettysburg.

In addition to this we had ascended that mountain in pursuit of the sharp-shooters, which but few men at this day are able to climb without the accoutrements, rifles, and knapsacks carried by those heroic men. Greater heroes never shouldered muskets than those Alabamians.

When we formed line of battle before the advance began, a detail was made of two men from each of the eleven companies of my regiment to take all the canteens to a well about one hundred yards in our rear and fill them with cool water before we went into the fight. Before this detail could fill the canteens the advance was ordered. It would have been infinitely better to have waited five minutes for those twenty-two men and the canteens of water, but generals never ask a colonel if his regiment is ready to move. The order was given and away we went. The water detail followed with the canteens of water, but when they got into the woods they missed us, walked right into the Yankee lines, and were captured, canteens and all. My men in the ranks, in the intense heat, suffered greatly for water. The loss of those twenty-two men and lack of the water contributed largely to our failure to take Little Round Top a few minutes later. About five minutes after I halted, Captain Terrell, assistant adjutant-general to General Law, rode up by the only pathway on the southeast side of the mountain and inquired why I had halted. I told him. He then informed me that General Hood was wounded, Law was in command of the division, and sent me his compliments, said for me to press on, turn the Union left, and capture Little Round Top, if possible, and to lose no time.

I then called his attention to my position. A precipice on the east and north, right at my feet; a very steep, stony, and wooded mountain-side on the west. The only approach to it by our enemy, a long wooded slope on the northwest, where the pathway to the observatory now is. Within half an hour I could convert it into a Gibraltar that I could hold against ten times the number of men that I had, hence in my judgment it should be held and occupied by artillery as soon as possible, as it was higher than the other mountain and would command the entire field. Terrell replied that probably I was right, but that he had no authority to change or originate orders, which I very well knew; but with his sanction I would have remained at that point until I could have heard from Law or some superior in rank. I inquired for Law. Terrell said that as senior brigadier he was commanding the division, and along the line to the left. He then repeated that General Law had sent him to tell me to lose no time, but to press forward and drive everything before me as far as possible. General Meade did not then know the importance of the Round Tops. He admitted before the Committee of Congress on the Conduct of the War that it was the key-point to his position. He soon discovered its importance, and at the very moment we occupied it, he sent couriers to General Sykes to occupy it with his division as speedily as possible. I felt confident that Law did not know my position, or he would not order me from it. I had not seen him or any other general officer after I received Stoughton's fire, and did not see any general or staff officer, other than Terrell, until the morning of July 3; and I am confident that no general and but the one staff officer ascended Great Round Top.

From an examination of the reports of the generals on each side and the testimony taken by the joint committee of Congress, there appears to have been confusion and inaccuracy of statement about Round Top Mountain, and a failure to discriminate between them. There are two mountains, Great, or Big Round Top, and Little Round Top. They are from apex to apex one thousand yards apart, and Big Round Top is southeast of Little Round Top and 120 feet higher. Many of the generals in their reports speak of "Round Top" without indicating which. A reader who is

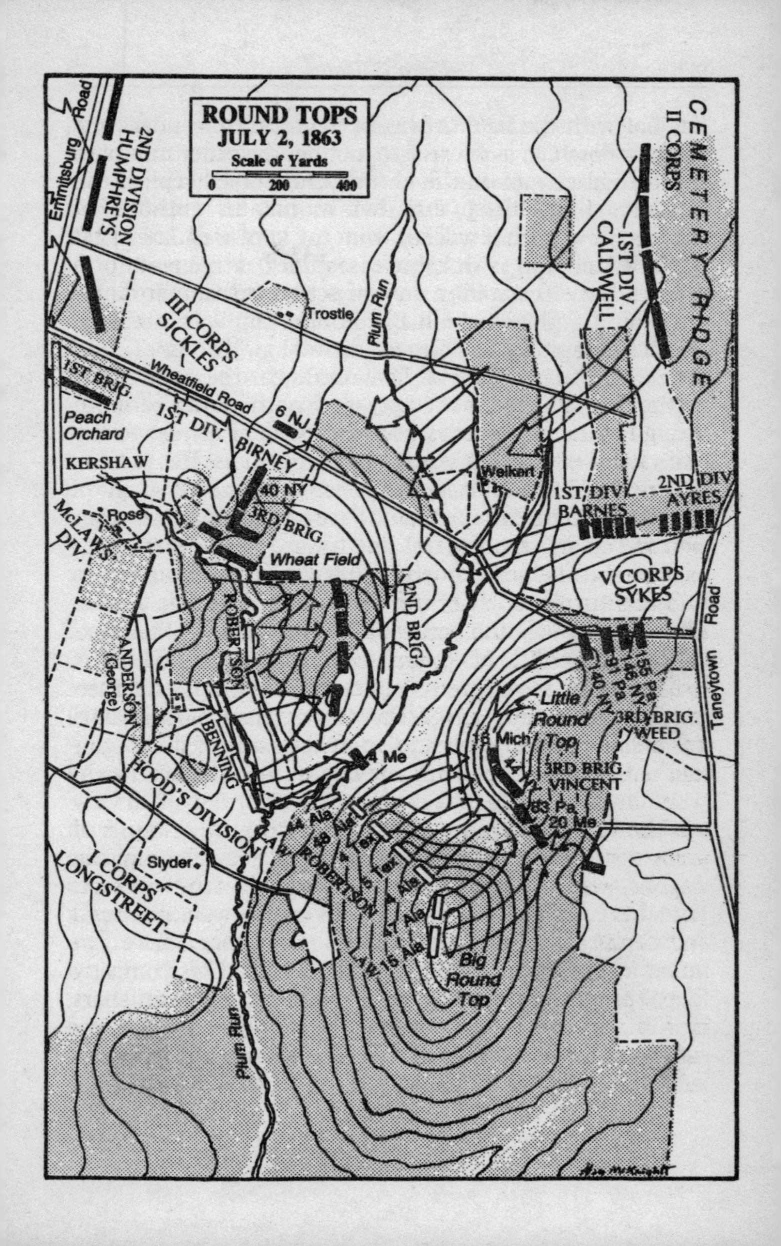

ROUND TOPS
JULY 2, 1863
Scale of Yards
0 200 400
Emmitsburg Road
2ND DIVISION HUMPHREYS
II CORPS
CEMETERY RIDGE
1ST DIV. CALDWELL
III CORPS SICKLES
Trostle
Plum Run
1ST BRIG.
Wheatfield Road
Peach Orchard
1ST DIV. BIRNEY
6 NJ
KERSHAW
Weikert
40 NY
3RD BRIG.
Rose
McLAWS' DIV.
1ST DIV. BARNES
2ND DIV AYRES
Wheat Field
V CORPS SYKES
ROBERTSON
2ND BRIG.
Taneytown Road
ANDERSON (George)
155 Pa
146 NY
91 Pa
140 NY
Little Round Top
3RD BRIG. WEED
16 Mich
BENNING
4 Me
3RD BRIG. VINCENT
HOOD'S DIVISION
83 Pa
20 Me
44 Ala
48 Ala
4 Tex
5 Tex
4 Ala
47 Ala
15 Ala
LAW
ROBERTSON
Slyder
I CORPS LONGSTREET
Big Round Top
Plum Run

familiar with the field or was in the fight can understand pretty well which is referred to, but one unacquainted with the topography of the field will find some difficulty in understanding which of these twin mountains is meant. For the benefit of such, I will say from my knowledge of it that Little Round Top is in most cases the one referred to in reports. Notwithstanding my conviction of the importance of holding and occupying Big Round Top with artillery, which I endeavored to communicate to Law through Terrell (he never reached General Law until near the close of the battle), I considered it my duty to obey the order communicated to me by Terrell, whom I knew to be a trustworthy and gallant officer; but it was against my judgment to leave that strong position. It looked to me to be the key-point of the field, as artillery on it would have commanded the other Round Top and the Federal line toward Gettysburg as far as it extended along Cemetery Ridge; but the order was to find and turn the left of the Union line, and that was on Little Round Top; the battle was raging below. I therefore caused both regiments to face to the left and moved to the left, so as to avoid the precipice in our front, and then ordered the line by the right flank forward and passed to the left-oblique entirely down the northern side of the mountain without encountering any opposition whatever.

While descending in rear of Vincent's Spur, in plain view was the Federal wagon-trains, and less than three hundred yards distant was an extensive park of Federal ordnance wagons, which satisfied me that we were then in their rear. I ordered Captain Shaaf to deploy his company, A, surround and capture the ordnance wagons, have them driven in under a spur of the mountain, and detached his company for the purpose. Advancing rapidly, without any skirmishers in front, the woods being open without undergrowth, I saw no enemy until within forty or fifty steps of an irregular ledge of rocks—a splendid line of natural breastworks running about parallel with the front of the Forty-seventh regiment and my four left companies, and then sloping back in front of my center and right at an angle of about thirty-five or forty degrees. Vincent's brigade, consisting of the Sixteenth Michigan on the right, Forty-fourth New York, Eighty-third Pennsylvania, and Twentieth Maine regiments, reached this position ten minutes before my arrival, and they piled a few rocks from boulder to boulder, making the zigzag line more complete, and were concealed behind it ready to receive us. From behind this ledge, unexpectedly to us, because concealed, they poured into us the most destructive fire I ever saw. Our line halted, but did not break. The enemy were formed in line as named from their right to left. We received the fire of the three left regiments. As men fell their comrades closed the gap, returning the fire most spiritedly. I could see through the smoke men of the Twentieth Maine in front of my right wing running from tree to tree back westward toward the main body, and I advanced my right, swinging it around, overlapping and turning their left.

At the dedication of the monument on Little Round Top to the Forty-fourth New York regiment on July 3, 1893, in delivering the oration, Captain Nash, describing the assaults made upon Vincent's brigade, which held that spur of the mountain during the battle of the afternoon of July 2, 1863, among other things said:

> In the meantime the enemy sent a strong flanking column to envelop and turn the left of the brigade held by the Twentieth Maine. Success there opened to him—vantage ground from which to operate on the flank and rear of our entire army. While his regiment was under a heavy fire, with great presence of mind Colonel Chamberlain changed direction of his left wing and took intervals to the left to meet the new emergency. For an hour the terrible contest at this point ensued, the edge of the fight rolling backward and forward like a wave.

The flanking column referred to by Captain Nash was mine.

At the erection of monuments to the Twentieth Maine Regiment on Little Round Top, October 3, 1889, Capt. Howard L. Prince, the historian of that regiment, said in his oration, among other things, that—

> Again and again was this mad rush repeated, each time to be beaten off by the ever-thinning line that desperately clung to its ledge of rock, refusing to yield except as it involuntarily shrunk for a pace or two at a time from the storm of lead which swept its front. Colonel Oates himself advanced close to our lines at the head of his men, and at times the hostile forces were actually at hand-to-hand distance. Twice the rebels were followed down the slope so sharply that they were obliged to use the bayonet, and in places small squads of their men in their charges reached our actual front. The reports of both commanders are authority for these statements. The front surged backward and forward like a wave. At times our dead and wounded were in front of our line, and then by a superhuman effort our gallant lads would carry the combat forward beyond their prostrate forms. Continually the gray lines crept up by squads under protecting trees and boulders, and the firing became at closer and closer range. And even the enemy's line essayed to reach around the then front of blue that stretched out in places in single rank and could not go much farther without breaking. So far had they extended, that their bullets passed beyond and into the ranks of the other regiments farther up the hill, and Captain Woodward, commanding the Eighty-third, sent his adjutant to ask if the Twentieth had been turned. Colonel Chamberlain assured him that he was holding his ground, but would like a company, if possible, to extend his line. Captain Woodward was unable to do this, but by shortening his line somewhat, he was able to cover the right of the Twentieth

> and enable it to take a little more ground to the left. Meanwhile the brigade in front of the hill was hard pushed to hold its own, and the heavy roar of musketry in the fitful lulls of our guns came to the anxious ears of our commander and told too plainly what would be the result if our line gave way. Not a man in that devoted band but knew that the safety of the brigade, and perhaps of the army, depended on the steadfastness with which that point was held, and so fought on and on, with no hope of assistance, but not a thought of giving up. Already nearly half of the little force is prostrate. The dead and the wounded clog the footsteps of the living.

General Chamberlain, who was colonel of the Twentieth Maine, afterwards made general for his conduct on that occasion, and after the war Governor of Maine, in his address, delivered on the same occasion, said:

> All can see what would have become of our brigade swallowed up; of Weed's struck in the rear; of Hazlitt's guns taken in the flank and turned to launch their thunderbolts upon our troops, already sore pressed in the gorge at our feet, and the fields upon the great front and right. Round Top lost—the day lost—Gettysburg lost—who can tell what for loss thence would follow!

Captain Prince, of the Twentieth Maine, in his oration above referred to claims that "fifty dead bodies of the Fifteenth Alabama men were buried in the front of his regiment and about one hundred of the badly wounded were left behind to become prisoners." His is an over-estimate of the number of the dead from the Fifteenth Alabama. There were present in the seven companies of the Forty-seventh, as shown by the muster roll, an aggregate of but 154 men. Only four or five of these were killed and about twenty wounded. If they buried fifty dead that included those from the Forty-seventh companies with the Fifteenth dead. He was certainly mistaken as to the number badly wounded, including both regiments, for several of these—fully one-half—went to the Confederate rear.

Prince also said: "Four hundred prisoners, mostly from the Fifteenth and Forty-seventh Alabama, were sent to the rear." This is an egregiously mistaken statement. I have examined the muster rolls of the companies of the Fifteenth, made soon after the battle, in which the names were given of the captured without wounds, and there was a total of but eighty-four, most of them being with Adjutant Waddell when the retreat was ordered, which they did not hear. If every man in the seven companies of the Forty-seventh which went into the action (only one hundred and fifty-four) were included it would make but two hundred and thirty-eight, and we know that at least one hundred and twenty-odd of the Forty-seventh escaped and were afterwards in line all night. Deduct the killed and wounded from those companies, and Captain Prince has but little over half the number of prisoners which he says were taken from those regiments and sent to the rear. General Chamberlain fell into the same error. All of us, on both sides, who were in such hot places as that were made to see double and are disposed to exaggerate in favor of our respective sides, and do it honestly in most cases.

If I had had one more regiment we would have completely turned the flank and have won Little Round Top, which would have forced Meade's whole left wing to retire. Had the Forty-eighth Alabama not been transferred to the left, it would have driven the sharp-shooters, and then following my advance, we would have gotten in the rear of the Federal line and have completely turned the tide of battle in favor of the Confederates. With the five companies of skirmishers which had gone to the east of the mountain they might have made my assault successful. Another lost opportunity.

I knew that the left of the Forty-seventh was disconnected, I knew not how far from the right of the Fourth Alabama, and consequently was out-flanked on its left and without support. The seven companies of that regiment present confronted the Eighty-third Pennsylvania and was enfiladed by the left-oblique fire of the left wing of the Forty-fourth New York, which was very destructive, and drove the men from the obstructions behind which they were sheltering. Lieutenant-Colonel Bulger, in command of the Forty-seventh Alabama companies, a most gallant old gentleman over sixty years of age, fell severely wounded, and soon afterwards his seven companies, after behaving most gallantly, broke, and in confusion retreated southward toward the position of the other regiments of the brigade and reached their right. I aided their gallant Major Campbell in his efforts to hold them, but having no support on the left, they could not be rallied and held to the position. When the Fifteenth was driven back, Colonel Bulger was left sitting by a tree, sword in hand, shot through one lung and bleeding profusely. A captain in the Forty-fourth New York approached and demanded his sword. The old Colonel said, "What is your rank?" The reply was, "I am a captain." Bulger said, "Well, I am a lieutenant-colonel, and I will not surrender my sword except to an officer of equal rank." The captain then said, "Surrender your sword, or I will kill you." Colonel Bulger promptly replied, "You may kill and be d—d! I shall never surrender my sword to an officer of lower rank." The captain was so amused at the old Colonel's high notions of military etiquette that he went for his colonel, Rice, to whom the sword was gracefully surrendered. Rice's statement of the circumstances caused Colonel Bulger to be better cared for than he would otherwise have been, which probably saved his life.* When exchanged in the summer of 1864 he was promoted to the colonelcy of his regiment, went to the front, and served with it for a short time, and was then honorably retired. He was not made a brigadier-general, as reported in Vol. VII of Confederate Military History, but returned to his home in Dadeville, Alabama, and was elected to the State Senate in August, 1864, where he served until the surrender. He was in the Secession Convention in 1861, voted against secession, and refused to sign the ordinance. But when war came as a consequence, he raised a company and fought heroically through the struggle. He was unskilled in tactics and lacking in disciplinary power, but he possessed such a high order of courage that he was greatly respected by his men, who stood bravely with him until he fell. He died in 1900, about 95 years of age.

Just as the Forty-seventh companies were being driven back, I ordered my regiment to change direction to the left, swing around, and drive the Federals from the ledge of rocks, for the purpose of enfilading their line, relieving the Forty-seventh—gain the enemy's rear, and drive him from the hill. My men obeyed and advanced about half way to the enemy's position, but the fire was so destructive that my line wavered like a man trying to walk against a strong wind, and then slowly, doggedly, gave back a little; then with no one upon the left or right of me, my regiment exposed, while the enemy was still under cover, to stand there and die was sheer folly; either to retreat or advance became a necessity. The Lieutenant-Colonel, I. B. Feagin, had lost his leg at Plum Run; the heroic Captain Ellison

*General Chamberlain denies this statement and says that Bulger surrendered to him. Rice and Bulger are both dead and there is now no living witness to verify the statement. The writer derived his information from Colonel Bulger.

had fallen; while Captain Brainard, one of the bravest and best officers in the regiment, in leading his company forward, fell, exclaiming, "O God! that I could see my mother," and instantly expired. Lieutenant John A. Oates, my dear brother, succeeded to the command of the company, but was pierced through by a number of bullets, and fell mortally wounded. Lieutenant Cody fell mortally wounded, Captain Bethune and several other officers were seriously wounded, while the carnage in the ranks was appalling. I again ordered the advance, and knowing the officers and men of that gallant old regiment, I felt sure that they would follow their commander anywhere in the line of duty. I passed through the line waving my sword, shouting, "Forward, men, to the ledge!" and was promptly followed by the command in splendid style. We drove the Federals from their strong defensive position; five times they rallied and charged us, twice coming so near that some of my men had to use the bayonet, but in vain was their effort. It was our time now to deal death and destruction to a gallant foe, and the account was speedily settled. I led this charge and sprang upon the ledge of rock, using my pistol within musket length, when the rush of my men drove the Maine men from the ledge along the line now indicated by stone markers on the east end of Vincent's Spur. I have seen a statement from General Chamberlain that his right was not forced back beyond the point or angle of the rocky ledge, where the right marker of his regiment stands. My recollection is quite different. At this angle and to the southwest of it is where I lost the greatest number of my men. The Twentieth Maine was driven back from this ledge, but not farther than to the next ledge on the mountain-side. I recall a circumstance which I recollect. I, with my regiment, made a rush forward from the ledge. About forty steps up the slope there is a large boulder about midway the Spur. The Maine regiment charged my line, coming right up in a hand-to-hand encounter. My regimental colors were just a step or two to the right of that boulder, and I was within ten feet. A Maine man reached to grasp the staff of the colors when Ensign Archibald stepped back and Sergeant Pat O'Connor stove his bayonet through the head of the Yankee, who fell dead. I witnessed that incident, which impressed me beyond the point of being forgotten. There never were harder fighters than the Twentieth Maine men and their gallant Colonel. His skill and persistency and the great bravery of his men saved Little Round Top and the Army of the Potomac from defeat. Great events sometimes turn on comparatively small affairs. My position rapidly became untenable. The Federal infantry were reported to be coming down on my right and certainly were closing in on my rear, while some dismounted cavalry were closing the only avenue of escape on my left rear. I sent my sergeant-major with a request to Colonel Bowles, of the Fourth Alabama, the next in line to the left, to come to my relief. He returned within a minute and reported that none of our troops were in sight, the enemy to be between us and the Fourth Alabama, and swarming the woods south of Little Round Top. The lamented Captain Park, who was afterwards killed at Knoxville, and Captain Hill, killed near Richmond in 1864, came and informed me that the enemy were closing in on our rear. I sent Park to ascertain their number. He soon returned, and reported that two regiments were coming up behind us, and just then I saw them halt behind a fence, some two hundred yards distant, from which they opened fire on us. These, I have since learned from him, were the battalions of Stoughton's sharp-shooters, each of which carried a flag, hence the impression that there were two regiments. They had been lost in the woods, but, guided by the firing, came up in our rear. At Balaklava Captain Nolan's six hundred had cannon to the right of them, cannon to the left of them, cannon in front of them, which volleyed and thundered. But at this moment the Fifteenth Alabama had infantry in front of them, to the right of them, dismounted cavalry to the left of them, and infantry in the rear of them. With a withering and deadly fire pouring in upon us from every direction, it seemed that the regiment was doomed to destruction. While one man was shot in the face, his right-hand or left-hand comrade was shot in the side or back. Some were struck simultaneously with two or three balls from different directions. Captains Hill and Park suggested that I should order a retreat; but this seemed impracticable. My dead and wounded were then nearly as great in number as those still on duty. They literally covered the ground. The blood stood in puddles in some places on the rocks; the ground was soaked with the blood of as brave men as ever fell on the red field of battle. I still hoped for reenforcements or for the tide of success to turn my way. It seemed impossible to retreat and I therefore replied to my captains, "Return to your companies; we will sell out as dearly as possible." Hill made no reply, but Park smiled pleasantly, gave me the military salute, and said, "All right, sir." On reflection a few moments later I saw no hope of success and did order a retreat, but did not undertake to retire in order. I sent Sergeant-Major Norris (who is now a physician residing in Brazil) and had the officers and men advised the best I could that when the signal was given that we would not try to retreat in order, but every one should run in the direction from whence we came, and halt on the top of the Big Round Top Mountain. I found the undertaking to capture Little Round Top too great for my regiment unsupported. I waited until the next charge of the Twentieth Maine was repulsed, as it would give my men a better chance to get out unhurt, and then ordered the retreat. The historian of that regiment claims that its charge drove us from the field. This is not true; *I ordered the retreat*. He was, I believe, the chaplain, and not present to see it. Doubtless he was at prayer a safe distance in the rear. Colonel Chamberlain also reported it and doubtless believed it, but it was just as I state—I ordered the retreat.

When the signal was given we ran like a herd of wild cattle, right through the line of dismounted cavalrymen. Some of the men as they ran through seized three of the cavalrymen by the collar and carried them out prisoners. As we ran, a man named Keils, of Company H, from Henry County, who was to my right and rear had his throat cut by a bullet, and he ran past me breathing at his throat and the blood spattering. His wind-pipe was entirely severed, but notwithstanding he crossed the mountain and died in the field hospital that night or the next morning.

Captain De B. Waddell, who was then adjutant of the regiment, when we had reached our most advanced position, about one hundred and fifty yards from the top of Little Round Top, where the New York monument now stands, came and asked me to let him take forty or fifty men from the right wing of the regiment and advance to some rocks from which to enfilade the Union line, the Twentieth Maine and Eighty-third Pennsylvania. I authorized it and he had about fifty men behind a ledge of rocks or ridge of ground, and doing effective work when I ordered the retreat. The firing was so heavy that he did not hear the order, but said he saw me and the men near me start and knew that it was a retreat. Sergeant-Major Norris when communicating to commanders of companies that I would order a retreat did not so inform Waddell. He gave the order and broke to run. He saw two of his men fall. He escaped, but his men were captured. When he reached the foot of the mountain he there met Company A coming out of the woods to the east of the position from which we had just retreated. This was the company whose captain I had ordered, as we advanced down the north side of Great Round Top, to deploy his company in open order to surround and capture the train of ordnance wagons. Captain Shaaff claimed that there were Union troops in the woods east of the wagons and he feared capture of his company if he attempted to capture the wagons, and desisted in consequence. He should then have rejoined the regiment at once, but did not. The troops in the woods were Stoughton's sharp-shooters, and perhaps Morrell's company of the Twentieth Maine. Waddell caused the company to take a stand a short distance up the mountain-side, where by their fire they checked and turned back the Maine men who were pursuing my regiment. When I visited the battle-field after the war I could not understand how the trees on that side of Round Top near its base were scarred on each side by bullets, and why monuments, or markers, were set up there, as I thought no battle occurred there. Afterwards Captain Waddell (now an Episcopal clergyman at Meridian, Mississippi) explained it.

The absence of Company A from the assault on Little Round Top, the capture of the water detail, and the number overcome by heat who had fallen out on scaling the rugged mountain, reduced my regiment to less than four hundred officers and men who made that assault. All these facts I did not know when I made my report nor when I wrote the article for the Southern Historical Society papers in 1878, but close investigation since the war revealed them to me. In the hasty manner of writing my report I took as a basis of the strength of my regiment its last muster before we began the march to Pennsylvania. I also wrote the article after the war on the same basis, which was a mistake. When approaching the top of the mountain in retreat I made an attempt to halt and reform the regiment; but the men were helping wounded and disabled comrades, and scattered in the woods and among the rocks, so that it could not then be done. I was so overcome by heat and exertion that I fainted and fell, and would have been captured but for two stalwart, powerful men of the regiment, who carried me to the top of the mountain, where Dr. Reeves, the assistant surgeon, poured water on my head from a canteen until it revived me. I never can forget those two men, for I dreaded a prison more than death. When I revived I turned over the command of the regiment to Captain Hill temporarily, with directions to retire to the open field at the foot of the mountain on the line of our advance. This was between sunset and dark; the fighting along our line had pretty well ceased. It had been terrific all along Longstreet's front. His seventeen thousand men had done the best fighting of any equal number of troops during the war, but had not accomplished anything in the way of substantial results.

Lee's plan for Longstreet's attack was up the Emmitsburg Road, beginning with the right brigade, which was Law's, where I was. Had General Longstreet been where the attack began, he would have seen the necessity of protecting my flank from the assault of United States sharp-shooters. Had that been done, I would, with the six hundred veterans I had, have reached Little Round Top before Vincent's brigade did and would easily have captured that place, which would have won the battle. Or had he seen the Fifteenth and Forty-seventh regiments when they reached the top of Great Round Top, and ordered a battery and another regiment to aid me in holding that mountain, it would have been held, which Meade admitted, in his testimony on the conduct of the war, was the key to his position. With that in our possession he could not have held any of the ground which he subsequently held to the last, for it was the key-point of his position. Instead of this, General Longstreet was near the other end of his line, more than a mile away from his right, and never knew that those regiments passed over the top of Big Round Top until years after the battle, when he saw it in print.

Though he may not have approved Lee's plan, it was his duty to have loyally and to the best of his ability executed that plan. Had he done so, I have no doubt of the success of the attack. General Lee was at fault for failing to have Longstreet's two divisions, then on the field (except Law's brigade), seize the Round Tops in the forenoon, when there were no Union troops on them. When the assault was made at 3.30 P.M. neither of these mountains were occupied in force, but Sickles's corps was advanced beyond and obstructed a direct attack on Little Round Top. Longstreet was responsible and at fault for the negligent and bungling manner in which it was done. The change made in his line by General Sickles, which was unknown to General Lee, greatly impaired his plan; but notwithstanding his shrewd change and its tendency to thwart the plan, yet had Longstreet skilfully and loyally, instead of sullenly and disapprovingly, executed it, he would have won the battle. When he found the change in Sickles's lines, of which he knew that General Lee was not aware, he should have adopted General Hood's suggestion to turn the flank and attack in the rear; but because Lee had ordered him to attack in a particular way, he would not change, though he knew that if Lee himself had been present he would have changed the order of attack when he discovered the change in Sickles's line which made it necessary.

General Longstreet in his book (p. 408) throws all the blame on Lee for not riding with him and personally directing his attack, as follows:

> We were left to our own resources in finding ground upon which to organize for battle. The enemy had changed position somewhat after the march was ordered, but as we

> were not informed of his position before the march, we could not know of the change. The Confederate commander did not care to ride near us, to give information of a change to assist in preparing for attack, nor to inquire if new and better combinations might be made.

General Lee mistakenly supposed that Longstreet understood the situation, position of the enemy, etc., and possessed the ability and patriotism sufficient to make that attack wisely without his presence.

General Longstreet disapproved the plan of attack because Lee was departing from the policy, declared by him before he moved from Virginia, of an aggressive defensive campaign, which Longstreet approved. He may have been right; it may have been best for Lee to have flanked Meade out of his strong position and have forced him to attack and thus to have acted on the defensive. Lee gave his reasons why he did not pursue that course, which were well-nigh conclusive. Longstreet had no right to sulk because of this change of policy. Sulking was disloyalty to his chief. If his conduct was not half-hearted and wilful, then the only explanation of it is that he was a failure as a general, and no one believes that. Hood saw the necessity, and insisted on a change of the plan of attack, but because Lee had ordered it, without a knowledge of Sickles's change of lines, Longstreet obeyed Lee's order literally—although Hood showed him the necessity of a change—and by his mulishness lost the greatest battle of the war. General Law fully concurred in Hood's views. A supposition that Hood's request would be granted may account for Law's skirmishers passing around Big Round Top to the east and thus missing the battle.

Early on the morning of the 2d General Meade expected Lee to attack him on his right, and determined to attack Lee before the latter moved against him. At 9.30 A.M. he ordered Slocum, who commanded the Twelfth and Fifth Corps, constituting the right wing of the Union army, to get ready to attack, and that he would give the signal as soon as the Sixth Corps arrived within supporting distance. Slocum—whom General Sherman afterwards said was as capable of commanding 80,000 men as he was—carefully examined the ground in his front, with its uneven surface, woods, hills and streams, and reported to Meade adversely and advised against making the attack. General Meade then surveyed the field with the view of attacking by his front, or left, and then summoned his corps commanders to a conference. Sickles did not come, but sent word that his corps, on the extreme left, was threatened with an attack and that he could not leave. Thereupon Meade sent him a peremptory order to attend the conference at once. Sickles then went, and as he rode up, Longstreet's guns opened upon his lines. Meade told him not to dismount, but return to his command. Meade reenforced him heavily and saved him from utter rout. The assault of Longstreet was the opening of the battle of that day. Slocum's decision and advice were wise. Had Slocum made that attack it would have been on Ewell's corps, which would have allowed Longstreet's and Hill's corps to advance against the Third and Second—Sickles's and Hancock's corps—which were inferior numerically, and they would have been driven back against Meade's attacking column, which Ewell could have held at bay for a time. Lee would have thus gained the advantage of position and Meade would inevitably have lost the battle. Slocum's advice and Sickles's wise disposition of his corps saved Meade from dishonor and the Army of the Potomac from defeat—two New York Union Democrats.

Inasmuch as General Lee did not have Longstreet seize the Round Tops in the forenoon, he had better have awaited the results of that conference; and had it been to attack him it would have been to his advantage, for as

Stonewall Jackson said on his death bed, "My troops sometimes fail to drive the enemy from their position, but theirs always fail to drive my men from their position." But of course Lee was not aware of that conference.

The Yankees did not occupy the top of Big Round Top until after dark. It was dark when my regiment reached the valley, and here we bivouacked for the night. After all had gotten up, I ordered the roll of the companies to be called. When the battle commenced, four hours previously, mine was the strongest and finest regiment in Hood's division. Its effectives numbered about five hundred officers and men. Now two hundred and twenty-three enlisted men answered at roll-call, and more than one-half of the officers had been left on the field—only nineteen answered to their names; but some of the officers and men came up in the course of the night and next morning, who had been overcome by the heat during the advance the previous evening.

Some of the men that night voluntarily went back across the mountain, and in the darkness penetrated the Federal lines, for the purpose of removing some of our wounded. They reached the scene and started out with some of the wounded officers, but were discovered and shot at by the Federal pickets, and had in consequence to leave the wounded, but succeeded in getting back to the regiment, and brought to me Lieutenant Cody's knife and pocket-book. These men reported to me that Big Round Top was, even at that late hour, occupied by only a thin skirmish line. I am sorry that I do not remember the names of those brave men who voluntarily went within the enemy's lines to relieve and save from capture wounded comrades.

Soon after the advance began the gallant Lieut.-Col. Isaac B. Feagin was shot through the knee, which necessitated amputation of the limb. The major was voluntarily with the wagon-train, and consequently I had no field officer to assist me. I discovered some time before we reached Gettysburg that my brother, Lieut. John A. Oates, had fallen behind some distance, and was reported sick. I sent back a horse for him and he came up. Just before we advanced I went to him where he was lying on the ground in rear of his company, and saw at once that he was sick. I thereupon told him not to go into the action, but when we advanced to remain where he was, because he was unable to bear the fatigue. He replied, with the most dogged and fiery determination, "Brother, I will not do it. If I were to remain here people would say that I did it through cowardice; no, sir, I am an officer and will never disgrace the uniform I wear; I shall go through, unless I am killed, which I think is quite likely." These were the last words ever passed between us. When he fell, struck by several balls, Lieut. Isaac H. Parks, who had been his school-fellow, ran to him and dragged him behind a large stone, and just as Parks let him down another ball struck one of his hands and carried away his little finger. Parks was for many years after the war a prominent lawyer at Rutledge, Crenshaw County, Alabama, and represented his county in both branches of the legislature, and in the Constitutional Convention of 1875, and died in 1900. Lieutenant Cody, a boy about eighteen years old, the best officer I ever saw of his age, except Major Latimer, of the artillery, fell near my brother, mortally wounded. When we retreated they, with most of our wounded and eighty-four men who were not, were taken prisoners, and the wounded were removed to the Federal field hospital, where they were as well cared for as wounded soldiers in the hands of an enemy ever are. Cody lived twenty-one and my brother twenty-three days. A Miss Lightner, a Virginia lady and Southern sympathizer, nursed them to the last, and Doctor Reid, of the One Hundred and Fifty-fifth Pennsylvania Regiment, did all that he could for them and had them decently buried when they died. He sent to me by flag of truce my brother's old gold watch, his pocket-book, and money. I endeavored for years after the war to find Doctor Reid, without success, but finally obtained his address, Lancaster, Pennsylvania, and had a very pleasant and satisfactory correspondence with him. I had theretofore never had an opportunity of expressing to him the full measure of my gratitude for his attention to my brother and Lieutenant Cody. The dear, good ministering angel, Miss Lightner, has long since passed beyond the arena of bloody battles and grim death, to reap that priceless reward which is promised to the charitable and the good. Some of our wounded were not treated so well. Some were not removed from the places where they fell for two or three days. Sergeant Johns, of Company B, had one of his thighs broken, and lay where he fell, in all the hard rain of the 3d and 4th days of July, and was not removed until the battle was over and Lee on his way back to Virginia. He lay on his back, could not turn, and kept from drowning by putting his hat over his face. He recovered, and was alive several years after the war, and living in Texas.

Capt. J. Henry Ellison was a son of the Rev. Dr. Ellison, a distinguished Methodist divine. When I gave the order to change direction to the left to drive the Twentieth Maine Regiment, he did not hear it with distinctness. He stepped toward me, and placing his hand behind his ear inquired, "What is the order, Colonel?" I repeated it. He turned to his company and cried out, "Forward, my men; forward!" and fell shot through the head. I saw the ball strike him; that is, I was looking at him when it did. He fell upon his left shoulder, turned upon his back, raised his arms, clenched his fists, gave one shudder, his arms fell, and he was dead. He wore that day a very fine captain's uniform which I had presented to him after my promotion, and I thought at the moment of his death that he was the handsomest and finest specimen of manhood that ever went down upon a field of carnage.

There was no better regiment in the Confederate Army than the Fifteenth Alabama, and when properly commanded, if it failed to carry any point against which it was thrown no other single regiment need try it. The long and rapid march, the climb of Great Round Top's rugged front without water impaired its power of endurance, but it fought hard and persistently until ordered to retreat. The other regiments of the brigade did their duty at Gettysburg, but the Fifteenth struck the hardest knot.

The following from the pen of Col. W. F. Perry describes "The Devil's Den" and the assault of his regiment, the Forty-fourth Alabama, upon it:

> Large rocks, from six to fifteen feet high, are thrown together in confusion over a considerable area, and yet so disposed as to leave everywhere among them winding passages carpeted with moss. Many of its recesses are never visited by the sunshine, and a cavernous coolness pervades the air within it.
>
> A short distance to the east the frowning bastions of Little Round Top rise 200 feet above the level of the plain. An abrupt elevation, thirty or forty feet high, itself buttressed with rocks, constitutes the western boundary of this strange formation.
>
> The view was imposing. Little Round Top, crowned with artillery, resembled a volcano in eruption; while the hillock near the Devil's Den resembled a small one. The distance between them, diminished by the view in perspective, appeared as a secondary crater near its base. It was evident that a formidable task was before us.
>
> The enemy were as invisible to us as we were to them. The presence of a battery of artillery of course implied the presence of a strong supporting force of infantry. Of its strength, its position, and the nature of its defenses we were in total ignorance. We were soon to learn. As the line

emerged from the woods into the open space mentioned above, a sheet of flame burst from the rocks less than fifty yards away. A few scattering shots in the beginning gave warning in time for my men to fall down, and thus largely to escape the effect of the main volley. They doubtless seemed to the enemy to be all dead, but the volley of the fire which they immediately returned proved that they were very much alive.

No language can express the intensity of the solicitude with which I surveyed the strange, wild situation which had suddenly burst upon my view. Upon the decision of a moment depended the honor of my command, and perhaps the lives of many brave men. I knew that, if called upon, they would follow me, and felt confident that the place could be carried by an impetuous charge. But then what? There were no supporting troops in sight. A heavy force of the enemy might envelop and overpower us. It was certain that we should be exposed to a plunging, enfilading fire from Little Round Top. And yet, the demoralization and shame of a retreat, and an exposure to be shot in the back were not to be thought of.

Before the enemy had time to load their guns a decision was made. Leaping over the prostrate line before me, I shouted the order, "Forward!" and started for the rocks. The response was a bound, a yell, and a rush, and in ten seconds my men were pouring into the Den, and the enemy were escaping from the opposite side. A few prisoners were taken. Two soldiers of the Fourth Maine Regiment surrendered to me in person at the edge of the rocks as my line overtook and passed me.

In the charge the left wing of the regiment struck the hill on which the artillery were stationed, and the center and the right swept into the rocks east of it. Maj. George W. Carey led the left wing up the hill, and bounding over the rocks on its crest, landed among the artillerymen ahead of the line, and received their surrender. One of the officers of the battery, whom I met soon after, complimented his gallantry and that of his men in the highest terms. The

Major a few moments later found me near the foot of the hill, completely prostrated by heat and excessive exertion. He exhibited several swords as an evidence that the artillery had surrendered, and complained that guns from both sides were playing upon the position. This I knew to be true as to the Federal side. At the very entrance of the labyrinth a spherical caseshot from Round Top had exploded very near my head and thrown its deadly contents against a rock almost within my reach. He was ordered to hurry back and withdraw the men from the crest so that they could find shelter on the sides of the hill.

In a very short time he came back in great haste and informed me that a force of the enemy large enough to envelop our position was moving down upon us. I sprang to my feet with the intention of climbing the hill to see the situation and determine what to do; but found myself unable to stand without support. While we were anxiously discussing the situation a line of battle, moving in splendid style, swept in from Seminary Ridge upon the left, and met the threatening force. One of us remarked, "There is Benning; we are all right now." Benning's march was so directed that his right lapped upon my left, and poured over the hill upon which were the abandoned guns.

A furious battle now began along his entire line, as well as my own, which had pressed through to the north side of the rocks. It has always been to me a source of sincere regret that my disability, which continued until after nightfall, prevented me from seeing anything that occurred after the arrival of Benning's line.

My loss was comparatively light, considering the desperate character of the fighting. This was due to three causes: The happy dodge given the first volley of the enemy, the rush made upon them before they had time to reload, and the protection afterwards afforded by the rocks. The killed and wounded numbered ninety-two, a little over one-fourth of those who went into action.

Thus ended the second day's fighting.

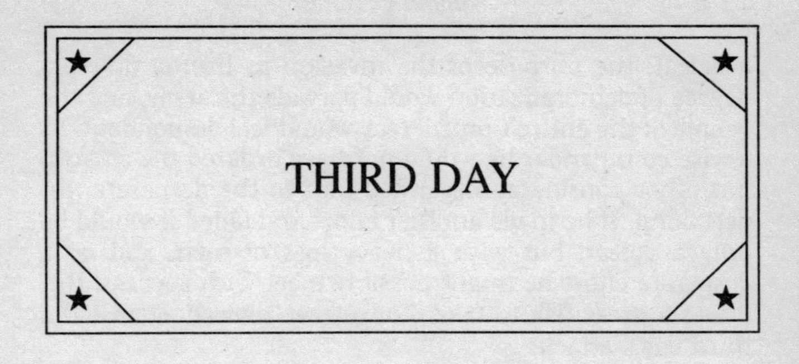

THIRD DAY

The Lessons of the Second Day's Fighting Not Heeded—The Arrival of Stuart, and What Was Expected of Him—The Greatest Artillery Duel the World Ever Knew—Pickett's Charge—The Cotton States Troops *Versus* the Border States—General Farnsworth's Attempt to Take a Confederate Battery—The Fifteenth Leaves the Field Without Orders—Awaiting An Attack—Responsibility for the Loss of the Battle—Some Deductions Based on Possibilities—Casualties of the Battle.

THE DESPERATE FIGHTING of the 2d had accomplished no substantial results. The great question with General Lee was whether to give up the contest on that field and withdraw or make a further effort. It was a momentous question. If he withdrew it was an acknowledgment, not that he was beaten, but that he had failed to beat Meade, which, the way things are accepted by the world, would be considered a defeat; the purpose of the invasion as having failed, a degree of demoralization would pervade the army, and the people of the entire Confederacy would feel despondent. As a wise commander he would not have ordered the assault, but other considerations urged him to the desperate undertaking. If he made another effort and failed it would be only a defeat, but with a heavy loss of men, and by a desperate effort he might possibly meet with success. But it was a great risk to take. Longstreet advised against the third day's attack.

One of the prominent characteristics of General Lee was his boldness and the hazardous moves he many times made. Meade during the night of the 2d strengthened his already strong and almost impregnable position. The disadvantage of Lee's position was that at least a mile of open wheat field interposed between it and the position held by the Union troops.

To traverse this open space under the fire of massed artillery and a double line of infantry behind a stone wall was too hazardous and success too near impossible. General Longstreet says in his book that he strenuously advised against it and still insisted on turning Meade's left and flanking him out of position. Lee, with all his robust daring and adventurous spirit, should not have ordered the impossible, as was apparent to the skilled observer. But about nightfall of the 2d General Stuart reported to his chief. Lee then resolved to try the desperate venture and directed him to move all of his available cavalry during that night through the woods in rear and to the left of Ewell's corps and get to a position from which after the Confederate artillery ceased its fire he could charge right into the rear of the Federal line and endeavor to meet the head of the assaulting column of Pickett. General Stuart made his way as far as practicable that night. But at daylight his movement was discovered and his column was soon confronted by a superior force of cavalry under General Gregg, supported by infantry and artillery. Stuart maneuvered for position, but could not get an advantageous one. The men and horses of the splendid brigades of Hampton, Fitzhugh Lee and William H. F. Lee were tired, fatigued and worn down by their long ride, constant vigils and loss of sleep, but this occasion was to be the culmination of their most superhuman efforts. If they could make a grand charge in the rear which would enable the Pickett assault in front to cut the Union army in twain, the cup of Stuart's glory and that of his alert and invincible cavalry would be full to overflowing. This was the immense stake to be won if possible.

In front all the forenoon was spent in placing batteries and arranging the charging column, under Longstreet's direction, who was habitually slow; he had no faith in the success of the battle from the first and did not wish to direct this grand assault.

Pickett's division arrived early that morning and were the only fresh troops which had not been engaged. That division belonged to Longstreet's corps and to him was assigned the duty of arranging and conducting the proposed assault. He did not approve it—his heart was not in it. One hundred and fifty guns—more than one-half of all that were in Lee's army—were put in position under the direction of General Alexander, chief of artillery of Longstreet's corps.

A little after 12 o'clock, at a given signal, all these guns opened fire upon the Federals along Cemetery Ridge and were at once replied to by at least an equal number. It was the most powerful cannonade that ever occurred in the world's history of warfare. The ground fairly trembled, the air was sulphurous and full of smoke, caissons were blown up, guns dismounted, horses killed and for two hours the earth was torn in holes by the bursting shells. The bombardment at Toulon in 1793 under young Napoleon was more terrible in its destructiveness, but with less than one-third as many guns.

The Union General Sickles said: "Lee's 200 guns, answered by as many on our side, made but little impression on our lines." The reason was that their infantry were all protected by the stone fence, and earthworks thrown up the night before, and most of their men lay behind the crest of the ridge. Soon after the great battle of the batteries ceased and as the smoke lifted Pickett's division of 5,000 men—fifteen Virginia regiments, formed in column of brigades—supported on the right by Wilcox's five Alabama regiments and on the left by Pender's division of North Carolinians, began a rapid advance against the center of the Union line. The column was at least three-quarters of a mile wide, three lines deep, and contained 15,000 men.

All was silent until this immense column, moving rapidly forward to the assault, came within range of the Federal line, when a terrible artillery fire was opened on the determined men. They were soon in range of the small arms; as men fell the ranks closed up and kept right on. General Sickles said: "Longstreet's column advancing toward Cemetery Ridge was torn by our artillery and crushed by the fire of Hancock's infantry and disappeared like ocean waves dashing against a rock-ribbed shore."

When about half the distance had been traversed, without sending any order to Wilcox, Pickett changed his column by the left flank, half a brigade's length, which made a gap between him and Wilcox of about two hundred yards. Why he did this the writer was never able to learn and Wilcox said years afterwards that it was never explained to him. General Longstreet states in his book that it was because the Union line on their right overlapped the Confederate assaulting column. It was a fatal mistake.

General Pickett himself halted at a barn about three hundred yards from the position of the Union troops and remained there until his division was repulsed. This opening exposed Pickett's right flank to the fire of Stanard's Vermont brigade. General Stanard changed front forward on first company of the first battalion and brought his whole brigade in line exactly on the flank of Pickett's column. Wilcox was too hotly engaged in front to turn on Stanard. Pickett's men rushed forward to, and some of them over, the stone fence, behind which lay two or three lines of battle. It is called "Pickett's charge" because he commanded the division of direction, but Brigadier-General Armistead, whose brigade was in support, led the charge when near the works and he was killed inside the Union line while holding up his cap on the point of his sword as a guide to his men. That spot is marked by a stone monument with raised letters on it, "High tide of the rebellion." Garnett's brigade came gallantly up to the stone wall and he was killed; Kemper's next, who was wounded and captured. Pickett's column was broken. Trimble, who succeeded General Pender when that officer was killed or mortally wounded in the advance with Pettigrew, came up on a line with Pickett's men, but was shot, from which he lost his leg, and the whole column was repulsed with heavy loss. He was then sixty-five years of age. He lived near thirty years after and died in Baltimore, an utterly unreconstructed rebel, in 1889.

Pickett lost all of his brigadiers and field officers except one major. Only 1,300 of the 5,000 returned from the charge. But I do not wish to be understood as asserting that they were all killed or wounded, for many hundreds of them—a majority—surrendered unhurt. The point assaulted was a very strong one by nature, which had been made still stronger by the engineers and pioneer corps the night before. Meade had double lines of infantry, hundreds of pieces of artillery, strong reserves, and was defended by batteries under the command of able and experienced officers. It was a perfect Gibraltar. The assault was made most gallantly by troops who had never been whipped upon any field and had often won victories against double their number. They had the utmost confidence in General Lee and the officers nearer to them. But no troops can long withstand a heavy fire in front and on the flank at the same time. Had it been otherwise possible for Pickett's column to have bisected Meade's army, that gap between him and Wilcox was fatal.

With that open space between him and Wilcox, Pickett invited ruin and it came. General Hancock was standing near the left of the line of Stanard's Vermont brigade of fresh troops, and his eagle eye saw the exposure of Pickett's flank and he was quick to take advantage of it. The very object of a support on the flank of a charging column is to prevent just what occurred here. Pickett at the barn never tried to close the gap. Wilcox told the writer that he did not receive any order to keep closed on Pickett and that he kept straight ahead, because no order came to him. But he was a West Pointer, an educated and experienced soldier, and knew the danger of such a gap and should have, even without orders, conformed to the movement of Pickett's column. Longstreet, who was conducting the grand assault, should have so ordered him. Stanard, just as Hancock was wounded, changed front forward and formed his line squarely on the flank of Pickett's column and a few volleys made more than 1,500 of the men surrender. As soon as this was accomplished, Stanard's line about-faced and moved to the attack of Wilcox's flank, and this, with the fire which his brigade was receiving in front, drove him from the field with decimated ranks. The demoralization produced instantly by Stanard's maneuvers, with a heavy fire from a double line of infantry in front, was enough to repel the most determined assault of the bravest veterans. Years after the war General Stanard accompanied the writer to the field and showed him the ground upon which these maneuvers occurred. Stanard having lost one arm, I, being a member of Congress, voted to increase his pension from fifty to one hundred dollars per month.

The total casualties in Pickett's division—killed, wounded and captured—in round numbers was 2,900. The total number in Hood's division of the day before was 2,300, but only 450 of these were captured.

Pickett's men were good soldiers and the people of that State just as hospitable, patriotic and noble as any in the world, but they did not do all the hard fighting and perform all the desperate deeds of valor. The North Carolinians on the left of Pickett's column went as far at Gettysburg as the Virginians did, and were under as heavy a fire, but they were not flanked and a less number of them surrendered as prisoners.

Without the least prejudice I do believe now and thought so all along through the war, that the men from the Cotton States (and the farther west the more so) were better soldiers and harder fighters than those from the Border States.

The absence of philosophic reason for this apparent difference for a long time puzzled me, but I finally attributed it to the difference between the frontiersman and the citizen of more refined and regular habits of the older States. I therefore believe, having inspected the position since the war, that had Hood's division, with him to handle it and fresh as it was before the fight of the previous day, composed as it was of Georgians, Alabamians and Texans (one regiment being from Arkansas) made that charge, with proper supports, notwithstanding the double lines of Union soldiers with heavy reserves behind that stone fence, the position would have been carried and held. But in justice to Pickett's division, it must be admitted that at

Gettysburg Hood's was 2,500 men the stronger, two of Pickett's best brigades having been left in Virginia.

General Stuart tried hard to carry out Lee's instructions. He tried to charge into Meade's rear, but the resistance he met with was too great. It was a grand combat which ensued. Years after the battle General Sickles said: "General Stuart's cavalry sent by Lee to assault our rear while the Confederate army attacked in front was driven back by Gregg. Twelve thousand sabres flashing in the July sun, the tread of twelve thousand horses charging over the turf revealed the greatest cavalry combat ever seen on this continent." Many dusty gray and blue young riders, amidst the deadly roar of musketry, the sharp rattle of carbines, the flashing of sabres and the thunders of the artillery, embraced the sleep that knows no waking in this world. Hampton, Stuart's first lieutenant, was seriously wounded and his repulse was complete. Lee was not whipped, but his bold assaults upon Meade's front and rear had been repulsed with heavy losses—it may well be said irreparable ones, yet the morale of that superb army of earnest patriots was still unbroken. Their confidence in the skill of their commander remained unshaken, though he had ordered them to perform an impossibility—they had been repulsed and were torn and bleeding.*

On the morning of the 3d of July Law's brigade still constituted the right of the Confederate line and lay along the second foot, up near the abrupt rise on the south side of Big Round Top, my regiment on the right. The old rocks piled up as breastworks still mark the place where the brigade lay. Kilpatrick's Union cavalry were in the woods just on our right flank, which necessitated the extension of

*Longstreet said in his book (p. 404): "Forty thousand men, unsupported as we were, could not have carried the position at Gettysburg. * * * It is simply out of the question for a lesser force to march over broad, open fields and carry a fortified front occupied by a greater force of seasoned troops."

a line of pickets for some distance southward and nearly at right angles to our line. Sharp-shooters from the top of the mountain made it a very precarious business for our men to go down to our rear for water. A member of the Fourth Alabama, on picket and acting as a scout on our southern line, overheard in the woods some loud talk between Generals Kilpatrick and Farnsworth and reported it to General Law at once, by which he was enabled to prepare for what was coming. It seems that Kilpatrick ordered Farnsworth to take a squadron, or battalion of cavalry, and charge through our skirmish line and capture a six-gun North Carolina battery in our rear, Captain Riley, a burly old Irishman, commanding. Farnsworth protested against it until Kilpatrick said, "By God, if you are afraid to go, I will lead the charge myself!" This so piqued Farnsworth, who had but recently been promoted, that he resolved to lead the charge, and did so. He first encountered the First Texas Regiment lying behind a low fence, which was charged over, the Texas regiment having been deployed as skirmishers, and he went for the battery; but the fire from it and a Georgia regiment and a cooking detail on the south caused him to circle around to the west side of the battery, but here he found the Fourth Alabama advancing to meet him. He turned and assailed the battery again, which kept up a constant eruption of grape and canister. His men attacked with their sabres, and a gunner knocked two of them off their horses with a rammer. I had been ordered from the right to move with all possible expedition to the relief of the battery. This I did, rear in front. I did not take time to counter-march, but threw out a few skirmishers as we moved.

We passed through an open space and crossed Plum Run, the same little muddy stream I described in detailing our first advance, and as we rose the ascent in a copse of woods some eight or ten cavalrymen came in between us and the battery. One of its guns just at this moment fired a double charge of canister-shot at the cavalry, which, missing them, came over our heads and through the ranks, making a noise resembling that of the wings of a covey of young partridges, but did us no damage. The officer commanding the cavalry, with pistol in hand, ordered the skirmishers to surrender, to which they replied with a volley. The cavalry commander, his horse, and one of his men fell to the ground, and the others dashed away. Lieutenant Adrian, commanding the skirmishers, with a carbine in hand, advanced and said to the wounded officer, who still grasped his pistol and was trying to rise, notwithstanding he had received three severe and perhaps mortal wounds, "Now you surrender." With an oath he swore he would not do it, and placing his pistol to his own body shot himself through the heart. I halted my regiment and allowed the men to rest where they were. The lieutenant with the skirmishers was Adrian, of the Forty-fourth Alabama Regiment, who was only temporarily with us, having left his own regiment with the carbine, as he said, to try to capture a horse from the cavalry.

I had the facts above related as to the death of Farnsworth stated to me then and there by Adrian, and from what I saw at a distance of not more than fifty steps I am satisfied of their truth. I did not go to the dead man at once, but sat down to rest. One of my skirmishers soon came and said, "Colonel, don't you want that Yankee major's shoulder straps?" holding them up before me. He supposed that the dead man's rank was that of major because he had but one star on each shoulder strap—a single star on the coat collar indicating that rank among the Confederates. I took them and saw at once he was a general, and went to the body. The men were coming up to it in little squads and looking at the dead man in silent amazement on account of Lieutenant Adrian's statement. Upon examination I found letters in his breast-pocket addressed to Gen. E. J. Farnsworth. I read enough to see that one of the letters was from his wife. I then destroyed them to prevent their falling into the hands of irresponsible parties. The monument which has been erected to him of cannon balls is at least one hundred and fifty yards north of where he fell. A short time after this incident, now late in the afternoon, I was ordered to take up an advanced position in the woods facing east and at right angles to our line at the base of Round Top, but separated from it by a half mile or more southward. The rain, which invariably succeeds a heavy battle, came pouring down. There was a strong line of dismounted cavalrymen within one hundred yards of our front. Night drew on, and I had not received any order. I was there in obedience to an order. The surroundings presented the most weird and lonely appearance. The dead lay scattered through the drear and sombre woods; the fast-scudding clouds overhead shut out all save just enough light, at short intervals, to get a glimpse of the solemn scenes around us. Not a sound was heard; the stillness was awful. I knew, intuitively, that there was something wrong. I felt it, and could not have given any other reason for my apprehension. I started to ride back through the woods toward the place where we had left our comrades, to ascertain the state of affairs. Before I had gone a hundred yards I heard a gun or pistol cap explode a short distance from me. I turned, rode back, and called for Sergt. Wm. R. Holley, of my old company, a brave soldier, but a very cautious, watchful, prudent, and sensible man. (He died at his home in Henry County in 1880.) I told Holley in a low tone what had occurred, and ordered him to creep through the woods, observing everything right and left closely, until he could discover what was there, and then report to me. I rode back a short distance and waited. The leaves were wet, and he glided noiselessly forward; I could not hear him walk. Within a short time

Holley returned and reported in his usual broad accent, "A line of Yankees out thar. I went up close to some of them; they are thar sho." I was satisfied of the truth of it. My videtes reported the enemy still near, within one hundred yards in front of us. It was after nightfall, very dark, with Yankees near to us in front and rear. No orders came, and I was satisfied none would come, except from our enemies, and that would be to surrender whenever they found us isolated from the main body of our troops. I resolved to act upon my own judgment, abandon the post without orders, and get out of there. I knew the penalty for disobedience of orders and abandoning my post in the presence of the enemy—it was infamous death if I made a mistake. I was sure of my position, and I took the responsibility, grave as it was. I therefore drew in the videttes from my left and front, faced the regiment to the right, and ordered the men silently to march after me. No man spoke above a whisper nor made any noise. After performing a considerable circuit, the rain pouring down at intervals, we got into the open field and marched westward until we heard troops in our front building breastworks. I did not know which side, but ventured, and to our great relief found our place in the line of Longstreet's corps, and thus escaped from a most perilous situation. We were fortunate, too, in reaching that line at our brigade.

I then learned that late that evening the greater portion of the Union army had been massed to move against Longstreet and crush him, and that just as the movement began General Lee ordered him to retire on a line with Hill's corps, and fortify his position. This the troops were then busily engaged in doing. If any order was ever sent to me to withdraw, I never received it. Colonel Sheffield, of the Forty-eighth Alabama, was commanding the brigade. He said that when the retrograde movement began he sent Tom Sinclaire, brigade courier, with an order to me to withdraw, but the courier was captured and did not reach me. The Union army had advanced, and I was nearly surrounded, and happened to take the only safe retreat. Had I obeyed orders I and all of those with me would have finished our service as prisoners of war, a thing I always dreaded more than the bullets of the enemy.

The next day, July 4, we celebrated by awaiting an attack of the Federals, but they came not. Thus far the Confederates had done all the attacking. They awaited our assaults. Now that they were on their own soil they acted strictly on the defensive, and thereby obtained the advantage of selecting their position. That was just what Longstreet desired Lee to do. But his supplies might soon have been exhausted, and he was too far from his base to readily or easily replenish; hence his defensive policy was annulled by Meade's defensive or waiting policy. Under the circumstances it was masterful in Meade. Lee could not wait; he had to be moving; he could not wait when so far from his base of supplies, and Meade perceived the situation.

As Meade would not assault him in the open field, on the morning of July 5 Lee began his retreat toward the Potomac. There was no hurry, no demoralization. The troops marched slowly, and frequently halted to give time to the wagon-trains and the wounded. The high-tide of the Confederacy had reached its flood. This day began its ebb, which reached low-water mark at Appomattox nearly two years thereafter.

When our march began I rode to our field hospital and saw as many of our wounded as I could before leaving. The sadness of parting with Colonel Feagin I will never forget, but he could not be removed. He had barely rallied from the shock of amputating his leg. He suffered a second amputation while in prison. But he stood it bravely, was ultimately exchanged, honorably retired, lived many years after the war, was sheriff of Barbour, and the Probate Judge of Bullock County, and died in 1901. Showers continued on the 5th, and after marching about three miles we stopped, built fires, and dried by them for two hours. Hood's division was not molested by the enemy on its retreat, but the Union cavalry captured many of our wounded and burned many Confederate wagons. When we reached Williamsport we found the Federal cavalry, and a rise in the river had broken and carried away or destroyed a part of the pontoons, and the river was not fordable. Lee formed his line of battle some miles below Williamsport and opposite to Falling Waters. It ran from the river above to the river below, across a semi-circular or horse-shoe bend, with his wagon trains, ordnance, and stores within and the cavalry well to the front. We threw up an entrenchment with a piece of artillery between every two regiments of infantry; and thus for several days Lee waited and tried to provoke an attack from General Meade. The latter was urged by the Washington Government to attack. Now that he had defeated Lee and had him at bay, not to allow him to escape was the urgent injunction of the Washington authorities. But Meade was too smart to throw away the morale of Gettysburg. He had been reenforced until all of his losses had been restored. His army was now over 100,000 strong. (See his testimony before the Joint Committee of Congress on the Conduct of the War.) Meade summoned his chief generals for a council of war.

There Lee stood, right before them, with his back to the Potomac, offering battle every day and every hour. A defeat would destroy him, and he had not more than forty thousand men in line. Some of the Union generals were anxious for a fight, but the majority thought otherwise, and Meade did the smartest thing of his life when he decided against an attack. There would have been no stragglers, and every Confederate would have fought as in a death struggle. We all desired his attack. But Meade would not come on. After days had elapsed, the rains continuing, Lee transferred his army to the Virginia shore. One corps forded the Potomac at Williamsport and the others crossed over a pontoon bridge near Falling Waters. General Pettigrew was killed, and by mismanagement of subordinates and a ruse of the Yankee cavalry, Lee lost 2,000 prisoners. Thus ended the Pennsylvania campaign, the second invasion of Union territory.

General Lee's army was never much stronger numerically, nor its morale better, than at Gettysburg. The rank and file were never more confident of success. He was over-confident. At Waterloo Napoleon and his army were radiant and confident of success. But in each case the unlooked-for came. The French became panic-stricken and fled in disgrace, while the Confederates remained cool, steady, and free from panic.

Generals Early, Pendleton, and Fitzhugh Lee have charged in publications that Longstreet was responsible for the loss of the battle. He has with much ingenuity attempted a refutation of the charge, and has, perhaps to the minds of most readers, at least partially succeeded. Their charge is based upon his alleged disobedience of orders to attack and capture the Round Tops early on the morning of July 2, and his inactivity and tardiness in making the attack that day. Longstreet has proven in his book, by a letter from Colonel Taylor, who was Lee's Adjutant-General, that he did not give Longstreet a written order. Taylor says that General Lee never gave written orders to his corps commanders, but informed them orally of what he wished them to do. And as to the charge of tardiness, all that he heard Lee say was that "Longstreet is a magnificent fighter after he becomes engaged, but he is so slow." And General Hood said to Longstreet that General Lee was anxious for him to attack. Longstreet was awaiting the arrival of Pickett's division, and said that he did not like to go into a battle with one boot off.

General Early also charges Longstreet with failing to give the commanding general that hearty and cordial support which was essential to success. All of these charges Longstreet denied. As to the first of the charges, so far as a written order is concerned, he has answered successfully. But no doubt Lee expressed to him a desire that he should early on the 2d occupy the Round Tops and the Devil's Den, which he knew that Longstreet could easily do with his seven brigades then present, which had not fired a gun in that battle.

Modesty dictates to me, a mere subordinate officer, with limited opportunities for observing what was transpiring on the field of strife, excepting on one part of it, to enter cautiously upon a critical discussion of the conduct of a corps commander in that great battle so far as my personal knowledge extends, but the truth of history can only be vindicated by bringing all of the testimony before the impartial and intelligent reader. Mine, as to the humble part I bore, is of no great importance; but from the position I happened to occupy, subsequent investigation, and several visits to that field since the war, I can truly say that I do know some facts which have an important bearing on the question of responsibility for the failure of the Confederates to win the battle. The truth of history and a sense of duty to the heroic conduct and sacrifices of the noble men I had the honor to command, and all Confederates who participated in the battle, demand that the whole truth be told, and hence I will contribute all that I know to that end. I was a close observer then, and have examined reports and studied that battle carefully since to obtain the truth. The campaign may have been an unwise or ill-advised one; but General Lee in his nobleness of soul put that question beyond the pale of discussion by assuming more than was chargeable to him, the entire responsibility for the failure. I have not sufficient personal knowledge of the charge against General Longstreet to be a witness against him, but have formed my conclusions from those things of which I was cognizant and the statement of facts and arguments of the respective parties. General Longstreet's book, "From Manassas to Appomattox," in giving his account of this great battle in its general tone bears strong evidence to my mind of the truth of General Early's charge against him. General Longstreet had advised against the campaign and the battle, and his heart was not in it. He desired Lee to turn Meade's left flank and to thus force him out of his strong position. He knew, too, that an army cannot fight long without rations. To have rations on hand often taxes the greatest ingenuity of the commanding general. Did Lee order Longstreet to attack the Round Tops and the Devil's Den on the morning of the 2d? If so, why did not Longstreet obey? If Lee did not give him a positive order, or if Lee did, and Longstreet disobeyed it, the onus was on Lee as well as Longstreet, because he had the power as commanding general to have enforced it.

General Lee made his great mistake when he did not, on the morning of the 2d, throw Longstreet's troops on the Federal left and capture the Round Tops and the Devil's Den, which were not then occupied in force. He never recovered from it. He knew the importance of the points, and had the power to have ordered Longstreet's troops to take them independently of his wishes. Lee was a great general and a good man. He wished to avoid wounding the feelings of his old army comrade and friend. He was too lenient with his corps commanders. He never gave one a written order, says Taylor, but merely expressed his desire as to what should be done, leaving to each the largest discretion. When Longstreet did attack he obeyed literally the order to attack up the Emmitsburg Road, when he knew that circumstances had changed after Lee had given him the order. And in the forenoon, when General Hood told him that Lee was seemingly anxious for him to attack that morning, Longstreet replied that he was awaiting the arrival of Pickett. He was then subordinating Lee's wishes to his own preferences. Lee should have relieved him from command and have ordered his troops under Hood or McLaws to make the advance at once before those strong positions were occupied by the Federals. Instead, he indulged Longstreet's preference and his tardiness until Law's brigade arrived, when Lee gave him a positive order to move and how to attack, which Longstreet obeyed reluctantly, as indicated by his stubborn refusal to modify or change, notwithstanding the circumstances, then unknown to Lee, required it. Longstreet deserved to have been arrested and dismissed from the service as the least penalty his conduct merited. When Lee made his official report of the campaign and his failure to win the battle of Gettysburg, he said, "It was all my fault," and tendered his resignation, which Davis refused to accept, saying that there was no one who could fill Lee's place.

The surrender of Vicksburg on Independence Day was a strong appeal to the superstitions of men on both sides. It seemed ominous of ultimate success of the Union cause. The next morning the beginning of Lee's retreat and the bisection of the Confederacy by the fall of Vicksburg and Port Hudson, the greatest reverses which had occurred, sounded the death-knell of the Confederacy; but neither its governmental authorities, the soldiers, or citizens would see it or believe it. The Union soldiers were enthused, the Confederates depressed, though still ready to fight and die game for Dixie.

Gettysburg furnishes to the student of military history a more interesting chapter than the battles of Waterloo, Jena, Marengo, Austerlitz, or any of the great battles fought by Napoleon Bonaparte.

The great interest manifested in the battle since the war

is attributable to the fact that it was, and is, regarded as the turning-point in the great struggle—the war between the Southern States and the Union. The Confederacy, in fact, had but little chance of success after the spirit of volunteering subsided; but none of us were ready to admit it, and those who continued to fight manfully for the cause and win victories, almost from fate itself, began to despair when Lee turned back from Gettysburg.

Had he won that battle his objective point was Philadelphia, Pennsylvania, and he could not have been checked. Washington and Baltimore would have fallen, and the thousands of prisoners who would have been released from Fort McHenry, Point Lookout, and other prisons, and the volunteers from Maryland who would have joined Lee, would have made him resistless, and negotiations for peace would have followed. The independence of the Confederacy so near, and yet so far. The fatalists and the predestinarians believe that it was not to have been, but the writer cannot agree with them. It was not, yet it might have been—it was possible. Had the civil government of the Confederacy been equal to the military it would have been a success, and the independence of the Confederacy firmly established.

The strategy and movements of troops on each side were for a purpose and constituted an interesting study. Lee's strategy was superb, but the execution of his plans was bungling. Stonewall Jackson was dead, and there was no executive officer of equal ability to take his place.

The fighting was of details—a piecemeal. No solid assault was made against the entire Federal line, nor was support given at all points when necessary.

The Federal army held the interior line nearly in horseshoe shape and but four miles long. Meade could easily transfer troops from one point to another to support his line wherever attacked. The Confederate line around the outside was six and a half miles long, which rendered it next to impossible to transfer troops from one point to another, one, two, three, or five miles apart, and Lee had practically no reserves. These disadvantages of position and Meade's army 20,000 stronger, constitute a wonderfully fine tribute to the valor and devotion of the Confederates, and to the skill, strategy and persistency of Lee. If he had had 50,000 negro troops or half that number commanded by white officers, which was practicable, he would have worsted Meade, have gone to Philadelphia and have won the independence of the Confederacy.

It is remarkable how small an occurrence or omission, trivial in itself, often turns the tide of battle, and changes governments and the maps of nations. Victor Hugo says that at Waterloo the shake of a peasant's head dethroned the Emperor Napoleon and changed the map of Europe. No battle in the world's history ever had greater consequences dependent upon it, nor so many mishaps, or lost opportunities—especially on the side of the Confederates—as that of Gettysburg. That was the O'Hane of the Confederacy.

Had Meade drawn on his heavy reserves immediately after Lee's repulse on the third day and sent 40,000 men to intercept his communications, block the mountain passes and thus obstruct his line of retreat toward the Potomac and Virginia, and when he began to move have pressed hard on his rear, he would have crippled Lee much worse than he did and with some probability of his destruction. But that general was so delighted that he did not get whipped at Gettysburg and so carried away with the renown of having repulsed and turned Lee homeward that he thought it wise to let well enough alone and thus he lost a great opportunity.

1. Had Stuart been less enthusiastic, not have gone so far east and have kept between the two armies, Lee would

have been more fully advised of every movement of his adversary, would have been better able to anticipate him, have selected his battle-ground and have had the cavalry fresh and in good plight in the battle and protecting his communications.

2. Had Ewell followed up the success of the first day, have driven the broken and defeated corps beyond the strong position of Cemetery Ridge that evening, or if he had occupied Culp's Hill before the Union troops did, which was easy enough done at any time until occupied by the Twelfth Corps after 9 o'clock P.M., no further fighting would have occurred at Gettysburg. General Lee ordered him to occupy Culp's Hill, but it could not be done after the Twelfth Corps arrived. Ramseur ascended with his brigade before dark, but was withdrawn.
3. Had Longstreet's attack on the 2d been made early in the forenoon, when there were no Federal troops on either of the Round Tops, instead of at 3.30 o'clock in the afternoon, he would easily have captured both mountain tops—the key-point of the entire Federal position—and Lee would have had a complete victory.
4. If the Forty-eighth Alabama had not been transferred to the left, but had remained to protect the rear, it would have taken care of the sharp-shooters, Colonel Oates's flanking column would have captured Little Round Top before Vincent's brigade arrived and it would have won the battle for the Confederates. No troops were then on Little Round Top but Hazlett's battery and Berdan's sharp-shooters, and they would have been captured or swept aside by the flankers in five minutes.
5. When Colonel Oates's two regiments reached the top of Great Round Top, had they been reenforced with artillery it would have commanded Little Round Top

and a part of Cemetery Ridge, which would have been untenable, and have enabled the Confederates to win the field.

6. Had not Lieutenant-Colonel Bulger fallen, which, in part, caused his companies to retreat, in ten minutes Oates's command would have captured Little Round Top, which would have given the Confederates the key-point and have enabled them to win the battle.
7. General Ayres commanded a division of regulars extending from Little Round Top westward. He told the writer that he lost eight hundred men in forty minutes and made a hurried retreat by regiments to Cemetery Ridge, the Confederates in such hot pursuit that some were mixed up with his men. If they had been volunteers instead of regulars, he said he could not have halted them in such a panic and have formed a new line, Wofford's Georgia brigade would have taken that part of Cemetery Ridge and Little Round Top would have fallen into Confederate hands like a mellow apple from its stem.
8. If, on the evening of the 2d, when Hays's and Hoke's brigades charged and took Cemetery Heights they had been supported, Lee would have won the field. Available Confederate troops were near, but were not thrown forward. Hancock brought up Carroll's brigade as a reenforcement, drove the Confederates and recaptured the line. For this fine work an equestrian statue to him stands on the spot.
9. If Major-General Edward Johnson had known on the night of the 2d that when his advance halted he was in the rear and within three hundred steps of the immense ordnance train of the Union army on the Baltimore Pike, he could have captured it and forced them to retreat.

10. If, late on the evening of the 2d, when Wright, with his Georgia brigade, reached the crest of Cemetery Ridge,—where he looked down the slope at and beyond Meade's quarters,—he had been supported by Posey's and other inactive brigades, that ridge might have been held and the battle won.
11. That same evening, when Wilcox's brigade also reached the top of that ridge, and occupied a part of it which had been evacuated by a brigade of Union troops, had he been supported he would have formed such a breach in their line that if improved might have won the battle.
12. If, on the 3d, the charging column had remained compact, with no opening for Stanard's maneuvers, or had Stuart reached the rear so as to have made his co-operative charge, a great victory might have been won.

These reflections only show us lost opportunities in that great struggle.

Gettysburg dead gathered for burial

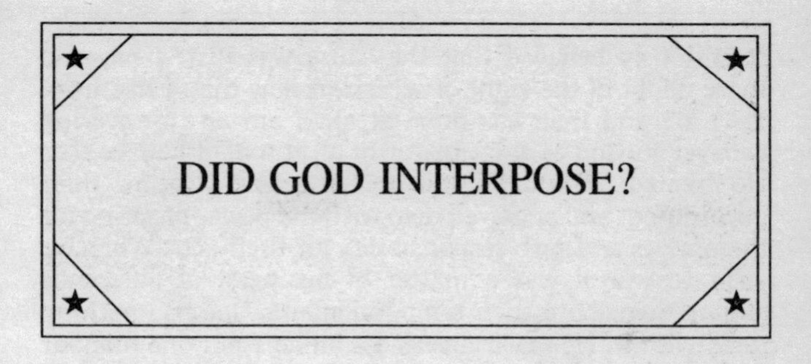

DID GOD INTERPOSE?

I AM NOT A fatalist nor a believer in destiny, and hence cannot say of Gettysburg as Victor Hugo said of Waterloo, "That God passed over the battle-field" and ordered the defeat of the Confederates. Their cause was just and nothing in it offensive to the Great Creator of us all. Under His laws, which are perfect and ample for the government of the world, it was given unto men to originate, formulate and regulate their governmental affairs in their own way, being responsible under those laws for individual acts as in every department of life. I do not worship a God who takes sides in battle and gives the victory to the heaviest battalions, greatest numbers and best equipped with arms and implements of war without regard to whether the cause be just or unjust. I can judge as well of the justice involved between nations when they go to war as I can of the laws of Nature and Nature's God. I am not infallible and may be mistaken in either, but nevertheless I can judge of the one as well as of the other. I would never go to war unless I conscientiously believed that the cause was just. I have no more doubt of the right of secession now than I had from 1861–65 and that was none at all. I am an unwavering believer in God as the Creator of all things. I believe that He created immutable and unchangeable laws for their government and endowed men with the power of acting for themselves and with responsibility for their acts. When we went to war it was a matter of business, of difference among men about their temporal affairs. God had nothing to do with it. He never diverted a bullet from one man, or caused it to hit another, nor directed who should fall or who should escape, nor how the battle should terminate. If I believed in such interposition of Providence I would be a fatalist. I believe in the justice and infinite wisdom of the Great Creator. His laws are perfect creations and any violation of them must be atoned for—the punishment cannot be averted. Unless individuals have freedom of action there is no justice in punishment. Courts of justice all over the world punish criminal acts voluntarily performed, which shows that all nations believe in the free agency of man.

To the religious, the superstitious and the fatalist the results may have appeared as Divine direction, to have been so ordered by Providence (which I do not believe); but, be it true or false, it is my purpose only to give the facts with appropriate suggestions of probable consequences and the statement of causes apparent.

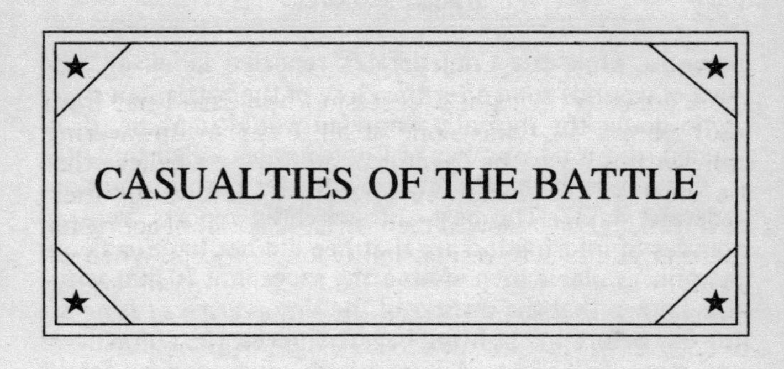

CASUALTIES OF THE BATTLE

THE REPORTS OF casualties during the Pennsylvania campaign as to each army are greater than those of the battle of Gettysburg, because the latter is included therein.

These reports are not perfectly accurate on either side, and from the nature of the case could not well be, but the following aggregate statements, compiled from such reports, is the nearest approach to accuracy obtainable, and applies only to that battle and not to the campaign:

Casualties in the Confederate Army.

Killed.	Wounded.	Captured.	Total.
2,592	12,706	5,150	20,448

In the Union Army.

Killed.	Wounded.	Captured.	Total.
5,091	14,529	5,365	24,985

The Federals reported in their list of killed all who were mortally wounded, or subsequently to the battle died of wounds, while the Confederates reported killed all who died of wounds soon after the close of the battle; but there is no doubt the mortally wounded would increase, if included, the total number of Confederates killed to 3,000.

Casualties in the Union army greater than in the Confederate, 4,537. The best authenticated reports from all sources of information are that Lee did not have in Pennsylvania available men of his army exceeding 70,000, while it is known that the muster of the Union army of June 30, the day before the fighting began, showed 105,000 officers and men of all arms. Making a large allowance for details of all kinds, it cannot be claimed that Meade had on the field, and within striking distance, an available force of less than 90,000 men, so that his army was at least 20,000 stronger than Lee's during the great battle.

The greater percentage of losses in the Union army is just about in proportion to the greater numbers of that army on the field.

It will be seen that the whole number of men of each side, Union and Confederate, aggregated 160,000, and the aggregate of losses was 53,433, or nearly one-third, which was heavier than the battle of Waterloo or of any of the great European battles of modern times.

During the three days' fighting the aggregate amount of lead and iron shot at each other by the two armies was five hundred and sixty-six tons. It is surprising that so many survived.

THE BATTLE OF GETTYSBURG

★ ★ ★

by
Lieutenant Frank A. Haskell

Lieutenant Frank A. Haskell, U.S.A.
(State Historical Society of Wisconsin)

At the headquarters, Second *Corps d'armée*,
Army of the Potomac, near Harper's Ferry,
July 16, 1863.

THE GREAT BATTLE of Gettysburg is now an event of the past. The composition and strength of the armies, their leaders, the strategy, the tactics, the result, of that field are today, by the side of those of Waterloo, matters of history. A few days ago these things were otherwise. This great event did not so "cast its shadow before" as to moderate the hot sunshine that streamed upon our preceding march or to relieve our minds of all apprehension of the result of the second great Rebel invasion of the soil north of the Potomac.

No, not many days since, at times we were filled with fears and forebodings. The people of the country, I suppose, shared the anxieties of the army somewhat in common with us, but they could not have felt them as keenly as we did. We were upon the immediate theater of events as they occurred from day to day, and were of them. We were the army whose province it should be to meet this invasion and repel it; on us was the immediate responsibility for results, most momentous for good or ill, but yet in the future. And so in addition to the solicitude of all good patriots, we felt that our own honor as men and as an army, as well as the safety of the Capitol and the country, was at stake.

And what if that invasion should be successful, and in the coming battle the Army of the Potomac should be overpowered? Would it not be? When our army was much larger than at present, had rested all winter, and, nearly perfect in all its departments and arrangements, was the most splendid army this continent ever saw, only a part of the Rebel force, which it now had to contend with, had defeated it—its leader, rather—at Chancellorsville! Now the Rebel had his whole force assembled; he was flushed with recent victory, was arrogant in his career of unopposed invasion at a favorable season of the year. His daring plans, made by no unskilled head, to transfer the war from his own to his enemy's ground were being successful. He had gone days' march from his front before Hooker moved or was aware of his departure. Then, I believe, the army in general, both officers and men, had no confidence in Hooker, in either his honesty or ability.

Did they not charge him personally with the defeat at Chancellorsville? Were they not still burning with indignation against him for that disgrace? And now again under his leadership they were marching against the enemy! And they knew of nothing, short of the Providence of God, that could—or would—remove him. For many reasons, during the marches prior to the battle we were anxious and, at times, heavy at heart.

But the Army of the Potomac was no band of schoolgirls. They were not the men likely to be crushed or utterly discouraged by any mere circumstances in which they might find themselves placed. They had lost some battles; they had gained some. They knew what defeat was, and what was victory. But here is the greatest praise that I can bestow upon them or upon any army: with the elation of victory, or the depression of defeat, amidst the hardest toils of the campaign, under unwelcome leadership—at all times, and under all circumstances, they were a reliable army still. The Army of the Potomac would do as it was told, always.

Well-clothed and well-fed, there never could be any ground for complaint on these heads; but a mighty work was before them. Onward they moved, night and day were blended, over many a weary mile, through dust and through mud, in the broiling sunshine, in the flooding rain, over steeps, through defiles, across rivers, over last year's battlefields, where the skeletons of our dead brethren by hundreds lay bare and bleaching, weary, without sleep for days, tormented with the newspapers and their rumors that the enemy was in Philadelphia, in Baltimore, in all places where he was not; yet these men could still be relied upon, I believed, when the day of conflict should come. "*Haec olim meminisse juvabit!*" We did not then know this. I mention them now that you may see that in those times we had several matters to think about—and to do—that were not as pleasant as sleeping upon a bank of violets in the shade.

In moving from near Falmouth, Virginia, the army was formed in several columns and took several roads. The Second Corps, the rear of the whole, was the last to move and left Falmouth at daybreak on the fifteenth of June, and pursued its march through Aquia, Dumfries, Wolf Run Shoals, Centerville, Gainesville, Thoroughfare Gap (this last we left on the twenty-fifth, marching back to Haymarket, where we had a skirmish with the cavalry and horse artillery of the enemy), Gum Spring, crossing the Potomac at Edward's Ferry, thence through Poolesville, Frederick, Liberty, and Union Town. We marched from near Frederick to Union Town, a distance of thirty-two miles, from eight o'clock A.M. to nine P.M., on the twenty-eighth. I think this is the longest march accomplished in so short a time by a corps during the war. On the twenty-eighth, while we were near this latter place, we breathed a full breath of joy and of hope. The Providence of God had been with us (we ought not to have doubted it): General Meade commanded the Army of the Potomac.

Not a favorable time, one would be apt to suppose, to change the general of a large army on the eve of battle, the result of which might be to destroy the government and country! But it should have been done long before. At all events, any change could not have been for the worse, and the administration, therefore, hazarded little in making it now. From this moment my own mind was easy concerning results. I now felt that we had a clearheaded, honest soldier to command the army, who would do his best always—that there would be no repetition of Chancellorsville. Meade was not as much known in the army as many of the other corps commanders, but the officers who knew all thought highly of him, a man of great modesty, with none of those qualities which are noisy and assuming and hankering for cheap newspaper fame—not at all of the "gallant" Sickles stamp. I happened to know much of General Meade. He and General Gibbon had always been very intimate, and I had seen much of him. I think my own notions concerning General Meade at this time were shared quite generally by the army. At all events, all who knew him shared them.

By this time, by reports that were not mere rumors, we

began to hear frequently of the enemy and of his proximity. His cavalry was all about us making little raids here and there, capturing now and then a few of our wagons and stealing a good many horses, but doing us really the least amount possible of harm, for we were not by these means impeded at all; and this cavalry gave no information at all to Lee that he could rely upon of the movements of the Army of the Potomac. The infantry of the enemy was at this time in the neighborhoods of Hagerstown, Chambersburg, and some had been at Gettysburg—possibly was there now. Gettysburg was a point of strategic importance: a great many roads, some ten or twelve at least, concentrated there, so the army could easily converge to—or, should a further march be necessary—diverge from this point. General Meade therefore resolved to try to seize Gettysburg and, accordingly, gave the necessary orders for the concentration of his different columns there. Under the new auspices the army brightened and moved on with a more elastic step towards the yet undefined field of conflict.

The First Corps (General Reynolds), already having the advance, was ordered to push forward rapidly and take and hold the town, if he could. The rest of the army would assemble to his support. Buford's cavalry cooperated with this corps, and on the morning of the first of July found the enemy near Gettysburg (and to the west) and promptly engaged him. The First Corps, having bivouacked the night before south of the town, came up rapidly to Buford's support, and immediately a sharp battle was opened with the advance of the enemy. The first division (General Wadsworth) was the first of the infantry to become engaged, but the other two, commanded respectively by generals Robinson and Doubleday, were close at hand and forming the line of battle to the west and northwest of the town, at a mean distance of about a mile away. The battle continued for some hours with various success, which was on the whole with us until near noon. At this time a lull occurred, which was occupied by both sides in supervising and reestablishing the hastily formed lines of the morning. New divisions of the enemy were constantly arriving and taking up positions, for this purpose marching in upon the various roads that terminate at the town, from the west and north.

The position of the First Corps was then becoming perilous in the extreme, but it was improved at a little before noon by the arrival upon the field of two divisions of the Eleventh Corps (General Howard)—these divisions commanded respectively by generals Schurz and Barlow, who by order posted their commands to the right of the First Corps with their right retired, forming an angle with the line of the First Corps. Between three and four o'clock in the afternoon the enemy, now in overwhelming force, resumed the battle with spirit. The portion of the Eleventh Corps, making but feeble opposition to the advancing enemy, soon began to fall back (General Barlow was badly wounded), and their retreat quickly degenerated into a disgraceful rout and panic. Back in disorganized masses they fled into the town, hotly pursued, and in houses, in barns, in yards and cellars, throwing away their arms, they sought to hide like rabbits, and were there captured, unresisting, by hundreds.

The First Corps, deprived of this support (if support it could be called), outflanked upon either hand and engaged in front, was compelled to yield the field. Making its last stand upon what is called "Seminary Ridge," not far from the town, it fell back in considerable confusion through the southwest part of the town, making brave resistance, however, but with considerable loss. The enemy did not see fit to follow—or to attempt to—further than the town; and so the fight of the first of July closed here. I suppose our losses during the day would exceed four thousand, of whom a large number were prisoners. Such usually is the kind of loss sustained by the Eleventh Corps. You will remember that the old "Iron Brigade" is in the First Corps and consequently shared this fight, and I hear their conduct praised on all hands.

In the 2nd Wisconsin, Colonel Fairchild lost his left arm, Lieutenant Colonel Stevens was mortally wounded, and Major Mansfield was wounded. Lieutenant Colonel Callis of the 7th Wisconsin and Lieutenant Colonel Dudley of the 19th Indiana were badly, dangerously, wounded, the latter by the loss of his right leg above the knee.

I saw "*John Burns*," the only citizen of Gettysburg who fought in the battle, and I asked him what troops he fought with. He said: "O, I pitched in with them Wisconsin fellers." I asked what sort of men they were, and he answered: "They fit terribly—the Rebs couldn't make any thing of them fellers." And so the brave compliment the brave. This man was touched by three bullets from the enemy but not seriously wounded.

But the loss of the enemy today was severe also—probably in killed and wounded as heavy as our own, but not so great in prisoners. Of these latter the "Iron Brigade" captured almost an entire Mississippi brigade, however.

Of the events so far of the first of July, I do not speak from personal knowledge. I shall now tell my introduction to these events.

At eleven o'clock A.M. on that day, the Second Corps was halted at Taneytown (which is thirteen miles from Gettysburg, south), and there awaiting orders the men were allowed to make coffee and rest. At between one and two o'clock in the afternoon, a message was brought to General Gibbon requiring his immediate presence at the headquarters of General Hancock, who commanded the corps. I went with General Gibbon, and we went at a rapid gallop to General Hancock.

At General Hancock's headquarters the following was learned: the First Corps had met the enemy at Gettysburg and had possession of the town; General Reynolds was badly—it was feared mortally—wounded; the fight of the First Corps still continued; by General Meade's order, General Hancock was to hurry forward and take command upon the field of all troops there or which should arrive there; the Eleventh Corps was near Gettysburg when the messenger, who told of the fight, left there, and the Third Corps was marching up, by order, on the Emmitsburg Road; General Gibbon—he was not the ranking officer of the Second Corps after Hancock—was ordered to assume the command of the Second Corps.

All this was sudden, and for that reason, at least, exciting; but there were other elements in this information that aroused our profoundest interest. The great battle that we had so anxiously looked for during so many days had at length opened; it was a relief, in some sense, to have these accidents of time and place established. What would be the result? Might not the enemy fall upon and destroy the First Corps before succor could arrive?

General Hancock with his personal staff at about two o'clock P.M. galloped off towards Gettysburg. General Gibbon took his place in command of the corps, appointing me his Acting Assistant Adjutant General. The Second Corps took arms at once and moved rapidly towards the field. It was not long before we began to hear the dull booming of the guns; and, as we advanced, from many an eminence or opening among the trees, we could look out upon the white battery smoke puffing up from the distant field of blood and drifting up to the clouds. At these sights and sounds the men looked more serious than before and were more silent, but they marched faster and straggled less.

At about five o'clock P.M., as we were riding along at the

head of the column, we met an ambulance accompanied by two or three mounted officers. We knew them to be staff officers of General Reynolds. Their faces told plainly enough what load the vehicle carried: it was the dead body of General Reynolds. Very early in the action, while seeing personally to the formation of his lines under fire, he was shot through the head by a musket or rifle bullet and killed almost instantly. His death at this time affected us much, for he was one of the *soldier* generals of the army, a man whose soul was in his country's work, which he did with a soldier's high honor and fidelity.

I remember seeing him often at the first battle of Fredericksburg (he then commanded the First Corps), and while Meade's and Gibbon's divisions were assaulting the enemy's works, he was the very beau ideal of the gallant general. Mounted upon a superb black horse with his head thrown back and his great black eyes flashing fire, he was everywhere upon the field, seeing all things and giving commands in person. He died as many a friend—and many a foe—to the country have died in this war.

Just as the dusk of evening fell, from General Meade the Second Corps had orders to halt where the head of the column then was and to go into position for the night. The second division (Gibbon's) was accordingly put in position upon the left of the (Taneytown) road, its left near the southeastern base of "Round Top"—of which mountain more anon—and the right near the road; the third division was posted upon the right of the road, abreast of the second; and the first division in rear of these two, all facing towards Gettysburg. Arms were stacked and the men lay down to sleep—alas, many of them their last but the great final sleep upon the earth.

Late in the afternoon as we came near the field, from some slightly wounded men we met and occasional stragglers from the scene of operations in front, we got many rumors and much disjointed information of battle, of lakes of blood, of rout and panic and undescribable disaster, from all of which the narrators were just fortunate enough to have barely escaped, the sole survivors. These stragglers are always terrible liars!

About nine o'clock in the evening, while I was yet engaged in showing the troops their positions, I met General Hancock, then on his way from the front to General Meade, who was back towards Taneytown; and he, for the purpose of having me advise General Gibbon for his information, gave me a quite detailed account of the situation of matters at Gettysburg and of what had transpired subsequently to his arrival there.

He had arrived and assumed command there just when the troops of the First and Eleventh corps, after their repulse, were coming in confusion through the town. Hancock is just the man for such an emergency as this. Upon horseback, I think he was the most magnificent looking general in the whole Army of the Potomac at that time. With a large, well-shaped person, always dressed with elegance, even upon that field of confusion, he would look as if he was "*monarch of all he surveyed*," and few of his subjects would dare to question his right to command or do aught else but to obey. His quick eye, in a flash, saw what was to be done; and his voice and his royal right hand at once commenced to do it. General Howard had put one of his divisions (Steinwehr's) with some batteries in position upon a commanding eminence at the "Cemetery," which, as a reserve, had not participated in the fight of the day; and this division was now, of course, steady. Around this division the fugitives were stopped, and the shattered brigades and regiments, as they returned, were formed upon either flank and faced towards the enemy again. A show of order at least speedily came from chaos; the rout was at an end.

The First and Eleventh corps were in line of battle again (not very systematically formed, perhaps) in a splendid position and in a condition to offer resistance should the enemy be willing to try them. These formations were all accomplished long before night. Then some considerable portion of the Third Corps (General Sickles) came up by the Emmitsburg Road and was formed to the left of the Taneytown Road on an extension of the line that I have mentioned; and all the Twelfth Corps (General Slocum), arriving before night, the divisions were put in position to the right of the troops already there to the east of the Baltimore Pike. The enemy was in the town and behind it (and to the east and west) and appeared to be in strong force and was jubilant over his day's success. Such was the posture of affairs as evening came on of the first of July.

General Hancock was hopeful and in the best of spirits; and from him I also learned that the reason of halting the Second Corps in its present position was that it was not then known where for the coming fight the lines of battle would be formed—up near the town, where the troops then were, or further back towards Taneytown. He would give his views upon the subject to General Meade, which were in favor of the line near the town (the one that was subsequently adopted) and General Meade would determine.

The night before a great pitched battle would not ordinarily, I suppose, be a time for much sleep to generals and their staff officers. We needed it enough, but there was work to be done. This war makes strange confusion of night and day! I did not sleep at all that night. It would, perhaps, be expected, on the eve of such great events, that one should have some peculiar sort of feelings, something extraordinary, some great arousing and excitement of the sensibilities and faculties commensurate with the event itself. This certainly would be very poetical and pretty, but so far as I was concerned, and I think I can speak for the army in this matter, there was nothing of the kind. Men who had volunteered to fight the battles of the country—have met the enemy in many battles and had been constantly before them, as had the Army of the Potomac—were too old soldiers and long ago too well had weighed chances and probabilities to be so disturbed now. No, I believe the army slept soundly that night and well; and I am glad the men did, for they needed it.

At midnight General Meade and staff rode by General Gibbon's headquarters on their way to the field; and in conversation with General Gibbon, General Meade announced that he had decided to assemble the whole army before Gettysburg and offer the enemy battle there. The Second Corps would move at the earliest daylight to take up its position.

At three o'clock A.M. of the second of July the sleepy soldiers of the corps were aroused. Before six the corps was up to the field and halted temporarily by the side of the Taneytown Road upon which it had marched, while some movements of other troops were being made to enable it to take position in the order of battle. The morning was thick and sultry, the sky overcast with low, vapory clouds. As we approached all was astir upon the crests near the cemetery, and the work of preparation was speedily going on. Men looked like giants there in the mist, and the guns of the frowning batteries so big that it was a relief to know that they were our friends.

Without a topographical map, some description of the ground and localities is necessary to a clear understanding of the battle. With the sketch that I have rudely drawn without scale or compass, I hope you may understand my description. The line of battle as it was established on the evening of the first and morning of the second of July was in the form of the letter "U," the troops facing outwards, and the "cemetery," which is at the point of the sharpest curvature of the line, being due south of the town of Gettysburg. "Round Top," the extreme left of the line, is a small, woody, rocky elevation, a very little west of south of the town and nearly two miles from it. The sides of this are in places very steep, and its rocky summit is almost inaccessible. A short distance north of this is a smaller elevation called "Little Round Top." On the very top of "Little Round Top," we had heavy rifled guns in position during the battle. Near the right of the line is a small woody eminence named "Culp's Hill." Three roads come up to the town from the south, which near the town are quite straight, and at the town the external ones unite, forming an angle of about sixty or more degrees. Of these, the farthest to the east is the "Baltimore Pike," which passes by the east entrance to the cemetery; the farthest to the west is the "Emmitsburg Road," which is wholly outside of our line of battle but near the cemetery [and] is within a hundred yards of it; the "Taneytown Road" is between these, running nearly due north and south by the eastern base of "Round Top," by the western side of the cemetery, and uniting with the Emmitsburg Road between the cemetery and the town. High ground near the cemetery is named "Cemetery Ridge."

The Eleventh Corps (General Howard) was posted at the cemetery, some of its batteries and troops actually among the graves and monuments, which they used for shelter from the enemy's fire—its left resting upon the Taneytown road and extending thence to the east, crossing the Baltimore Pike, and then bending backwards towards the southeast. On the right of the Eleventh came the First Corps—now, since the death of General Reynolds, commanded by General Newton—formed in a line curving still more towards the south. The troops of these two corps were reformed on the morning of the second in order that each might be by itself and to correct some things not done well during the hasty formations here the day before.

To the right of the First Corps, and on an extension of the same line along the crest and down the southeastern slope of Culp's Hill, was posted the Twelfth Corps (General Slocum), its right, which was the extreme right of the line of the army, resting near a small stream called "Rock Run." No changes that I am aware of occurred in the formation of this corps on the morning of the second.

The Second Corps, after the brief halt that I have mentioned, moved up and took position, its right resting upon the Taneytown Road at the left of the Eleventh Corps and extending the line thence (nearly a half a mile) almost due south towards Round Top, with its divisions in the following order, from right to left: the third (General Alexander Hays), the second (Gibbon's; General Harrow, temporarily), the first (General Caldwell). The formation was in line by brigade in column, the brigades being in column by regiment, with forty paces interval between regimental lines. The second and third divisions having each one, and the first division two brigades (there were four brigades in the first) similarly formed in reserve, one hundred and fifty paces in rear of the line of their respective divisions. That is, the line of the corps, exclusive of its reserves, was the length of six regiments, deployed, and the intervals between them—some of which were left wide for the posting of the batteries and consisted of four common deployed lines, each of two ranks of men, and a little more than one-third was in reserve.

The five batteries, in all twenty-eight guns, were posted as follows: Woodruff's Regular (six twelve-pound Napoleons, brass) between the two brigades in line of the third division; Arnold's "A" 1st Rhode Island (six three-inch Parrotts, rifled) and Cushing's Regular (four three-inch ordnance, rifled) between the third and second division; Hazard's (commanded during the battle by Lieutenant Brown) "B" 1st Rhode Island and Rorty's New York (each six twelve-pound Napoleons, brass) between the second and first divisions.

I have been thus specific in the description of the posting and formation of the Second Corps because they were works that I assisted to perform and also that the other corps were similarly posted with reference to the strength of the lines and the intermixing of infantry and artillery. From this, you may get a notion of the whole.

The Third Corps (General Sickles), the remainder of it arriving upon the field this morning, was posted upon the left of the Second, extending the line still in the direction of Round Top with its left resting near "Little Round Top." The left of the Third Corps was the extreme left of the line of battle until changes occurred, which will be mentioned in the proper place. The Fifth Corps (General Sykes), coming on the Baltimore Pike about this time, was massed there near the line of battle and held in reserve until sometime in the afternoon, when it changed position as I shall describe.

I cannot give a detailed account of the cavalry, for I saw but little of it. It was posted near the wings and watched the roads and the movements of the enemy upon the flanks of the army, but further than this participated but little in the battle. Some of it was also used for guarding the trains which were far to the rear. The artillery reserve, which consisted of a good many batteries (though I cannot give the number or the number of guns) was posted between the Baltimore Pike and the Taneytown Road on very nearly the center of a direct line passing through the extremities of the wings. Thus it could be readily sent to any part of the line. The Sixth Corps (General Sedgwick) did not arrive upon the field until sometime after noon; but it was now not very far away and was coming up rapidly upon the

Baltimore Pike. No fears were entertained that "Uncle John," as his men call General Sedgwick, would not be in the right place at the right time.

These dispositions were all made early, I think before eight o'clock in the morning; skirmishers were posted well out all around the line and all put in readiness for battle. The enemy did not yet demonstrate himself. With a look at the ground now, I think you may understand the movements of the battle. From Round Top, by the line of battle, round to the extreme right, I suppose is about three miles. From this same eminence to the cemetery extends a long ridge or hill—more resembling a great wave than a hill, however—with its crest, which was the line of battle, quite direct between the points mentioned. To the west of this—that is, towards the enemy—the ground falls away by a very gradual descent across the Emmitsburg Road and then rises again forming another ridge nearly parallel to the first but inferior in altitude, and something over a thousand yards away. A belt of woods extends, partly along this second ridge and partly farther to the west, at distances of from one thousand to thirteen hundred yards away from our line. Between these ridges, and along their slopes—that is, in front of the Second and Third corps—the ground is cultivated and is covered with fields of wheat (now nearly ripe), with grass and pastures, with some peach orchards, with fields of waving corn, and some farmhouses and their outbuildings along the Emmitsburg Road. There are very few places within the limits mentioned where troops or guns could move concealed. There are some oaks of considerable growth along the position of the right of the Second Corps; a group of small trees (sassafras and oak) in front of the right of the second division of this corps, also; and considerable woods immediately in front of the left of the Third Corps and also to the west of, and near, Round Top.

At the cemetery, where is Cemetery Ridge, to which the line of the Eleventh Corps conforms, is the highest point in our line, except Round Top. From this the ground falls quite abruptly to the town, the nearest point of which is some five hundred yards away from the line and is cultivated and checkered with stone fences. The same is the character of the ground occupied by, and in front of the left of, the First Corps, which is also on a part of Cemetery Ridge. The right of this corps, and the whole of the Twelfth, are along Culp's Hill and in woods, and the ground is very rocky, and in places in front precipitous—a most admirable position for defense from an attack in front, where, on account of the woods, no artillery could be used with effect by the enemy. Then these last three mentioned corps had—by taking rails, by appropriating stone fences, by felling trees, and digging the earth during the night of the first of July—made for themselves excellent breastworks, which were a very good thing indeed.

The position of the First and Twelfth corps was admirably strong, therefore. Within the line of battle is an irregular basin, somewhat wooded and rocky in places, but presenting few obstacles to the moving of troops and guns from place to place along the lines and also affording the advantage that all such movements, by reason of the surrounding crests, were out of view of the enemy. On the whole this was an admirable position to fight a defensive battle—good enough, I thought when I saw it first, and better, I believe, than could be found elsewhere in a circle of many miles. Evils, sometimes at least, are blessings in disguise; for the repulse of our forces and the death of Reynolds on the first of July, with the opportune arrival of Hancock to arrest the tide of fugitives and fix it on these heights, gave us this position. Perhaps the position gave us the victory.

On arriving upon the field, General Meade established

his headquarters at a shabby little farmhouse on the left of the Taneytown Road, the house nearest the line and a little more than five hundred yards in rear of what became the center of the position of the Second Corps—a point where he could communicate readily and rapidly with all parts of the army. The advantages of the position, briefly, were these: the flanks were quite well protected by the natural defences there—Round Top up the left, and rocky, steep, untraversable ground upon the right. Our line was more elevated than that of the enemy; consequently our artillery had a greater range and power than theirs. On account of the convexity of our line, every part of the line could be reinforced by troops having to move a shorter distance than if the line were straight; further, for the same reason, the line of the enemy must be concave and consequently longer, and with an equal force, thinner, and so weaker than ours. Upon those parts of our line which were wooded neither we nor the enemy could use artillery; but they were so strong by nature, aided by art, as to be readily defended by a small against a very large body of infantry. Where the line was open, it had the advantage of having open country in front; consequently the enemy here could not surprise us. We were on a crest, which besides the other advantages that I have mentioned, had this: the enemy must advance to the attack up an ascent and must therefore move slower, and be (before coming upon us) longer under our fire, as well as more exhausted. These and some other things rendered our position admirable for a defensive battle.

So before a great battle was ranged the Army of the Potomac. The day wore on, the weather still sultry and the sky overcast, with a mizzling effort at rain. When the audience has all assembled time seems long until the curtain rises; so today. "Will there be a battle today?" "Shall we attack the Rebel?" "Will he attack us?" These and similar questions, later in the morning, were thought or asked a million times.

Meanwhile on our part all was put in the last state of readiness for battle. Surgeons were busy riding about selecting eligible places for hospitals, and hunting streams and springs and wells. Ambulances and the ambulance men were brought up near the lines, and stretchers gotten ready for use. Who of us could tell but that he would be the first to need them? The provost guards were busy driving up all stragglers and causing them to join their regiments. Ammunition wagons were driven to suitable places and pack mules bearing boxes of cartridges, and the commands were informed where they might be found. Officers were sent to see that the men had each his hundred rounds of ammunition. Generals and their staffs were riding here and there among their commands to see that all was right. A staff officer or an orderly might be seen galloping furiously in the transmission of some order or message. All, all was ready. And yet the sound of no gun had disturbed the air or ear today.

And so the men stacked their arms; in long bristling rows they stood along the crests and were at ease. Some men of the Second and Third corps pulled down the rail fences near and piled them up for breastworks in their front. Some loitered; some went to sleep upon the ground; some, a single man carrying twenty canteens slung over his shoulder, went for water; some made them a fire and boiled a dipper of coffee; some with knees cocked up enjoyed the soldier's peculiar solace, a pipe of tobacco; some were mirthful and chatty; and some were serious and silent. Leaving them thus (I suppose of all arms and grades there were about a hundred thousand of them somewhere about that field) each to pass the hour according to his duty or his humor, let us look to the enemy.

Here let me state that according to the best information

that I could get, I think a fair estimate of the Rebel force engaged in this battle would be a little upwards of a hundred thousand men of all arms. Of course, we cannot now know, but there are reasonable data for this estimate. At all events, there was no great disparity of numbers in the two opposing armies. We thought the enemy to be somewhat more numerous than we, and he probably was. But if ninety-five men should fight with a hundred and five, the latter would not always be victors, and slight numerical differences are of much less consequence in great bodies of men.

Skillful generalship and good fighting are the jewels of war. These concurring are difficult to overcome; and these, not numbers, must determine this battle. During all the morning—and the night, too—the skirmishers of the enemy had been confronting those of the Eleventh, First, and Twelfth corps. At the time of the fight of the first, he was seen in heavy force north of the town; he was believed to be now in the same neighborhood in full force. But from the woody character of the country, and thereby the careful concealment of troops which the Rebel is always sure to effect, during the early part of the morning almost nothing was actually seen by us of the invaders of the North. About nine o'clock in the morning, I should think, our glasses began to reveal them at the west and northwest of the town, a mile and a half away from our lines. They were moving towards our left, but the woods of Seminary Ridge so concealed them that we could not make out much of their movements.

About this time some rifled guns in the cemetery at the left of the Eleventh Corps opened fire, almost the first shots of any kind this morning, and when it was found they were firing at a Rebel line of skirmishers, merely, that were advancing upon the left of that and the right of the Second Corps, the officer in charge of the guns was ordered to cease firing and was rebuked for having fired at all. These skirmishers soon engaged those of the right of the Second Corps, who stood their ground and were reinforced to make the line entirely secure. The Rebel skirmish line kept extending further and further to their right, toward our left. They would dash up close upon ours and sometimes drive them back a short distance, in turn to be repulsed themselves; and so they continued to do until their right was opposite the extreme left of the Third Corps. By these means they had ascertained the position and extent of our line, but their own masses were still out of view.

From the time that the firing commenced, as I have mentioned, it was kept up among the skirmishers until quite noon, often briskly, but with no definite results further than those mentioned and with no considerable show of infantry on the part of the enemy to support. There was a farmhouse and outbuildings in front of the third division of the Second Corps at which the skirmishers of the enemy had made a dash and dislodged ours posted there; and from there their sharpshooters began to annoy our line of skirmishers, and even the main line, with their long range rifles. I was up to the line, and a bullet from one of the rascals hid there hissed by my cheek so close that I felt the movement of the air distinctly. And so I was not at all displeased when I saw one of our regiments go down and attack and capture the house and buildings and several prisoners after a spirited little fight, and, by General Hays's order, burn the buildings to the ground.

About noon the Signal Corps, from the top of Little Round Top, with their powerful glasses, and the cavalry at our extreme left, began to report the enemy in heavy force making dispositions of battle to the west of Round Top and opposite to the left of the Third Corps. Some few prisoners had been captured, some deserters from the enemy had come in, and from all sources by this time we had much

General G. K. Warren at the Signal Station on Little Round Top

important and reliable information of the enemy, of his dispositions and apparent purposes. The Rebel infantry consisted of three army corps, each consisting of three divisions: Longstreet, Ewell (the same whose leg Gibbon's shells knocked off at Gainesville on the twenty-eighth of August last year), and A. P. Hill—each in the Rebel service having the rank of lieutenant general—were the commanders of these corps. Longstreet's division commanders were Hood, McLaws, and Pickett; Ewell's were Rodes, Early, and Johnson; and Hill's were Pender, Heth, and Anderson. Stuart and Fitz Lee commanded divisions of the Rebel cavalry. The rank of these division commands, I believe, was that of major general. The Rebel had about as much artillery as we did; but we never thought much of this arm in the hands of our adversaries. They have courage enough, but not the skill, to handle it well. They generally fire far too high, and their ammunition is usually of a very inferior quality. And of late we have begun to despise the enemy's cavalry, too; it used to have enterprise and dash, but in the late cavalry contests ours has always been victor, and so now we think about all this *chivalry* is fit for is to steal a few of our mules occasionally and their Negro drivers.

This army of the Rebel infantry, however, is good. To deny this is useless—I never had any desire to—and if one should count up it would possibly be found that they have gained more victories over us than we have over them; and they will now, doubtless, fight well, even desperately. And it is not horses or cannon that will determine the result of this confronting of the two armies, but the men with the muskets must do it; the infantry must do the sharp work.

So we watched all this posting of forces as closely as possible, for it was a matter of vital interest to us, and all information relating to it was hurried to the commander of the army. The Rebel line of battle was concave, bending around our own, with the extremities of the wings opposite to, or a little outside of, ours. Longstreet's corps was upon their right; Hill's in the center. These two Rebel corps occupied the second or inferior ridge to the west of our position, as I have mentioned, with Hill's left bending towards, and resting near, the town; and Ewell's was upon their left, his troops being in, and to the east of, the town. This last corps confronted our Twelfth, First, and the right of the Eleventh Corps. When I have said that ours was a good *defensive* position, this is equivalent to saying that that of the enemy was not a good *offensive* one; for these are relative terms and cannot be both predicated of the respective positions of the two armies at the same time. The reasons that theirs was not a good offensive position are the same [ones] already stated in favor of ours for defense. Excepting occasionally for a brief time during some movement of troops, as when advancing to attack, their men and guns were kept constantly and carefully, by woods and inequalities of ground, out of our view.

Noon is past, one o'clock is past, and save the skirmishing that I have mentioned, and an occasional shot from our guns at something or other of the nature of which the ones who fired it were ignorant, there was no fight yet. Our arms were still stacked, and the men were at ease. As I looked upon those interminable rows of muskets along the crests, and saw how cool and good spirited the men were who were lounging about on the ground among them, I could not, and did not, have any fears as to the result of the battle. The storm was near, and we all knew it well enough by this time, which was to rain death upon these crests and down these slopes; and yet the men who could not and would not escape it were as calm and cheerful, generally, as if nothing unusual was about to happen! You see, these men were veterans and had been in such places so often that they were accustomed to them. But I was well pleased with the tone of the men today; I could almost see the foreshadowing of victory upon their faces, I thought. And I thought, too, as I had seen the mighty preparations go on to completion for this great conflict—the marshaling of these two hundred thousand men and the guns, of the hosts that now but a narrow valley divided—that to have been in such a battle and to survive on the side of the victors would be glorious. Oh, the world is most unchristian yet!

Somewhat after one o'clock P.M., the skirmish firing had nearly ceased now, [and] a movement of the Third Corps occurred which I shall describe. I cannot conjecture the reason of this movement. From the position of the Third Corps, as I have mentioned, to the second ridge west, the distance is about a thousand yards; and there the Emmitsburg Road runs near the crest of the ridge. General Sickles commenced to advance his whole corps from the general line straight to the front, with a view to occupy this second ridge along and near the road. What his purpose could have been is past conjecture. It was not ordered by General Meade, as I heard him say, and he disapproved of it as soon as it was made known to him. Generals Hancock and Gibbon, as they saw the move in progress, criticized its propriety sharply, as I know, and foretold quite accurately what would be the result. I suppose the truth probably is that General Sickles supposed he was doing for the best; but he was neither born nor bred a soldier. But one can scarcely tell what may have been the motives of such a man—a politician, and some other things, exclusive of the *Barton Key* affair; a man after show, and notoriety, and newspaper fame, and the adulation of the mob! O, there is a grave responsibility on those in whose hands are the lives of ten thousand men and on those who put stars upon men's shoulders, too! Bah! I kindle when I see some things that I have to see. But this move of the Third Corps was an important one: it developed the battle; the results of the move to the corps itself we shall see. O, if this corps had kept its strong position upon the crest and, supported by the rest of the army, had waited for the attack of the enemy!

It was magnificent to see those ten or twelve thousand men—they were good men—with their batteries and some squadrons of cavalry upon the left flank, all in battle order in several lines with flags streaming, sweep steadily down the slope, across the valley, and up the next ascent towards their destined position! From our position we could see it all. In advance Sickles pushed forward his heavy line of skirmishers, who drove back those of the enemy across the Emmitsburg Road, and thus cleared the way for the main body. The Third Corps now became the absorbing object of interest of all eyes. The Second Corps took arms; and the first division of this corps was ordered to be in readiness to support the Third Corps should circumstances render support necessary. As the Third Corps was the extreme left of our line, as it advanced, if the enemy was assembling to the west of Round Top with a view to turn our left, as we had heard, there would be nothing between the left flank of the corps and the enemy; and the enemy would be square upon its flank by the time it had attained the road.

So when this advance line came near the Emmitsburg Road, and we saw the squadrons of cavalry mentioned come dashing back from their position as flankers, and the smoke of some guns, and we heard the reports away to Sickles left, anxiety became an element of our interest in these movements. The enemy opened slowly at first and from long range; but he was square upon Sickles's left flank. General Caldwell was ordered at once to put his division—the first of the Second Corps, as mentioned—in motion, and to take post in the woods at the west slope of Round Top in such a manner as to resist the enemy should he attempt to come around Sickles's left and gain his rear. The division moved as ordered and disappeared from view in the woods towards the point indicated at between two and three o'clock P.M.; and the reserve brigade—the first (Colonel Heath, temporarily commanding)—of the second division, was therefore moved up and occupied the position vacated by the third division. About the same time the Fifth Corps could be seen marching by the flank from its position on the Baltimore Pike and in the openings of the woods heading for the same locality where the first division of the Second Corps had gone. The Sixth Corps had now come up and was halted upon the Baltimore Pike. So the plot thickened.

As the enemy opened upon Sickles with his batteries (some five or six in all, I suppose, firing slowly), Sickles with as many replied and with much more spirit. The artillery fire became quite animated soon; but the enemy was forced to withdraw his guns farther and farther away, and ours advanced upon him. It was not long before the cannonade ceased altogether, the enemy having retired out of range, and Sickles, having temporarily halted his command pending this, moved forward again to the position he desired, or nearly that. It was now about five o'clock, and we shall soon see what Sickles gained by his move.

First we hear more artillery firing upon Sickles left—the enemy seems to be opening again and, as we watched, the Rebel batteries seem to be advancing there. The cannonade is soon opened again, and with great spirit upon both sides. The enemy's batteries press those of Sickles and pound the shot upon them, and this time they, in turn, begin to retire to positions nearer the infantry. The enemy seems to be fearfully in earnest this time. And what is more ominous than the thunder or the shot of his advancing guns, this time, in the intervals between his batteries, far to Sickles's left, appear the long lines and the columns of the Rebel infantry, now unmistakably moving out to the attack. The position of the Third Corps becomes at once one of great peril, and it is probable that its commander by this time began to realize his true situation.

All was astir now on our crest: generals and their staffs were galloping hither and thither, the men were all in their places, and you might have heard the rattle of ten thousand ramrods as they drove home and "thugged" upon the little globes and cones of lead. As the enemy was advancing upon Sickles's flank, he commenced a change, or at least a partial one, of front by swinging back his left and throwing forward his right in order that his lines might be parallel to those of his adversary, his batteries meantime doing what they could to check the enemy's advance; but this movement was not completely executed before new Rebel batteries opened upon Sickles's right flank—his former front—and in the same quarter appeared the Rebel infantry, also. Now came the dreadful battle picture of which we for a time could be but spectators. Upon the front and right flank of Sickles came sweeping the infantry of Longstreet and Hill. Hitherto there had been skirmishing and artillery practice—now the battle begins; for amid the heavier smokes and larger tongues of flame of the batteries now began to appear the countless flashes, and the long fiery sheets of the muskets, and the rattle of the volleys mingled with the thunder of the guns. We see the long gray lines come sweeping down upon Sickles's front and mix with the battle smoke; now the same colors emerge from the bushes and orchards upon his right and envelop his flank in the confusion of the conflict.

O, the din, and the roar, and those thirty thousand Rebel wolf cries! What a hell is there down that valley!

These ten or twelve thousand men of the Third Corps fight well, but it soon becomes apparent that they must be swept from the field or perish there where they are doing so well, so thick and overwhelming a storm of Rebel fire involves them. It was fearful to see, but these men, such as ever escape, must come from that conflict as best they can. To move down and support them there with other troops is out of the question, for this would be to do as Sickles did, to relinquish a good position and advance to a bad one. There is no other alternative—the Third Corps must fight itself out of its position of destruction! What was it ever put there for?

In the meantime some other dispositions must be made to meet the enemy in the event that Sickles is overpowered. With this corps out of the way, the enemy would be in a position to advance upon the line of the Second Corps, not in a line parallel with its front, but they would come obliquely from the left. To meet this contingency the left of the second division of the Second Corps is thrown back slightly and two regiments—the 15th Massachusetts (Colonel Ward) and the 82nd New York (Lieutenant Colonel Huston)—are advanced down to the Emmitsburg Road to a favorable position nearer us than the fight has yet come, and some new batteries from the artillery reserve are posted upon the crest near the left of the Second Corps. This was all General Gibbon could do—other dispositions were made, or were now being made upon the field, which I shall mention presently. The enemy is still giving Sickles fierce battle—or rather the Third Corps, for Sickles has been borne from the field minus one of his legs and General Birney now commands—and we of the Second Corps, a thousand yards away, with our guns and men are, and must be, still idle spectators of the fight.

The Rebel, as anticipated, tries to gain the left of the Third Corps, and for this purpose is now moving into the woods at the west of Round Top. We knew what he would find there. No sooner had the enemy gotten a considerable force into the woods mentioned, in the attempted execution of his purpose, than the roar of the conflict was heard there, also. The Fifth Corps and the first division of the Second were there at the right time and promptly engaged him; and there, too, the battle soon became general and obstinate.

Now the roar of battle has become twice the volume that it was before, and its range extends over more than twice the space. The Third Corps has been pressed back considerably, and the wounded are streaming to the rear by hundreds, but still the battle there goes on with no considerable abatement on our part. The field of actual conflict extends now from a point to the front of the left of the Second Corps away down to the front of Round Top, and the fight rages with the greatest fury. The fire of artillery and infantry and the yells of the Rebels fill the air with a mixture of hideous sounds. When the first division of the Second Corps first engaged the enemy, for a time it was pressed back somewhat, but under the able and judicious management of General Caldwell, and the support of the Fifth Corps, it speedily ceased to retrograde and stood its ground; and then there followed a time, after the Fifth Corps became well engaged, when from appearances we hoped the troops already engaged would be able to check entirely or repulse the further assault of the enemy. But fresh bodies of the Rebels continued to advance out of the woods to the front of the position of the Third Corps and to swell the numbers of the assailants of this already hard-pressed command. The men there begin to show signs of exhaustion; their ammunition must be nearly expended. They have now been fighting more than an hour and against greatly superior numbers. From the sound of the firing at the extreme left, and the place where the smoke rises above the treetops there, we know that the Fifth Corps is still steady and holding its own there; and as we see the Sixth Corps now marching and near at hand to that

Ewell's charge on the evening of July 2 upon East Cemetery Hill

point, we have no fears for the left. We have more apparent reason to fear for ourselves.

The Third Corps is being overpowered—here and there its lines begin to break, the men begin to pour back to the rear in confusion, the enemy are close upon them—and among them organization is lost to a great degree, guns and caissons are abandoned and in the hands of the enemy; the Third Corps, after a heroic, but unfortunate fight, is being literally swept from the field. That corps gone, what is there between the Second Corps and these yelling masses of the enemy? Do you not think that by this time we began to feel a personal interest in this fight? We did indeed. We had been mere observers of all this—the time was at hand when we must be actors in this drama.

Up to this hour General Gibbon had been in command of the Second Corps, since yesterday, but General Hancock, relieved of his duties elsewhere, now assumed command. Five or six hundred yards away the Third Corps was making its last opposition. And the enemy was hotly pressing his advantage there and throwing in fresh troops whose line extended still more along our front, when generals Hancock and Gibbon rode along the lines of their troops; and at once cheer after cheer—not Rebel, mongrel cries, but genuine cheers—rang out all along the line, above the roar of battle, for "Hancock," and "Gibbon," and "our generals." These were good. Had you heard their voices, you would have known these men would fight. Just at this time we saw another thing that made us glad: we looked to our rear, and there and all up the hillside, which was the rear of the Third Corps before it went forward, were rapidly advancing large bodies of men from the extreme right of our line of battle coming to the support of the part now so hotly pressed. There was the whole Twelfth Corps (with the exception of about one brigade, that is), the larger portions of the divisions of generals Williams and Geary;

the third division of the First Corps (General Doubleday) and some other brigades from the same corps, and some of them were moving at the double quick. They formed lines of battle at the foot of the hill by the Taneytown Road, and when the broken fragments of the Third Corps were swarming by them towards the rear, without halting or wavering they came sweeping up, and with glorious old cheers under fire took their places on the crest in line of battle to the left of the Second Corps. Now Sickles's blunder is repaired. Now, Rebel Chief, hurl forward your howling lines and columns! Yell out your loudest and your last, for many of your best will never yell, or wave the spurious flag, again!

The battle still rages all along the left, where the Fifth Corps is; and the west slope of Round Top is the scene of the conflict; and nearer us there was but short abatement, as the last of the Third Corps retired from the field, for the enemy is flushed with his success. He has been throwing forward brigade after brigade and division after division since the battle began, and his advancing line now extends almost as far to our right as the right of the second division of the Second Corps. The whole slope in our front is full of them; and in various formation, in line, in column, and in masses which are neither, with yells, and thick volleys, they are rushing towards our crest. The Third Corps is out of the way. Now we are in for it. The battery men are ready by their loaded guns. All along the crest is ready. Now Arnold and Brown. Now Cushing, and Woodruff, and Rorty (you three shall survive today)! They drew the cords that moved the friction primers, and gun after gun, along all the batteries, in rapid succession leaped where it stood and bellowed its canister upon the enemy. The enemy still advance. The infantry open fire—first the two advance regiments (the 15th Massachusetts and the 82nd New York), then here and there throughout the length of the long line at the points where the enemy comes nearest, and soon the whole crest, artillery and infantry, is one continued sheet of fire. From Round Top to near the cemetery stretches an uninterrupted field of conflict. There is a great army upon each side, now hotly engaged.

To see the fight, while it went on in the valley below us, was terrible: what must it be now when we are in it, and it is all around us in all its fury?

All senses for the time are dead but the one of sight. The roar of the discharges, over the yells of the enemy, all pass unheeded; but the impassioned soul is all eyes and sees all things that the smoke does not hide. How madly the battery men are driving home the double charges of canister in those broad-mouthed Napoleons, whose fire seems almost to reach the enemy. How rapidly these long blue-coated lines of infantry deliver their file fire down the slope.

But there is no faltering; the men stand nobly to their work. Men are dropping dead or wounded on all sides by scores and by hundreds; and the poor mutilated creatures—some with an arm dangling, some with a leg broken by a bullet—are limping and crawling towards the rear. They make no sound of complaint or pain, but are as silent as if dumb and mute. A sublime heroism seems to pervade all and the intuition that to lose that crest and all is lost. How our officers, in the work of cheering on and directing the men, are falling.

We have heard that General Zook and Colonel Cross, in the first division of our corps, are mortally wounded. They both commanded brigades. Now near us Colonel Ward of the 15th Massachusetts (he lost a leg at Ball's Bluff) and Lieutenant Colonel Huston of the 82nd New York are mortally struck while trying to hold their commands, which are being forced back. Colonel Revere (20th Massachusetts), grandson of old Paul Revere of the Revolution, is killed. Lieutenant Colonel Max Thoman, commanding 59th New York, is mortally wounded, and a host of others that I cannot name. These were of Gibbon's division. Lieutenant Brown is wounded among his guns. His position is a hundred yards in advance of the main line. The enemy is upon his battery, and he escapes but leaves three of his six guns in the hands of the enemy.

The fire all along our crest is terrific, and it is a wonder how anything human could have stood before it; and yet the madness of the enemy drove them on, clear up to the muzzles of the guns, clear up to the lines of our infantry. But the lines stood right in their places. General Hancock with his aides rode up to Gibbon's division under the smoke. General Gibbon, with myself, was near, and there was a flag dimly visible coming towards us from the direction of the enemy. "Here, what are these men falling back for?" said Hancock. The flag was no more than fifty yards away, but it was the head of a Rebel column, which at once opened fire with a volley. Lieutenant Miller, General Hancock's aide, fell twice struck, but the general was unharmed, and he told the 1st Minnesota, which was near, to drive these people away. That splendid regiment, the less than three hundred that are left out of fifteen hundred that it has had, swings around upon the enemy, gives them a volley in their faces, and advances upon them with the bayonet. The Rebels fled in confusion; but Colonel Colvill, Lieutenant Colonel Adams, and Major Downie, are all badly, dangerously, wounded; and many of the other officers and men will never fight again. More than two-thirds fell.

Such fighting as this cannot last long. It is now near sundown, and the battle has gone on wonderfully long already. But, if you will stop to notice it, a change has occurred. The Rebel cry has ceased, and the men of the Union begin to shout there, under the smoke, and their lines to advance. See, the Rebels are breaking! They are in confusion in all our front! The wave has rolled upon the rock, and the rock has smashed it. Let us shout, too!

First upon their extreme left the Rebels broke, where they had almost pierced our lines; thence the repulse extended rapidly to their right: they hung longest about Round Top, where the Fifth Corps punished them; but in a space of time incredibly short, after they first gave signs of weakness, the whole force of the Rebel assault along the whole line—in spite of waving red flags, and yells, and the entreaties of officers, and the pride of the chivalry—fled like chaff before the whirlwind, back down the slope, over the valley, across the Emmitsburg Road, shattered, without organization, in utter confusion, fugitive into the woods, and victory was with the arms of the Republic. The great Rebel assault, the greatest ever made upon this continent, has been made and signally repulsed, and upon this part of the field the fight of today is now soon over.

Pursuit was made as rapidly and as far as was practicable; but owing to the proximity of night, and the long distance which would have to be gone over before any of the enemy, where they would be likely to halt, could be overtaken, further success was not attainable today. When the Rebel rout first commenced, a large number of prisoners, some thousands at least, were captured; almost all their dead, and such of their wounded as could not themselves get to the rear, were within our lines. Several of their flags were gathered up, and a good many thousand muskets. Some nine or ten guns and some caissons lost by the Third Corps (and the three of Brown's battery—these last were in Rebel hands but a few minutes) were all safe now with us, the enemy having had no time to take them off.

Not less, I estimate, than twenty thousand men were killed or wounded in this fight. Our own losses must have been nearly half this number: about four thousand in the Third Corps, fully two thousand in the Second, and I think two thousand in the Fifth. And I think the losses of the First, Twelfth, and the little more than a brigade of the Sixth (all of that corps which were actually engaged) would reach nearly two thousand more. Of course, it will never be possible to know the numbers upon either side who fell in this particular part of the general battle, but from the position of the enemy, and his numbers, and the appearance of the field, his loss must have been as heavy as—I think much heavier than—our own; and my estimates are probably short of the actual loss.

The fight done, the sudden revulsions of sense and feeling follow, which more or less characterize all similar occasions. How strange the stillness seems! The whole air roared with the conflict but a moment since. Now all is silent, not a gunshot sound is heard, and the silence comes distinctly, almost painfully to the senses. And the sun purples the clouds in the west, and the sultry evening steals on as if there had been no battle and the furious shout and the cannon's roar had never shook the earth. And how look those fields? We may see them before dark: the ripening grain, the luxuriant corn, the orchards, the grassy meadows, and in their midst the rural cottage of brick or wood? They were beautiful this morning. They are desolate now, trampled by the countless feet of the combatants, plowed and scarred by the shot and shell, the orchards splintered, the fences prostrate, the harvests trodden in the mud. And more dreadful than the sight of all this, thickly strewn over all their length and breadth, are the habiliments of the soldier—the knapsacks, cast aside in the stress of the fight, or after the fatal lead had struck; haversacks, yawning with the rations the owner will never call for; canteens of cedar of the Rebel men of Jackson and cloth-covered tin of the men of the Union; blankets and trousers and coats and caps, and some are blue and some are gray; muskets, and ramrods, and bayonets, and swords, and scabbards, and belts, some bent and cut by the shot or shell; broken wheels, exploded caissons, and limber boxes, and dismantled guns (and all these are sprinkled with blood); horses, some dead, a mangled heap of carnage, some alive, with a leg shot clear off or other frightful wound, appealing to you with almost more than brute gaze, as you pass; and last, but not least numerous, many thousands of men. And there was no rebellion here now—the men of South Carolina were quiet by the side of those of Massachusetts, some composed with upturned faces sleeping the last sleep, some mutilated and frightful, some wretched, fallen, bathed in blood, survivors still and unwilling witnesses of the rage of Gettysburg.

And yet with all this before them, as darkness came on and the dispositions were made and the outposts thrown out for the night, the Army of the Potomac was quite mad with joy. No more lighthearted guests ever graced a banquet than were these men as they boiled their coffee and munched their soldiers' supper tonight. Is it strange?

Otherwise, they would not have been soldiers. And such sights, as all these will continue to be seen as long as war lasts in the world; and when war is done, then is the end, and the days of the millennium at hand.

The ambulances commenced their work as soon as the battle opened; the twinkling lanterns through the night and the sun of tomorrow saw them still with the same work unfinished.

I wish that I could write that with the coming on of the darkness ended the fight of today, but such was not the case. The armies have fought enough today and ought to sleep tonight, one would think. But not so, thought the Rebel.

Let us see what he gained by his opinion. When the

troops, including those of the Twelfth Corps, had been withdrawn from the extreme right of our line in the afternoon to support the left, as I have mentioned, thereby, of course, weakening that part of the line so left, the Rebel Ewell, either becoming aware of the fact or because he thought he could carry our right at all events, late in the afternoon commenced an assault upon that part of our line. His battle had been going on there simultaneously with the fight on the left, but not with any great degree of obstinacy on his part. He had advanced his men through the woods and in front of the formidable position lately held by the Twelfth Corps cautiously, and to his surprise, I have no doubt, found our strong defenses upon the extreme right entirely abandoned. These he at once took possession of and simultaneously made an attack upon our right flank, which was now near the summit of Culp's Hill and upon the front of that part of the line. That small portion of the Twelfth Corps, which had been left there, and some of the Eleventh Corps sent to their assistance, did what they could to check the Rebels; but the Eleventh Corps men were getting shot at there, and they did not like to stay. Matters began to have a bad look in that part of the field; a portion of the first division of the First Corps was sent there for support (the 6th Wisconsin among others), and this improved matters. But still as we had but a small number of men there, all told, the enemy with their great numbers were having there too much prospect of success; and it seems that, probably emboldened by this, Ewell had resolved upon a night attack, upon that wing of our army, and was making his dispositions accordingly. The enemy had not at sundown actually carried any part of our rifle pits there, save the ones abandoned; but he was getting troops assembled upon our flank. And all together, with our weakness there at that time, matters did not look as we would like to have them.

Such was then the posture of affairs when the fight upon our left that I have mentioned was done. Under such circumstances it is not strange that the Twelfth Corps, as soon as its work was done upon the left, was quickly ordered back to the right to its old position. There it arrived in good time; not soon enough, of course, to avoid the mortification of finding the enemy in the possession of a part of the works the men had labored so hard to construct, but in ample time before dark, to put the men well in the pits we already held and to take up a strong defensible position at right angles to, and in rear of, the main line in order to resist those flanking dispositions of the enemy. The army was secure again. The men in the works would be steady against all attacks in front as long as they knew that their flank was safe.

Until between ten and eleven o'clock at night, the woods upon the right resounded with the discharges of musketry. Shortly after or about dark, the enemy made a dash upon the right of the Eleventh Corps. They crept up the windings of a valley, not in a very heavy force, but from the peculiar mode in which this corps does outpost duty, quite unperceived in the dark until they were close upon the main line. It is said—I do not know it to be true—that they spiked two guns of one of the Eleventh Corps' batteries and that the battery men had to drive them off with their sabres and rammers, and that there was some fearful Dutch swearing on the occasion—"*donner wetter,*" among other similar impious oaths, having been freely used. The enemy here were finally repulsed by the assistance of Colonel Carroll's brigade of the third division of the Second Corps, and the 106th Pennsylvania from the second division of the same corps was, by General Howard's request, sent there to do outpost duty. It seems to have been a matter of utter madness and folly upon the part of the enemy to have continued their night attack, as they did upon the right.

Our men were securely covered by ample works; and even in most places a log was placed a few inches above the top of the main breastwork as a protection to the heads of the men as they thrust out their pieces beneath it to fire. Yet in the darkness the enemy would rush up, clambering over rocks and among trees, even to the front of the works, but only to leave their riddled bodies there upon the ground or to be swiftly repulsed headlong into the woods again. In the darkness the enemy would climb trees close to the works and endeavor to shoot our men by the light of the flashes; when discovered, a thousand bullets would whistle after them in the dark, and some would hit; and then the Rebel would make up his mind to come down.

Our loss was light, almost nothing in this fight. The next morning the enemy's dead were thick all along this part of the line. Near eleven o'clock, the enemy—wearied with his disastrous work—desisted; and thereafter until morning not a shot was heard in all the armies.

So much for the battle. There is another thing that I wish to mention of the matters of the second of July.

After evening came on (and from reports received, was known to be going satisfactorily upon the right), General Meade summoned his corps commanders to his headquarters for consultation. A consultation is held upon matters of vast moment to the country; and that poor little farmhouse is honored with more distinguished guests than it ever had before or than it will ever have again, probably.

Do you expect to see a degree of ceremony and severe military aspect characterize this meeting, in accordance with strict military rules and commensurate with the moment of the matters of their deliberation? Name it: "Major General Meade, Commander of the Army of the Potomac, with His Corps Generals, Holding a Council of War upon the Field of Gettysburg," and it would sound pretty well—and that was what it was; and you might make a picture of

Major-General George G. Meade

it and hang it up by the side of "Napoleon and His Marshals" and "Washington and His Generals," maybe, at some future time. But for the artist to draw his picture from, I will tell how this council appeared.

Meade, Sedgwick, Slocum, Howard, Hancock, Sykes, Newton, Pleasonton (commander of the cavalry), and Gibbon were the generals present. Hancock, now that Sickles is wounded, has charge of the Third Corps, and Gibbon again has the Second. Meade is a tall, spare man, with full beard, which with his hair, originally brown, is quite thickly sprinkled with gray, has a romanish face, very large nose, and a white large forehead, prominent and wide over the eyes, which are full and large and quick in their movements, and he wears spectacles. His *fibers* are all of the long and sinewy kind. His habitual personal appearance is quite careless, and it would be rather difficult to make him look well-dressed.

Sedgwick is quite a heavy man—short, thickset, and muscular, with florid complexion, dark, calm, straight-looking eyes, with full, heavyish features, which with his eyes, have plenty of animation when he is aroused; he has a magnificent profile—well cut, with the nose and forehead forming almost a straight line, curly short chestnut hair and full beard, cut short, with a little gray in it. He dresses carelessly, but can look magnificently when he is well-dressed. Like Meade, he looks—and is—honest and modest. You might see at once why his men, because they love him, call him "Uncle John," not to his face of course, but among themselves.

Slocum is small, rather spare, with black straight hair and beard, which latter is unshaven and thin, large, full, quick black eyes, white skin, sharp nose, wide cheek bones, and hollow cheeks, and small chin. His movements are quick and angular, and he dresses with a sufficient degree of elegance. Howard is medium in size, has nothing marked about him, is the youngest of them all, I think, has lost an arm in the war, has straight brown hair and beard, shaves his short upper lip, over which his nose slants down, dim blue eyes, and on the whole appears a very pleasant, affable, well-dressed little gentleman.

Hancock is the tallest, and most shapely, and in many respects is the best-looking officer of them all. His hair is very light brown, straight and moist, and always looks well; his beard is of the same color, of which he wears the moustache and a tuft upon the chin, complexion ruddy, features neither large nor small, but well-cut, with full jaw and chin, compressed mouth, straight nose, full deep blue eyes, and a very mobile, emotional countenance. He always dresses remarkably well, and his manner is dignified, gentlemanly, and commanding. I think if he were in citizens' clothes and should give commands in the army to those who did not know him, he would be likely to be obeyed at once and without any question as to his right to command.

Sykes is a small, rather thin man, well-dressed and gentlemanly, brown hair and beard which he wears full, with a red, pinched, rough-looking skin, feeble blue eyes, large nose, with the general air of one who is weary and a little ill-natured. Newton is a well-sized, shapely, muscular, well-dressed man, with brown hair, with a very ruddy, clean-shaved, full face, blue eyes, blunt, round features, walks very erect, curbs in his chin, and has somewhat of that smart sort of swagger, that people are apt to suppose characterizes soldiers. Pleasonton is quite a nice little dandy, with brown hair and beard, a straw hat with a little jockey rim, which he cocks upon one side of his head, with an unsteady eye that looks slyly at you, and then dodges.

Gibbon, the youngest of them all save Howard, is about the same size as Slocum, Howard, Sykes, and Pleasonton, and there are none of these who will weigh one hundred and fifty pounds. He is compactly made, neither spare nor corpulent, with ruddy complexion, chestnut brown hair, with a clean-shaved face, except his moustache, which is decidedly reddish in color, medium-sized, well-shaped head, sharp, moderately-jutting brows, deep-blue, calm eyes, sharp, slightly-aquiline nose, compressed mouth, full jaws and chin, with an air of calm firmness in his manner. He always looks well-dressed.

I suppose Howard is about thirty-five, and Meade about forty-five, years of age; the rest are between these ages, but not many are under forty. As they come to the council now there is the appearance of fatigue about them, which is not customary but is only due to the hard labors of the past few days. They all wear clothes of dark blue; some have top boots, and some not, and except the two-starred strap upon the shoulders of all save Gibbon, who has but one star, there was scarcely a piece of regular uniform about them all. There were their swords of various pattern, but no sashes; the army hat, but with the crown pinched into all sorts of shapes, and the rim slouched down, and shorn of all its ornaments but the gilt band (except Sykes who wore a blue cap and Pleasonton with his straw hat, with broad black band).

Then the mean little room where they met: its only furniture consisted of a large, wide bed in one corner; a small pine table in the center, upon which was a wooden pail of water, with a tin cup for drinking, and a candle, stuck to the table by putting the end in tallow melted down from the wick; and five or six straight-backed, rush-bottom chairs. The generals came in. Some sat, some kept walking or standing, two lounged upon the bed, some were constantly smoking cigars.

And thus disposed, they deliberated whether the army should fall back from its present position to one in rear which it is said was stronger; should attack the enemy on the morrow, wherever he could be found; or should stand there upon the horseshoe crest, still on the defensive, and await the further movements of the enemy. The latter proposition was unanimously agreed to. Their heads were sound. The Army of the Potomac would just halt right there and allow the Rebel to come up and smash his head against it to any reasonable extent he desired, as he had today. After some two hours the council dissolved, and the officers went their several ways.

Night, sultry and starless, droned on; and it was almost midnight that I found myself peering my way from the line of the Second Corps back down to the general's headquarters, which were an ambulance in the rear in a little peach orchard. All was silent now but the sound of the ambulances as they were bringing off the wounded; and you could hear them rattle here and there about the field and see their lanterns. I am weary and sleepy almost to such an extent as not to be able to sit my horse.

And my horse can hardly move; the spur will not start him. What can be the reason? I know that he has been touched by two or three bullets today, but not to wound or lame him to speak of. Then in riding by a horse that is hitched, in the dark I got kicked; had I not a very thick boot, the blow would have been likely to have broken my ankle. It did break my temper as it was, and as if it would cure matters I foolishly spurred my horse again. No use; he would not but walk. I dismounted. I could not lead him along at all; so out of temper, I rode at the slowest possible walk to the headquarters, which I reached at last. Generals Hancock and Gibbon were asleep in the ambulance. With a light I found what was the matter with "Billy." A bullet had entered his chest just in front of my left leg as I was mounted, and the blood was running down all his side and leg, and the air from his lungs came out of the bullet hole. I begged his pardon mentally for my cruelty in spurring him and should have done so in words, if he could have understood me. Kind treatment as is due to the wounded he could understand, and he had it. Poor Billy. He and I were first under fire together, and I rode him at the Second Bull Run, and the First and Second Fredericksburg, and at Antietam after brave "Joe" was killed; but I shall never mount him again—Billy's battles are over.

"George, make my bed here upon the ground, by the side of this ambulance. Pull off my sabre and my boots—that will do!" Was ever princely couch, or softest down, so soft as those rough blankets, there upon the unroofed sod? At midnight they received me for four hours delicious, dreamless oblivion of weariness and of battle. So to me ended the second of July.

At four o'clock on the morning of the third, I was awakened by General Gibbon's pulling me by the foot and saying: "Come, don't you hear that?" I sprang to my feet. Where was I? A moment and my dead senses and memory were alive again, and the sound of brisk firing of musketry to the front and right of the Second Corps and over at the extreme right of our line, where we heard it last in the night, brought all back to my memory. We surely were on the field of battle; and there were palpable evidences to my senses that today was to be another of blood.

Oh, for a moment the thought of it was sickening to every sense and feeling! But the motion of my horse as I galloped over the crest a few minutes later, and the serene splendor of the morning now breaking through rifted clouds and spreading over all the landscape, soon reassured me. Come day of battle, up Rebel hosts, and thunder with your arms; we are all ready to do and to die for the Republic!

I found a sharp skirmish going on in front of the right of the Second Corps between our outposts and those of the enemy; but save this (and none of the enemy but his outposts were in sight), all was quiet in all that part of the field. On the extreme right of the line the sound of musketry was quite heavy; and this I learned was brought on by the attack of the second division, Twelfth Corps (General Geary) upon the enemy in order to drive him out of our works which he had sneaked into yesterday, as I have mentioned. The attack was made at the earliest moment in the morning when it was light enough to discern objects to fire at.

The enemy could not use the works, but were confronting Geary in woods and had the cover of many rocks and trees; so the fight was an irregular one, now breaking out and swelling to a vigorous fight, now subsiding to a few scattering shots. And so it continued by turns until the morning was well advanced, when the enemy was finally wholly repulsed and driven from the pits, and the right of our line was again reestablished in the place it first occupied. The heaviest losses the Twelfth Corps sustained in all the battle occurred during this attack, and they were here quite severe. I heard General Meade express dissatisfaction at General Geary for making this attack as a thing not ordered and not necessary, as the works of ours were of no intrinsic importance and had not been captured from us by a fight; and Geary's position was just as good as they, where he was during the night. And I heard General Meade say that he sent an order to have this fight stopped; but I believe the order was not communicated to Geary until after the repulse of the enemy. Later in the forenoon the enemy again tried to carry our right by storm. We heard that old Rebel Ewell had sworn an oath that he would break our right. He had Stonewall Jackson's corps, and possibly imagined himself another Stonewall, but he certainly *hankered* after the right of our line—and so up through the woods, and over the rocks, and up the steeps he sent his storming parties; our men could see them now in the day time.

But all the Rebel's efforts were fruitless, save in one thing—slaughter to his own men. These assaults were made with great spirit and determination; but as the enemy would come up, our men lying behind their secure defenses would just singe them with the blaze of their muskets and riddle them, as a hail storm, the tender blades of corn. The Rebel oath was not kept, any more than his former one to support the Constitution of the United States. The Rebel loss was very heavy indeed here; ours but trifling. I regret that I cannot give more of the details of this fighting upon the right; it was so determined upon the part of the enemy, both last night and this morning—so successful to us. About all that I actually saw of it, during its progress, was the smoke; and I heard the discharges. My information is derived from officers who were personally in it. Some of our heavier artillery assisted our infantry in this by firing with the pieces elevated far from the rear, over the heads of our men, at a distance from the enemy of two miles, I suppose. Of course they could have done no great damage. It was nearly eleven o'clock that the battle in this part of the field subsided, not to be again renewed. All the morning we felt no apprehension for this part of the line, for we knew its strength and that our troops engaged—the Twelfth Corps and the first division (Wadsworth's) of the First—could be trusted.

For the sake of telling one thing at a time, I have anticipated events somewhat, in writing of this fight upon the right. I shall now go back to the starting point, four o'clock this morning, and, as other events occurred during the day—second to none in the battle in importance, which I think I saw as much of as any man living—I will tell you something of them, and what I saw, and how the time moved on.

The outpost skirmish that I have mentioned soon subsided. I suppose it was the natural escape of the wrath which the men had during the night hoarded up against each other and which, as soon as they could see in the morning, they could no longer contain but must let it off through their musket barrels at their adversaries. At the commencement of the war such firing would have awaked the whole army and roused it to its feet and to arms; not so now. The men upon the crest lay snoring in their blankets, even though some of the enemy's bullets dropped among them, as if bullets were harmless as the drops of dew around them. As the sun arose today the clouds became broken, and we had once more glimpses of sky and fits of sunshine, a rarity to cheer us. From the crest, save to the right of the Second Corps, no enemy, not even his outposts, could be discovered along all the position where he so thronged upon the Third Corps yesterday. All was silent there—the wounded horses were limping about the fields; the ravages of the conflict were still fearfully visible; the scattered arms and the ground thickly dotted with the dead—but no hostile foe.

The men were roused early, in order that their morning meal might be out of the way in time for whatever should occur. Then ensued the hum of an army not in ranks, chatting in low tones, and running about and jostling among each other, rolling and packing their blankets and tents. They looked like an army of rag gatherers, while shaking these very useful articles of the soldier's outfit—for you must know that rain and mud in conjunction have not had the effect to make them very clean, and the wear and tear of service have not left them entirely whole. But one could not have told by the appearance of the men that they were in battle yesterday and were likely to be again today. They packed their knapsacks, boiled their coffee, and munched their hard bread, just as usual—just like old soldiers who know what campaigning is; and their talk is far more concerning their present employment—some joke or drollery, than concerning what they saw or did yesterday.

As early as practicable the lines all along the left are revised and reformed, this having been rendered necessary by yesterday's battle and also by what is anticipated today.

It is the opinion of many of our generals that the Rebel will not give us battle today, that he had enough yesterday, that he will be heading towards the Potomac at the earliest practicable moment, if he has not already done so; but the better and controlling judgment is that he will make another grand effort to pierce or turn our lines, that he will either mass and attack the left again, as yesterday, or direct his operations against the left of our center—the position of the Second Corps—and try to sever our line. I infer that General Meade was of the opinion that the attack today would be upon the left (this from the dispositions he ordered); I know that General Hancock anticipated the attack upon the center.

The dispositions today upon the left are as follows: The second and third divisions of the Second Corps are in the positions of yesterday. Then on the left come Doubleday's (the third) division and Colonel Stannard's brigade of the First Corps; then Caldwell's (the first) division of the Second Corps; then the Third Corps, temporarily under the command of Hancock since Sickles's wound. The Third Corps is upon the same ground in part, and on the identical line, where it first formed yesterday morning, and where, had it stayed instead of moving out to the front, we should have many more men today and should not have been upon the brink of disaster yesterday. On the left of the Third is the Fifth Corps, with a short front and deep line; then comes the Sixth Corps (all but one brigade, which is sent over to the Twelfth). The Sixth, a splendid corps, almost intact in the fight of yesterday, is the extreme left of our line, which terminates to the south of Round Top

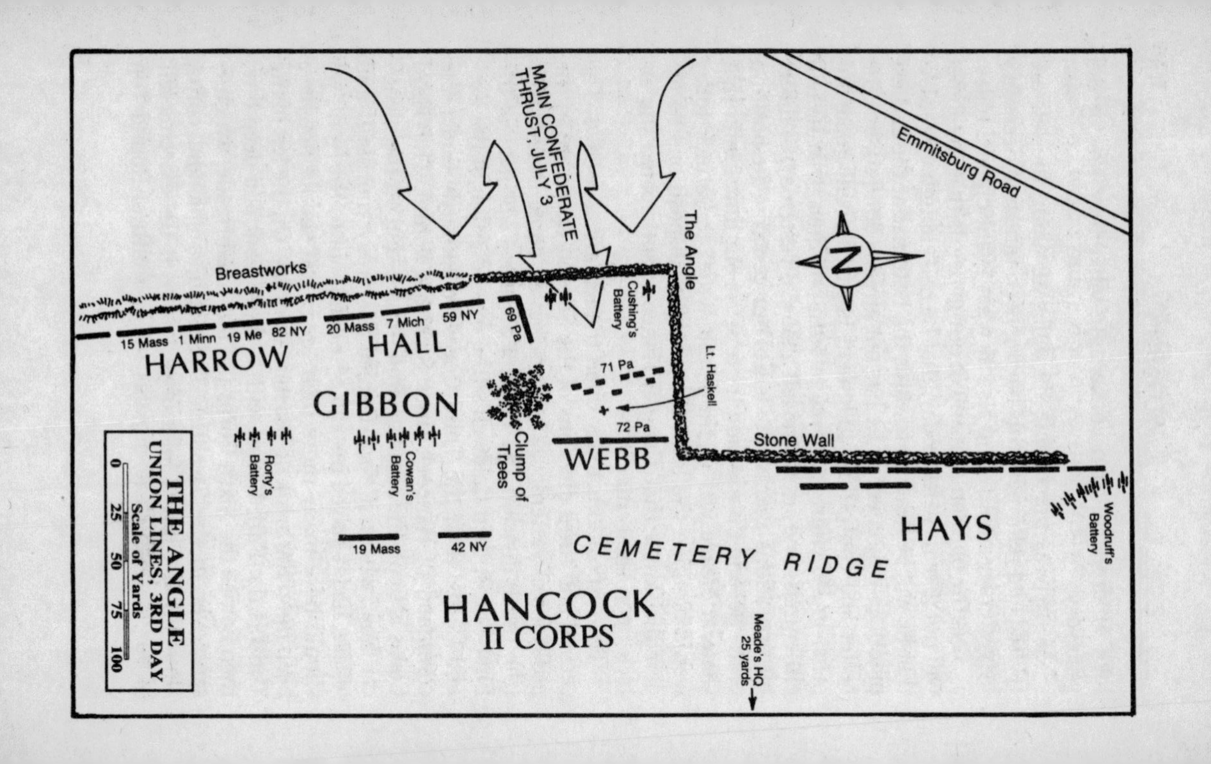

THE ANGLE
UNION LINES, 3RD DAY
Scale of Yards
0 25 50 75 100
Emmitsburg Road
N
MAIN CONFEDERATE THRUST, JULY 3
The Angle
Breastworks
Stone Wall
Cushing's Battery
Lt. Haskell
Woodruff's Battery
Rorty's Battery
Cowan's Battery
Clump of Trees
Meade's HQ 25 yards
15 Mass
1 Minn
19 Me
82 NY
20 Mass
7 Mich
59 NY
69 Pa
71 Pa
72 Pa
19 Mass
42 NY
HARROW
HALL
GIBBON
WEBB
HAYS
CEMETERY RIDGE
HANCOCK
II CORPS

and runs along its western base in the woods, and thence to the cemetery. This corps is burning to pay off the old scores made on the fourth of May there back of Fredericksburg. Note well the position of the second and third divisions of the Second Corps—it will become important.

There are nearly six thousand men and officers in these two divisions here upon the field. The losses were quite heavy yesterday; some regiments are detached to other parts of the field. So all told there are less than six thousand men now in the two divisions who occupy a line of about a thousand yards. The most of the way along this line upon the crest was a stone fence, constructed of small rough stones, a good deal of the way badly pulled down; but the men had improved it and patched it with rails from the neighboring fences and with earth, so as to render it in many places a very passable breastwork against musketry and flying fragments of shells.

These works are so low as to compel the men to kneel or lie down, generally to obtain cover. Near the right of the second division, and just by the little group of trees that I have mentioned there, this stone fence made a right angle and extended thence to the front about twenty or thirty yards, where with another, less than a right angle, it followed along the crest again. [*Here Haskell drew a small, rough sketch of the Angle and the clump of trees nearby.*] The lines were conformed to these breastworks and to the nature of the ground upon the crest, so as to occupy the more favorable places—to be covered and still be able to deliver effective fire upon the enemy should he come there. In some places a second line was so posted as to be able to deliver its fire over the heads of the first line behind the works; but such formation was not practicable all of the way. But all the force of these two divisions was in line, in position without reserves, and in such a manner that every man of them could have fired his piece at the same instance. The division flags—that of the second division being a white trefoil upon a square blue field and of the third division a blue trefoil upon a white rectangular field—waved behind the divisions at the points where the generals of division were supposed to be; the brigade flags, similar to these but with a triangular field, were behind the brigades; and the national flags of the regiments were in the lines of their regiments. To the left of the second division, and advanced something over a hundred yards, were posted a part of Stannard's brigade, two regiments or more, behind a small bush-crowned crest that ran in a direction oblique to the general line. These were well covered by the crest, and wholly concealed by the bushes, so that an advancing enemy would be close upon them before they could be seen. Other troops of Doubleday's division were strongly posted in rear of these in the general line.

I could not help wishing all the morning that this line of the two divisions of the Second Corps were stronger; it was, so far as numbers constitute strength, the weakest part of our whole line of battle. What if, I thought, the enemy should make an assault here today with two or three heavy lines, a great overwhelming mass; would he not sweep through that thin six thousand?

But I was not General Meade, who alone had power to send other troops there; and he was satisfied with that part of the line as it was. He was early on horseback this morning and rode along the whole line, looking to it himself, and with glass in hand, sweeping the woods and fields in the direction of the enemy, to see if aught of him could be discovered. His manner was calm and serious, but earnest. There was no arrogance of hope or timidity of fear discernible in his face; but you would have supposed he would do his duty, conscientiously all well, and would be willing to abide the result. You would have seen this in his face. He was well pleased with the left of the line today; it was so strong, with good troops. He had no apprehension for the right, where the fight now was going on, on account of the admirable position our forces there. He was not of the opinion that the enemy would attack the center (our artillery had such sweep there), and this was not the favorite point of attack with the Rebel; besides, should he attack the center, the general thought, he could reinforce it in good season. I heard General Meade speak of these matters to Hancock and some others at about nine o'clock in the morning, while they were up by the line near the Second Corps.

No further changes of importance, except those mentioned, were made in the disposition of the troops this morning, except to replace some of the batteries that were disabled yesterday by others from the artillery reserve and to brace up the lines well with guns, wherever there were eligible places, from the same source. The line is all in good order again, and we are ready for general battle.

Save the operations upon the right, the enemy—so far as we could see—was very quiet all the morning. Occasionally the outposts would fire a little and then cease. Movements would be discovered which would indicate the attempt on the part of the enemy to post a battery; our Parrotts would send a few shells to the spot, then silence would follow.

At one of these times a painful accident happened to us this morning: First Lieutenant Henry Ropes (20th Massachusetts in General Gibbon's division), a most estimable gentleman and officer—intelligent, educated, refined, one of the noble souls that came to the country's defense—while lying at his post with his regiment in front of one of the batteries, which fired over the infantry, was instantly killed by a badly made shell, which, or some portion of it, fell but a few yards in front of the muzzle of the gun. The same accident killed or wounded several others. The loss of

Ropes would have pained us at any time and in any manner; in this manner his death was doubly painful.

Between ten and eleven o'clock over in a peach orchard in front of the position of Sickles yesterday, some little show of the enemy's infantry was discovered. A few shells scattered the graybacks; they again appeared and, it becoming apparent that they were only posting a skirmish line, no further molestation was offered them. A little after this some of the enemy's flags could be discerned over near the same quarter, above the top and behind a small crest of a ridge; there seemed to be two or three of them—possibly they were guidons—and they moved too fast to be carried on foot. Possibly, we thought, the enemy is posting some batteries there. We knew in about two hours from this time better about the matter.

Eleven o'clock came. The noise of battle has ceased upon the right. Not a sound of a gun or musket can be heard on all the field. The sky is bright with only the white fleecy clouds floating over from the west. The July sun streams down its fire upon the bright iron of the muskets in stacks upon the crest and the dazzling brass of the Napoleons. The army lolls and longs for the shade, of which some get a hand's breadth from a shelter tent stuck upon a ramrod. The silence and sultriness of a July noon are supreme.

Now it so happened that just about this time of day a very original and interesting thought occurred to General Gibbon and several of his staff: that it would be a very good thing, and a very good time, to have something to eat. When I announce to you that I had not tasted a mouthful of food since yesterday noon—and that all I had had to drink since that time, but the most miserable muddy warm water, was a little drink of whiskey that Major Biddle, General Meade's aide-de-camp, gave me last evening, and a cup of strong coffee that I gulped down as I was first mounting this morning; and further, that save the four or five hours in the night, there was scarcely a moment, since that time but that I was in the saddle—you may have some notion of the reason of my assent to this extraordinary proposition. Nor will I mention the doubts I had as to the feasibility of the execution of this very novel proposal, except to say that I knew this morning that our larder was low—not to put too fine a point upon it, that we had nothing but some potatoes and sugar and coffee in the world. And I may as well say here that of such, in scant proportions, would have been our repast had it not been for the riding of miles by two persons, one an officer, to procure supplies; and they only succeeded in getting some few chickens, some butter, and one huge loaf of bread, which last was bought of a soldier because he had grown faint in carrying it, and was afterwards rescued—with much difficulty—and after a long race from a four-footed hog, which had got hold of and had actually eaten a part of it. "There is a divinity," etc.

Suffice it, this very ingenious and unheard of contemplated proceeding, first announced by the general, was accepted and at once undertaken by his staff. Of the absolute quality of what we had to eat, I could not pretend to judge. But I think an unprejudiced person would have said of the bread that it was good; so of the potatoes, before they were boiled; of the chickens, he would have questioned their age, but they were large and in good *running* orders; the toast was good and the butter; there were those who, when coffee was given them, called for tea, and *vice versa*, and were so ungracious as to suggest that the water that was used in both might have come from near a barn. Of course it did not. We all came down to the little peach orchard where we had stayed last night; and wonderful to see and tell, ever mindful of our needs, had it all ready, had our faithful John. There was an enormous pan of stewed chickens, and the potatoes, and toast, all hot, and the bread and the butter, and tea, and coffee.

There was satisfaction derived from just naming them all over. We called John an angel, and he snickered and said, he "*knowed*" we'd come. General Hancock is, of course, invited to partake, and without delay we commence operations. Stools are not very numerous—two in all—and these the two generals have by common consent. Our table was the top of a mess-chest; by this the generals sat. The rest of us sat upon the ground, cross-legged like the picture of a smoking Turk, and held our plates upon our laps. How delicious was the stewed chicken. I had a cucumber pickle in my saddle bags—the last of a lunch left there two or three days ago, which George brought—and I had half of it. We were just well at it, when General Meade rode down to us from the line, accompanied by one of his staff, and by General Gibbon's invitation they dismounted and joined us. For the general commanding the Army of the Potomac, George—by an effort worthy of the person and the occasion—finds an empty cracker box for a seat. The staff officer must sit upon the ground with the rest of us. Soon generals Newton and Pleasonton, each with an aide, arrive. By an almost superhuman effort a roll of blankets is found, which, upon a perch, is long enough to seat these generals both, and room is made for them. The aides sit with us. And fortunate to relate, there was enough cooked for us all, and from General Meade to the youngest second lieutenant we all had a most hearty and well-relished dinner. Of the "past" we were "secure."

The generals ate, and after lighted cigars, and under the flickering shade of a very small tree, discoursed of the incidents of yesterday's battle and of the probabilities of today. General Newton humorously spoke of General Gibbon as "this young North Carolinian" and how he was becoming arrogant and above his position because he commanded a corps. General Gibbon retorted by saying that General Newton had not been long enough in such a command (only since yesterday) to enable him to judge of such things. General Meade still thought that the enemy would attack his left again today, towards evening, but he was ready for them; General Hancock, that the attack would be upon the position of the Second Corps. It was mentioned that General Hancock would again resume command of the Second Corps from that time, so that General Gibbon would again return to the second division.

General Meade spoke of the provost guards, that they were good men, and that it would be better today to have them in the ranks than to stop stragglers and skulkers, as these latter would be good for but little even in the ranks; and so he gave the order that all the provost guards should at once temporarily rejoin their regiments. Then General Gibbon called up Captain Farrell (1st Minnesota), who commanded the provost guard of his division, and directed him for that day to join the regiment. "Very well, sir," said the captain as he touched his hat and turned away. He was a quiet, excellent gentleman, and thorough soldier. I knew him well and esteemed him. I never saw him again. He was killed in two or three hours from that time, and over half of his splendid company were either killed or wounded.

And so the time passed on, each general now and then dispatching some order or message by an officer or orderly, until about half-past twelve, when all the generals, one by one (first General Meade), rode off their several ways. And General Gibbon and his staff alone remained.

We dozed in the heat and lolled upon the ground, with half-open eyes. Our horses were hitched to the trees, munching some oats. A great lull rests upon all the field. Time was heavy; and for want of something better to do, I yawned and looked at my watch. It was five minutes before one o'clock. I returned my watch to its pocket and thought possibly that I might go to sleep, and stretched myself upon the ground accordingly. "*Ex uno disce omnes*." My attitude and purpose were those of the general and the rest of the staff.

What sound was that? There was no mistaking it! The distinct sharp sound of one of the enemy's guns, square over to the front, caused us to open our eyes and turn them in that direction, when we saw directly above the crest the smoke of the bursting shell and heard its noise. In an instant, before a word was spoken, as if that was the signal gun for general work, loud, startling, booming, the report of gun after gun, in rapid succession, smote our ears, and their shells plunged down and exploded all around us. We sprang to our feet. In briefest time the whole Rebel line to the west was pouring out its thunder and its iron upon our devoted crest. The wildest confusion for a few moments obtained among us. The shells came bursting all about. The servants ran terror-stricken for dear life and disappeared. The horses, hitched to the trees or held by the slack hands of orderlies, neighed out in fright and broke away and plunged riderless through the fields.

The general, at the first, had snatched his sword and started on foot for the front. I called for my horse; nobody responded. I found him tied to a tree nearby, eating oats, with an air of the greatest composure, which, under the circumstances, even then struck me as exceedingly ridiculous. He alone, of all beasts or men near, was cool. I am not sure but that I learned a lesson then from a horse. Anxious alone for his oats, while I put on the bridle and adjusted the halter, he delayed me by keeping his head down. So I had time to see one of the horses of our mess wagon struck and torn by a shell; the pair plunge, the driver has lost the rein—horses, driver, and wagon go into a heap by a tree. Two mules close at hand, packed with boxes of ammunition, are knocked all to pieces by a shell. General Gibbon's groom has just mounted his horse and is starting to take the general's to him, when the flying iron meets him and tears open his breast—he drops dead, and the horses gallop away. No more than a minute since the first shot was fired, and I am mounted and riding after the general. The mighty din that now rises to heaven and shakes the earth is not all of it the voice of the rebellion; for our guns, the guardian lions of the crest, quick to awake when danger comes, have opened their fiery jaws and begun to roar—the great hoarse roar of battle. I overtake the general half way up to the line. Before we reach the crest his horse is brought by an orderly.

Leaving our horses just behind a sharp declivity of the ridge, on foot we go up among the batteries. How the long streams of fire spout from the guns, how the rifled shells hiss, how the smoke deepens and rolls! But where is the infantry? Has it vanished in smoke? Is this a nightmare, or a juggler's devilish trick? All too real. The men of the infantry have seized their arms; and behind their works, behind every rock, in every ditch, wherever there is any shelter, they hug the ground, silent, quiet, unterrified, little harmed. The enemy's guns now in action are in position at their front of the woods along the second ridge, that I have before mentioned, and towards their right, behind a small crest in the open field, where we saw the flags this morning. Their line is some two miles long, concave on the side towards us, and their range is from one thousand to eighteen hundred yards. A hundred and twenty-five Rebel guns, we estimate, are now active firing twenty-four pound; twenty-, twelve-, and ten-pound projectiles; solid shot and shells, spherical, conical, spiral.

The enemy's fire is chiefly concentrated upon the position of the Second Corps. From the cemetery to Round Top, with over a hundred guns and to all parts of the enemy's line, our batteries reply—of twenty- and ten-pound Parrotts, ten-pound rifled ordnances, and twelve-pound Napoleons, using projectiles as various in shape and name as those of the enemy. Captain Hazard, commanding the artillery brigade of the Second Corps, was vigilant among the batteries of his command, and they were all doing well.

All was going on satisfactorily. We had nothing to do, therefore, but to be observers of the grand spectacle of battle. Captain Wessels, judge advocate of the division, now joined us, and we sat down just behind the crest, close to the left of Cushing's battery, to bide our time, to see, to be ready to act when the time should come, which might be at any moment. Who can describe such a conflict as is raging around us! To say that it was like a summer storm, with the crash of thunder, the glare of lightning, the shrieking of the wind, and the clatter of hailstones, would be weak. The thunder and lightning of these two hundred and fifty guns and their shells, whose smoke darkens the sky, are incessant, all pervading, in the air above our heads, on the ground at our feet—remote, near, deafening, ear-piercing, astounding; and these hailstones are massy iron charged with exploding fire. And there is little of human interest in a storm; it is an absorbing element of this. You may see flame and smoke, and hurrying men, and human passion, at a great conflagration; but they are all earthly and nothing more. These guns are great infuriate demons, not of the earth, whose mouths blaze with smoky tongues of living fire, and whose murky breath, sulphur-laden, rolls around them and along the ground, the smoke of Hades. These grimy men, rushing, shouting, their souls in frenzy, plying the dusky globes and the igniting spark, are in their league, and but their willing ministers.

We thought that at the Second Bull Run, at the Antietam, and at Fredericksburg on the eleventh of December, we had heard heavy cannonading; they were but holy day salutes compared with this. Besides the great ceaseless roar of the guns, which was but the background of the others, a million various minor sounds engaged the ear. The projectiles shriek long and sharp: they hiss, they scream, they growl, they sputter—all sounds of life and rage; and each has its different note, and all are discordant. Was ever such a chaos of sound before?

We note the effect of the enemy's fire among the batteries and along the crest. We see the solid shot strike axle, or pole, or wheel, and the tough iron and heart of oak snap and fly like straws. The great oaks there by Woodruff's guns heave down their massy branches with a crash, as if the lightning had smote them. The shells swoop down among the battery horses, standing there apart; a half a dozen horses start, they tumble, their legs stiffen, their vitals and blood smear the ground. And these shot and shells have no respect for men either. We see the poor fellows hobbling back from the crest, or unable to do so, pale and weak lying on the ground, with the mangled stump of an arm or leg, dripping their life blood away, or with a cheek torn open, or a shoulder smashed. And many, alas! hear not the roar as they stretch upon the ground with upturned faces and open eyes, though a shell should burst in their very ears. Their ear and their bodies this instant are only mud. We saw them but a moment since, there among the flame, with brawny arms and muscles of iron wielding the rammer and pushing home the cannon's plethoric load.

Strange freaks these round shot play! We saw a man coming up from the rear with his full knapsack on and some canteens of water held by the straps in his hands. He was walking slowly and with apparent unconcern, though the iron hailed around him. A shot struck the knapsack, and it and its contents flew thirty yards in every direction; the knapsack disappeared like an egg thrown spitefully against a rock. The soldier stopped and turned about in puzzled surprise, put one hand to his back to assure himself that the knapsack was not there, and then walked slowly on again unharmed, with not even his coat torn. Near us was a man crouching behind a small disintegrated stone, which was about the size of a common water bucket. He was bent up, with his face to the ground, in the attitude of a pagan worshiper before his idol. It looked so absurd to see him thus that I went and said to him: "Do not lie there like a toad. Why not go to your regiment and be a man!" He turned up his face with a stupid, terrified look upon me, and then without a word turned his nose again to the ground. An orderly, that was with me at the time, told me a few moments later that a shot struck the stone, smashing it in a thousand fragments, but did not touch the man, though his head was not six inches from the stone.

All the projectiles that came near us were not so harmless. Not ten yards away from us, a shell burst among some small bushes, where sat three or four orderlies holding horses; two of the men and one horse were killed. Only a few yards off a shell exploded over an open limber box in Cushing's battery, and almost at the same instant, another shell, over a neighboring box. In both the boxes the ammunition blew up with an explosion that shook the ground, throwing fire and splinters and shells far into the air and all around, and destroying several men. We watched the shells bursting in the air as they came hissing in all directions. Their flash was a bright gleam of lightning radiating from a point, giving place in the thousandth part of a second to a small, white, puffy cloud, like a fleece of the lightest, whitest wool. These clouds were very numerous. We could not often see the shell before it burst; but sometimes, as we faced towards the enemy and looked above our heads, the approach would be heralded by a prolonged hiss, which always seemed to me to be a line of something tangible terminating in a black globe, distinct to the eye, as the sound had been to the ear. The shell would seem to stop and hang unsuspended in the air an instant, and then vanish in fire and smoke and noise. We saw the missiles tear and plow the ground.

All in rear of the crest for a thousand yards, as well as among the batteries, was the field of their blind fury. Ambulances, passing down the Taneytown Road with wounded men, were struck. The hospitals near this road were riddled. The house which was General Meade's headquarters was shot through several times; and a great many horses of officers and orderlies were lying dead around it. Riderless horses, galloping madly through the fields, were brought up—or down, rather—by these invisible horse tamers, and they would not run any more. Mules with ammunition, pigs wallowing about, cows in the pastures, whatever was animate or inanimate in all this broad range, were no exception to their blind havoc. The percussion shells would strike, and thunder, and scatter the earth and their whistling fragments; the Whitworth bolts would pound, and ricochet, and howl far away sputtering, with the sound of a mass of hot iron plunged in water; and the great solid shot would smite the unresisting ground with a sounding "thud," as the strong boxer crashes his iron fist into the jaws of his unguarded adversary. Such were some of the sights and sounds of this great iron battle of missiles.

Our artillery men upon the crest budged not an inch nor intermitted; but, though caisson and limber were smashed, and guns dismantled, and men and horses killed, there amidst smoke and sweat, they gave back without grudge or loss of time in the sending in kind whatever the enemy sent—globe, and cone, and bolt, hollow or solid, an iron greeting to the rebellion, the compliments of the wrathful Republic.

An hour has droned its flight, since first the war began. There is no sign of weariness or abatement on either side.

So long it seemed, that the din and crashing around began to appear the normal condition of nature there, and fighting, man's element. The general proposed to go among the men and over to the front of the batteries, so at about two o'clock he and I started. We went along the lines of the infantry as they lay there flat upon the earth, a little to the front of the batteries. They were suffering little and were quiet and cool. How glad we were that the enemy were no better gunners and that they cut the shell fuses too long. To the question asked the men, "What do you think of this?" the replies would be: "O, this is bully"; "We are getting to like it"; "O, we don't mind this." And so they lay under the heaviest cannonade that ever shook the continent and among them a thousand times more jokes, than heads, were cracked.

We went down in front of the line some two hundred yards, and as the smoke had a tendency to settle upon a higher plain than where we were, we could see near the ground distinctly all over the field, as well back to the crest where were our own guns, as to the opposite ridge where were those of the enemy. No infantry was in sight save the skirmishers, and they stood silent, and motionless—a row of gray posts through the field on one side confronted by another of blue. Under the grateful shade of some elm trees, where we could see much of the field, we made seats of the ground and sat down. Here all the more repulsive features of the fight were unseen by reason of the smoke. Man had arranged the scenes and for a time had taken part in the great drama; but at last as the plot thickened, conscious of his littleness and inadequacy to the mighty part, he had stepped aside and given place to more powerful actors. So it seemed; for we could see no men about the batteries. On either crest we could see the great flaky streams of fire (and they seemed numberless) of the opposing guns and their white banks of swift convolving smoke;

but the sound of the discharges was drowned in the universal ocean of sound. Over all the valley, the smoke, a sulfury arch, stretched its lurid span; and through it always, shrieking on their unseen courses, thickly flew a myriad iron deaths.

With our grim horizon on all sides round-toothed thick with battery flame, under that dissonant canopy of warring shells, we sat and saw and heard in silence. What other expression had we that was not mean for such an awful universe of battle?

A shell struck our breastwork of rails up in sight of us, and a moment afterwards we saw the men bearing some of their wounded companions away from the same spot; and directly two men from there came down toward where we were and sought to get shelter in an excavation nearby, where many dead horses, killed in yesterday's fight, had been thrown. General Gibbon said to these men, more in a tone of kindly expostulation than of command: "My men, do not leave your ranks to try to get shelter here. All these matters are in the hands of God, and nothing that you can do will make you safer in one place than in another." The men went quietly back to the line at once. The general then said to me: "I am not a member of any church, but I have always had a strong religious feeling; and so in all these battles I have always believed that I was in the hands of God, and that I should be unharmed or not, according to his will. For this reason, I think it is, I am always ready to go where duty calls, no matter how great the danger."

Half-past two o'clock, an hour-and-a-half since the commencement, and still the cannonade did not in the least abate; but soon thereafter some signs of weariness and a little slackening of fire began to be apparent upon both sides. First we saw Brown's battery retire from the line, too feeble for further battle. Its position was a little to the front of the line. Its commander was wounded, and many of its men were so, or worse. Some of its guns had been disabled; many of its horses killed; its ammunition was nearly expended. Other batteries in similar case had been withdrawn before to be replaced by fresh ones, and some were withdrawn afterwards.

Soon after the battery named had gone, the general and I started to return, passing towards the left of the division and crossing the ground where the guns had stood. The stricken horses were numerous, and the dead and wounded men lay about; and as we passed these latter, their low piteous call for water would invariably come to us, if they had yet any voice left. I found canteens of water near—no difficult matter where a battle has been—and held them to livid lips, and even in the faintness of death, the eagerness to drink told of their terrible torture of thirst. But we must pass on.

Our infantry was still unshaken and in all the cannonade suffered very little. The batteries had been handled much more severely. I am unable to give any figures. A great number of horses had been killed; in some batteries more than half of all. Guns had been dismounted; a great many caissons, limbers, and carriages had been destroyed, and usually from ten to twenty-five men to each battery had been struck, at least along our part of the crest. All together the fire of the enemy had injured us much, both in the modes that I have stated and also by exhausting our ammunition and fouling our guns, so as to render our batteries unfit for further immediate use. The scenes that met our eyes on all hands among the batteries were fearful.

All things must end, and the great cannonade was no exception to the general law of earth. In the number of guns active at one time and in the duration and rapidity of their fire, this artillery engagement, up to this time, must stand alone and preeminent in this war. It has not been often or many times surpassed in the battles of the world.

Two hundred and fifty guns, at least, rapidly fired for two mortal hours! Cipher out the number of tons of gunpowder and iron that made those two hours hideous!

Of the injury of our fire upon the enemy, except the facts that ours was the superior position, if not better served and constructed artillery, and that the enemy's artillery, hereafter during the battle, was almost silent, we know little. Of course during the fight we often saw the enemy's caissons explode, and the trees sent, by our shot, crashing about his ears, but we can from these alone infer but little of general results.

At three o'clock almost precisely the last shot hummed, and bounded, and fell, and the cannonade was over. The purpose of General Lee in all this fire of his guns—we know it now; we did not at the time so well—was to disable our artillery and break up our infantry upon the position of the Second Corps, so as to render them less an impediment to the sweep of his own brigades and divisions over our crest and through our lines. He probably supposed our infantry was massed behind the crest and the batteries; and hence his fire was so high and his fuses to the shells were cut so long—too long. The Rebel general failed in some of his plans in this behalf, as many generals have failed before and will again.

The artillery fight over, men began to breathe more freely, and to ask: "What next I wonder?" The battery men were among their guns, some leaning to rest and wipe the sweat from their sooty faces, some were handling ammunition boxes and replenishing those that were empty. Some batteries from the artillery reserve were moving up to take the places of the disabled ones. The smoke was clearing from the crests. There was a pause between acts with the curtain down, soon to rise upon the great, final act and catastrophe of Gettysburg.

We had passed by the left of the second division, coming

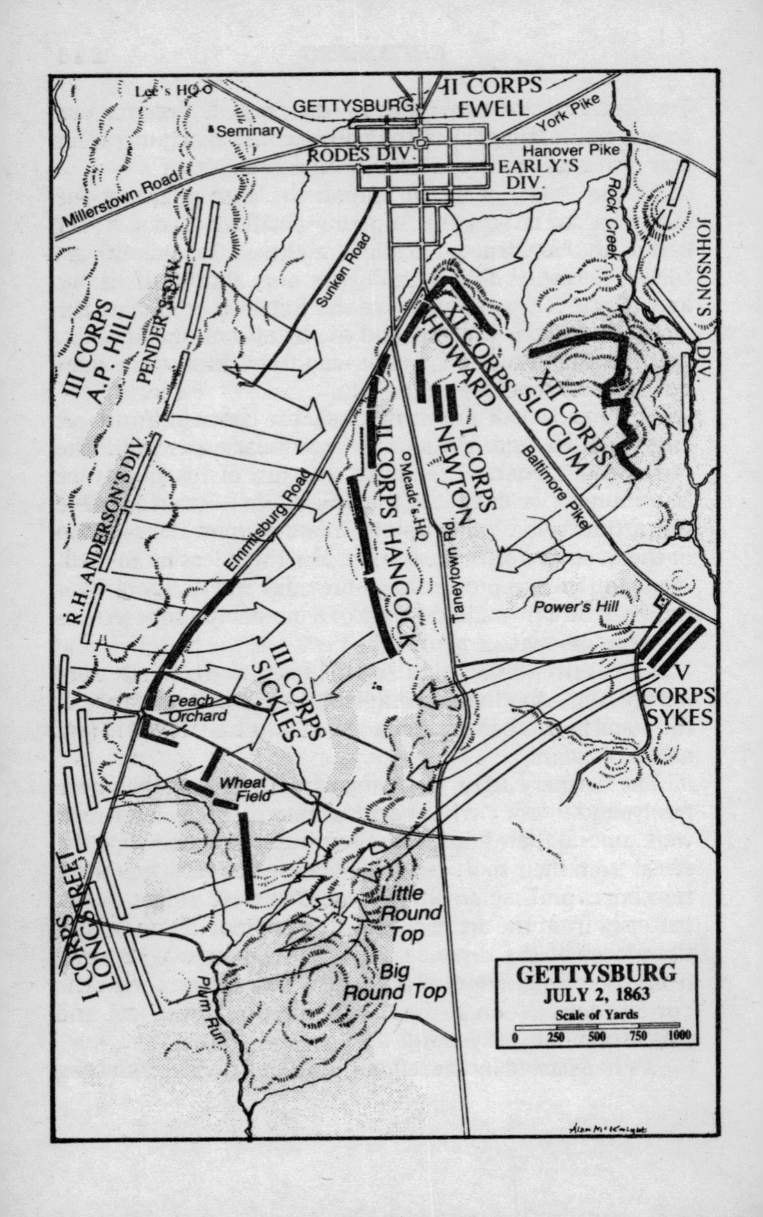

Lee's HQ
II CORPS
EWELL
GETTYSBURG
Seminary
York Pike
RODES DIV.
Hanover Pike
EARLY'S DIV.
Millerstown Road
Rock Creek
JOHNSON'S DIV.
Sunken Road
PENDER'S DIV.
III CORPS
A.P. HILL
XI CORPS
HOWARD
XII CORPS
SLOCUM
I CORPS
NEWTON
II CORPS HANCOCK
Meade's HQ
R.H. ANDERSON'S DIV.
Emmitsburg Road
Taneytown Rd.
Baltimore Pike
Power's Hill
III CORPS
SICKLES
V CORPS
SYKES
Peach Orchard
Wheat Field
Little Round Top
Big Round Top
I CORPS
LONGSTREET
Plum Run
GETTYSBURG
JULY 2, 1863
Scale of Yards
0
250
500
750
1000
Alan McKnight

from the first. When we crossed the crest, the enemy was not in sight, and all was still. We walked slowly along in rear of the troops, by the ridge cut off now from a view of the enemy, or his position, and were returning to the spot where we had left our horses. General Gibbon had just said that he inclined to the belief that the enemy was falling back and that the cannonade was only one of his noisy modes of covering the movement. I said that I thought that fifteen minutes would show that, by all his bowling, the Rebel did not mean retreat. We were near our horses when we noticed Brigadier General Hunt, chief of artillery of the army, near Woodruff's battery swiftly moving about on horseback and apparently, in a rapid manner, giving some orders about the guns. Thought we, what could this mean! In a moment afterwards we met Captain Wessels and the orderlies who had our horses; they were on foot leading the horses. Captain Wessels was pale, and he said, excited: "General, they say the enemy's infantry is advancing." We sprang into our saddles—a score of bounds brought us upon the all-seeing crest.

To say that none grew pale and held their breath at what we and they there saw would not be true. Might not six thousand men be brave and without shade of fear, and yet, before a hostile eighteen thousand, armed and not five minutes' march away, turn ashy white? None on that crest now need be told that *the enemy is advancing*. Every eye could see his legions, an overwhelming, resistless tide of an ocean of armed men sweeping upon us! Regiment after regiment, and brigade after brigade, move from the woods and rapidly take their places in the lines forming the assault. Pickett's proud division, with some additional troops, holds their right; Pettigrew's (Heth's), their left. The first line, at short interval, is followed by a second, and that a third succeeds; and the columns between support the lines. More than half a mile their front extends; more than a thousand yards the dull gray masses deploy, man touching man, rank pressing rank, and line supporting line. Their red flags wave; their horsemen gallop up and down; the arms of eighteen thousand men, barrel and bayonet, gleam in the sun, a sloping forest of flashing steel. Right on they move as with one soul, in perfect order, without impediment of ditch, or wall, or stream, over ridge and slope, through orchard and meadow and cornfield—magnificent, grim, irresistible.

All was orderly and still upon our crest—no noise and no confusion. The men had little need of commands, for the survivors of a dozen battles knew well enough what this array in front portended; and already in their places, they would be prepared to act when the right time should come. The click of the locks as each man raised the hammer to feel with his finger that the cap was on the nipple; the sharp jar as a musket touched a stone upon the wall when thrust in, aiming over it; and the clinking of the iron axles as the guns were rolled up by hand a little further to the front were quite all the sounds that could be heard. Cap-boxes were slid around to the front of the body; cartridge-boxes opened; officers opened their pistol holsters. Such preparation, little more, was needed. The trefoil flags, colors of the brigades and divisions, moved to their places in rear; but along the lines in front, the grand old ensign that first waved in battle at Saratoga in 1777, and which these people coming would rob of half its stars, stood up, and the west wind kissed it as the sergeants sloped its lance towards the enemy. I believe that not one above whom it then waved but blessed his God that he was loyal to it, and whose heart did not swell with pride towards it, as the emblem of the Republic, before that treason's flaunting rag in front.

General Gibbon rode down the lines, cool and calm, and in an unimpassioned voice he said to the men: "Do not hurry, men, and fire too fast; let them come up close before you fire, and then aim low, and steadily." The coolness of their general was reflected in the faces of his men. Five minutes had elapsed since first the enemy had emerged from the woods—no great space of time, surely, if measured by the usual standards by which men estimate duration, but it was long enough for us to note and weigh some of the elements of mighty moment that surrounded us: the disparity of numbers between the assailants and the assailed; that few as were our numbers, we could not be supported or reinforced until support would not be needed, or would be too late; that upon the ability of the two trefoil divisions to hold the crest and repel the assault depended not only their own safety or destruction but also the honor of the Army of the Potomac and defeat or victory at Gettysburg. Should these advancing men pierce our line and become the entering wedge, driven home, that would sever our army asunder, what hope would there be afterwards, and where the blood-earned fruits of yesterday?

It was long enough for the Rebel storm to drift across more than half the space that had at first separated it from us. None, or all, of these considerations either depressed or elevated us—they might have done the former, had we been timid; the latter, had we been confident and vain. But we were there waiting and ready to do our duty; that done, results could not dishonor us.

Our skirmishers open a spattering fire along the front, and fighting retire upon the main line—the first drops, the heralds of the storm, sounding on our windows. Then the thunders of our guns—first Arnold's, then Cushing's, and Woodruff's and the rest—shake and reverberate again through the air, and their sounding shells smite the enemy. The general said I had better go and tell General Meade of this advance: to gallop to General Meade's headquarters, to learn there that he had changed them to another part of the field, to dispatch to him by the Signal Corps (in General Gibbon's name) the message: "The enemy is advancing his infantry in force upon my front," and to be again upon the crest were but the work of a minute.

All our available guns are now active, and from the fire of shells, as the range grows shorter and shorter, they change to shrapnel, and from shrapnel to canister; but in spite of shells and shrapnel and canister, without wavering or halt, the hardy lines of the enemy continue to move on. The Rebel guns make no reply to ours, and no charging shout rings out today, as is the Rebel wont; but the courage of these silent men amid our shot seems not to need the stimulus of other noise. The enemy's right flank sweeps near Stannard's bushy crest, and his concealed Vermonters rake it with a well-delivered fire of musketry; the gray lines do not halt or reply, but withdrawing a little from that extreme, they still move on.

And so across all that broad open ground they have come, nearer and nearer, nearly half the way with our guns bellowing in their faces, until now a hundred yards, no more, divide our ready left from their advancing right. The eager men there are impatient to begin. Let them. First Harrow's breastworks flame, then Hall's, then Webb's. As if our bullets were the fire-coals that touched off their muskets, the enemy in front halts and his countless level barrels blaze back upon us. The second division is struggling in battle; the rattling storm soon spreads to the right, and the blue trefoils are vying with the white. All along each hostile front, a thousand yards, with narrowest space between, the volleys blaze and roll—as thick the sound as when a summer hailstorm pelts the city roofs, as thick the fire as when the incessant lightning fringes a summer cloud.

When the Rebel infantry had opened fire, our batteries soon became silent—and this without their fault, for they were foul[ed] by long previous use, they were the targets of the concentrated Rebel bullets, and some of them had expended all their canister. But they were not silent before Rorty was killed, Woodruff had fallen mortally wounded, and Cushing—firing almost his last canister—had dropped dead among his guns, shot through the head by a bullet. The conflict is left to the infantry alone.

Unable to find my general when I had returned to the crest after transmitting his message to General Meade, and while riding in the search (having witnessed the development of the fight from the first fire upon the left, by the main lines, until all of the two divisions were furiously engaged), I gave up hunting as useless. I was convinced General Gibbon could not be on the field: I left him mounted (I could easily have found him now had he so remained), but now, save myself, there was not a mounted officer near the engaged lines; and [I] was riding towards the right of the second division with purpose to stop there as the most eligible position to watch the further progress of the battle, there to be ready to take part, according to my own notions, whenever and wherever occasion was presented.

The conflict was tremendous, but I had seen no wavering in all our line. Wondering how long the Rebel ranks, deep though they were, could stand our sheltered volleys, I had come near my destination, when (Great Heaven! Were my senses mad?) the larger portion of Webb's brigade (my God, it was true), there by the group of trees and the angles of the wall, was breaking from the cover of their works, and without orders or reason, with no hand lifted to check them, was falling back a fear-stricken flock of confusion! The fate of Gettysburg hung upon a spider's single thread! A great magnificent passion came on me at the instant, not one that overpowers and confounds, but one that blanches the face and sublimes every sense and faculty. My sword that had always hung idle by my side—the sign of rank only—in every battle, I drew bright and gleaming, the symbol of command. Was not that a fit occasion and these fugitives the men on whom to try the temper of the Solingen steel? All rules and proprieties were forgotten, all considerations of person, and danger, and safety, despised; for as I met the tide of these rabbits, the damned red flags of the rebellion began to thicken and flaunt along the wall they had just deserted, and one was already waving over one of the guns of the dead Cushing.

I ordered these men to "*halt*," and "*face about*," and "*fire,*" and they heard my voice, and gathered my meaning, and obeyed my commands. On some unpatriotic backs, of those not quick of comprehension, the flat of my saber fell, not lightly; and at its touch their love of country returned; and with a look at me as if I were the destroying angel, as I might have become theirs, they again faced the enemy. General Webb soon came to my assistance. He was on foot, but he was active, and did all that one could do to repair the breach or to avert its calamity. The men that had fallen back, facing the enemy soon regained confidence in themselves and became steady. This portion of the wall was lost to us, and the enemy had gained the cover of the reverse side, where he now stormed with fire; but Webb's men, with their bodies in part protected by the abruptness of the crest, now sent back in the enemy's faces as fierce a storm. Some scores of venturesome Rebels that in their first push at the wall had dared to cross at the further angle, and those that had desecrated Cushing's guns, were promptly shot down, and speedy death met him who should raise his body to cross it again.

At this point little could be seen of the enemy by reason of his cover and the smoke (except the flash of his muskets and his wavering flags). Those red flags were accumulating at the wall every moment, and they maddened us as the same color does the bull. Webb's men are falling fast, and he is among them to direct and encourage; but however well they may now do, with that walled enemy in front (with more than a dozen flags to Webb's three), it soon becomes apparent that in not many minutes they will be overpowered or that there will be none alive for the enemy to overpower. Webb has but three regiments, all small—the 69th, 71st, and 72nd Pennsylvania (the 106th Pennsylvania, except two companies, is not here today)—and he must have speedy assistance or this crest will be lost. Oh, where is Gibbon? where is Hancock?—some general, anybody with the power and the will to support that wasting, melting line. No general came, and no succor! I thought of Hays upon the right; but from the smoke and war along his front, it was evident that he had enough upon his hands, if he staid the in-rolling tide of the Rebels there. Doubleday upon the left was too far off and too slow, and on another occasion I had begged him to send his idle regiments to support another line, battling with thrice its numbers, and this *"Old Sumter Hero"* had declined.

As a last resort I resolved to see if Hall and Harrow could not send some of their commands to reinforce Webb. I galloped to the left in the execution of my purpose, and as I attained the rear of Hall's line, from the nature of the ground there and the position of the enemy, it was easy to discover the reason and the manner of this gathering of Rebel flags in front of Webb. The enemy, emboldened by his success in gaining our line by the group of trees and the angle of the wall, was concentrating all his right against, and was further pressing, that point. There was the stress of his assault; there would he drive his fiery wedge to split our line. In front of Harrow's and Hall's brigades he had been able to advance no nearer than where he first halted to deliver fire; and these commands had not yielded an inch. To effect the concentration before Webb, the enemy

The charge of Pickett, Pettigrew, and Trimble (from a wartime sketch)

would march the regiment on his extreme right of each of his lines by the left flank to the rear of the troops, still halted and facing to the front, and so continuing to draw in his right, when they were all massed in the position desired, he would again face them to the front and advance to the storming. This was the way he made the wall before Webb's line blaze red with his battle flags, and such was the purpose there of his thick-crowding battalions.

Not a moment must be lost. Colonel Hall I found just in rear of his line, sword in hand, cool, vigilant, noting all that passed and directing the battle of his brigade. The fire was constantly diminishing now in his front in the manner by the movement of the enemy that I have mentioned: drifting to the right. "How is it going?" Colonel Hall asked me as I rode up. "Well, but Webb is hotly pressed and must have support or he will be overpowered. Can you assist him?" "Yes." "You cannot be too quick." "I will move my brigade at once." "Good." He gave the order, and in briefest time I saw five friendly colors hurrying to the aid of the imperiled three; and each color represented true, battle-tried men that had not turned back from Rebel fire that day nor yesterday, though their ranks were sadly thinned. To Webb's brigade, pressed back as it had been from the wall, the distance was not great, from Hall's right. The regiments marched by the right flank. Colonel Hall superintended the movement in person. Colonel Devereux coolly commanded the 19th Massachusetts—his major, Rice, had already been wounded and carried off. Lieutenant Colonel Macy of the 20th Massachusetts had just had his left hand shot off, and so Captain Abbott gallantly led over this fine regiment. The 42nd New York followed their excellent colonel, Mallon. Lieutenant Colonel Steele, 7th Michigan, had just been killed, and this regiment, and the handful of the 59th New York, followed their colors. The movement, as it did, attracting the enemy's fire, and executed in haste, as it must be, was difficult; but in reasonable time, and in order that is serviceable, if not regular, Hall's men are fighting gallantly side by side with Webb's before the all important point.

I did not stop to see all this movement of Hall's, but from him I went at once further to the left to the first brigade. General Harrow I did not see, but his fighting men would answer my purpose as well. The 19th Maine, the 15th Massachusetts, the 82nd New York, and the shattered old thunderbolt, the 1st Minnesota (poor Farrell was dying there upon the ground, where he had fallen) all men that I could find, I took over to the right at the *double quick*. As we were moving to and near the other brigades of the division, from my position on horseback, I could see that the enemy's right, under Hall's fire, was beginning to stagger and to break. "See," I said to the men, "see the "*chivalry*,' see the graybacks run!" The men saw, and as they swept to their places by the side of Hall's and opened fire, they roared; and this in a manner that said more plainly than words—for the deaf could have seen it in their faces, and the blind could have heard it in their voices—*the crest is safe*.

The whole division concentrated, and changes of position and new phases (as well on our part as on that of the enemy) having as indicated occurred for the purpose of showing the exact present posture of affairs, some further description is necessary. Before the second division, the enemy is massed, the main bulk of his force covered by the ground that slopes to his rear with his front at the stone wall. Between his front and us extends the very apex of the crest, all there are left of the White Trefoil Division. Yesterday morning there were three thousand eight hundred; this morning there were less than three thousand; at this moment there are somewhat over two thousand. Twelve regiments in three brigades are below or behind the crest in such a position that by the exposure of the head and upper part of the body, above the crest, they can deliver their fire in the enemy's faces along the top of the wall. By reason of the disorganization incidental (in Webb's brigade) to his men's having broken and fallen back as mentioned, in the two other brigades to their rapid and difficult change of position under fire, and in all the division, in part, to severe and continuous battle, formation of companies and regiments in regular ranks is lost; but commands, companies, regiments, and brigades are blended and intermixed: an irregular, extended mass—men enough, if in order to form a line of four or five ranks along the whole front of the division. The twelve flags of the regiments wave defiantly at intervals along the front; at the stone wall, at unequal distances from ours, of forty, fifty, or sixty yards, stream nearly double this number of the battle flags of the enemy.

These changes accomplished on either side, and the concentration complete, although no cessation or abatement in the general din of conflict since the commencement had at any time been appreciable, now it was as if a new battle—deadlier, stormier than before—had sprung from the body of the old, a young Phoenix of combat, whose eyes stream lightning, shaking his arrowy wings over the yet glowing ashes of his progenitor. The jostling swaying lines on either side boil, and roar, and dash their flamy spray—two hostile billows of a fiery ocean. Thick flashes stream from the wall; thick volleys answer from the crest. No threats or expostulation now—only example and encouragement. All depths of passion are stirred and all combative fire, down to their deep foundations. Individuality is drowned in a sea of clamor; and timid men, breathing the breath of the multitude, are brave. The frequent dead and wounded lie where they stagger and fall; there is no humanity for them now, and none can be spared to care for them. The men do not cheer or shout—they growl; and over that uneasy sea, heard with the roar of musketry, sweeps the muttered thunder of a storm of growls.

Webb, Hall, Devereux, Mallon, Abbott, among the men where all are heroes, are doing deeds of note. Now the loyal wave rolls up as if it would overleap its barrier, the crest. Pistols flash with the muskets. "Forward to the wall" is answered by the Rebel countercommand, "Steady, men," and the wave swings back. Again it surges, and again it sinks.

These men of Pennsylvania, on the soil of their own homesteads, the first and only to flee the wall, must be the first to storm it. "Major, *lead* your men over the crest; they will follow." "By the tactics, I understand my place is in rear of the men." "Your pardon, sir; I see *your* place is in rear of the men. I thought you were fit to lead." "Captain Suplee come on with your men." "Let me first stop this fire in the rear or we shall be hit by our own men." "Never mind the fire in the rear; let us take care of this in front first." "Sergeant, forward with your color. Let the Rebels see it close to their eyes once more before they die." The color sergeant of the 72nd Pennsylvania, grasping the stump of the severed lance in both his hands, waved the flag above his head and rushed towards the wall. "Will you see your color storm the wall alone?" One man only starts to follow. Almost half way to the wall, down go color bearer and color to the ground; the gallant sergeant is dead. The line springs. The crest of the solid ground, with a great roar, heaves forward its maddened load—men, arms, smoke, fire, a fighting mass. It rolls to the wall. Flash meets flash. The wall is crossed. A moment ensues of thrusts, yells, blows, shots, and undistinguishable conflict, followed by a shout, universal, that makes the welkin ring again; and the last and bloodiest fight of the great battle of Gettysburg is ended and won.

Brigadier-General Lewis A. Armistead, C.S.A.

Many things cannot be described by pen or pencil—such a fight is one. Some hints and incidents may be given but a description, a picture, never. From what is told, the imagination may for itself construct the scene; otherwise he who never saw can have no adequate idea of what such a battle is.

When the vortex of battle passion had subsided, hopes, fears, rage, joy, of which the maddest and the noisiest was the last, and we were calm enough to look about us. We saw that as with us the fight with the third division was ended, and that in that division was a repetition of the scenes immediately about us. In that moment the judgment almost refused to credit the senses. Are these abject wretches about us, whom our men are now disarming and driving together in flocks, the jaunty men of Pickett's division, whose sturdy lines and flashing arms, but a few moments since, were sweeping up the slope to destroy us? Are these red cloths, that our men toss about in derision, the "fiery Southern crosses," thrice ardent, the battle flags of the rebellion, that waved defiance at the wall? We know, but so sudden has been the transition, we yet can scarce believe.

Just as the fight was over, and the first outburst of victory had a little subsided, when all in front of the crest was noise and confusion—prisoners being collected, small parties in pursuit of them far down into the field, flags waving, officers giving quick, sharp commands to their men. I stood apart for a few moments, upon the crest, by that group of trees which ought to be historic forever, a spectator of the thrilling scene around. Some few musket shots were still heard in the third division; and the enemy's guns, almost silent since the advance of his infantry until the moment of his defeat, were dropping a few sullen shells among friend and foe upon the crest—rebellion fosters such humanity. Near me, saddest sight of the many of such a field, and not in keeping with all this noise, were mingled alone the thick dead of Maine, and Minnesota, and Michigan, and Massachusetts, and the Empire and the Keystone states, who, not yet cold, with the blood still oozing from their death wounds, had given their lives to the country upon that stormy field. So mingled upon that crest let their honored graves be.

Look with me, about us. These dead have been avenged already. Where the long lines of the enemy's thousands so proudly advanced, see now how thick the silent men of gray are scattered. It is not an hour since those legions were sweeping along so grandly. Now sixteen hundred of that fiery mass are strewn among the trampled grass, dead as the clods they load; more than seven thousand—probably eight thousand—are wounded: some there, with the dead, in our hands, some fugitive far towards the woods, among them generals Pettigrew, Garnett, Kemper, Armistead (the last three mortally, and the last one in our hands). "Tell General Hancock," he [i.e., Armistead] said to Lieutenant Mitchell, Hancock's aide-de-camp, to whom he handed his watch, "that I know I did my country a great wrong when I took up arms against her, for which I am sorry, but for which I cannot live to atone."

Four thousand, not wounded, are prisoners of war—more in number of the captured than the captors. Our men are still "gathering them in." Some hold up their hands or a handkerchief in sign of submission; some have hugged the ground to escape our bullets, and so are taken. Few made resistance after the first moment of our crossing the wall; some yield submissively with good grace, some with grim, dogged aspect, showing that but for the other alternative, they could not submit to this. Colonels and all less grades of officers, in the usual proportions, are among them, and all are being stripped of their arms. Such of them as escaped wounds and capture are fleeing routed and panic-stricken and disappearing in the woods. Small arms, more thousands than we can count, are in our hands, scattered over the field. And those defiant battle flags, some inscribed with: "First Manassas," the numerous battles of the Peninsula, "Second Manassas," "South Mountain," "Sharpsburg" (our Antietam), "Fredericksburg," "Chancellorsville," and many more names, our men have, and are showing about, *over thirty of them*.

Such was really the closing scene of the grand drama of Gettysburg. After repeated assaults upon the right and the left, where, and in all of which repulse had been his only success, this persistent and presuming enemy forms his chosen troops—the flower of his army—for a grand assault upon our center. The manner and the result of such assault have been told: a loss to the enemy of from twelve thousand to fourteen thousand, killed, wounded, and prisoners, and of over thirty battle flags. This was accomplished by not over six thousand men, with a loss on our part of not over two thousand five hundred, killed and wounded.

Would to heaven Generals Hancock and Gibbon could have stood there where I did and have looked upon that field! It would have done two men, to whom the country owes much, good to have been with their men in that moment of victory, to have seen the results of those dispositions which they had made and of that splendid fighting which men schooled by their discipline, had executed. But they are both severely wounded and have been carried from the field. One person did come then that I was glad to see there and that was no less than Major General Meade, whom the Army of the Potomac was fortunate enough to have at that time to command it. See how a great general looked upon the field, and what he said and did at the moment, and when he learned of his great victory. To appreciate the incident I give it should be borne in mind that one coming up from the rear of the line, as did General Meade, could have seen very little of our own men, who had now crossed the crest; and although he could have heard the noise, he could not have told its occasion, or by whom made, until he had actually attained the crest. One who did not know results, so coming, would have been quite as likely to have supposed that our line there had been carried and captured by the enemy, so many gray Rebels were on the crest as to have discovered the real truth. Such mistake was really made by one of our own officers, as I shall relate.

General Meade rode up, accompanied alone by his son, who is his aide-de-camp, an escort, if select, not large for a commander of such an army. The principal horseman was no bedizened hero of some holy day review, but he was a plain man, dressed in a serviceable summer suit of dark blue cloth, without badge or ornament save the shoulder straps of his grade, and a light, straight sword of a general, a general staff officer. He wore heavy, high-top boots and buff gauntlets; and his soft black felt hat was slouched down over his eyes. His face was very white, not pale, and the lines were marked, and earnest, and full of care.

As he arrived near me, coming up the hill, he asked in a sharp, eager voice: "How is it going here?" "I believe, General, the enemy's attack is repulsed," I answered. Still approaching, and a new light began to come in his face, of gratified surprise, with a touch of incredulity, of which his voice was also the medium, he further asked: "*What, is the assault entirely repulsed?*"—his voice quicker and more eager than before. "It is, sir," I replied. By this time he was on the crest; and when his eye had for an instant swept over the field, taking in just a glance of the whole—the masses of prisoners; the numerous captured flags, which the men were derisively flaunting about; the fugitives of the routed enemy, disappearing with the speed of terror in the woods—partly at what I had told him, partly at what he saw, he said impressively, and his face was lighted: "*Thank God.*" And then his right hand moved as if it would have caught off his hat and waved it; but this gesture he suppressed, and instead he waved his hand and said, "Hur-rah." The son, with more youth in his blood and less rank upon his shoulders, snatched off his cap and roared out his three "hurrahs" right heartily. The general then surveyed the field some minutes in silence. He at length asked who was in command. He had heard that Hancock and Gibbon were wounded, and I told him that General Caldwell was the senior officer of the corps and General Harrow of the division. He asked where they were, but before I had time to answer that I did not know, he resumed: "No matter; I will give my orders to you and you will see them executed." He then gave direction that the troops should be reformed as soon as practicable and kept in their places, as the enemy might be mad enough to attack again; he also gave directions concerning the posting of some reinforcements which he said would soon be there, adding: "*If the enemy does attack, charge him in the flank, and sweep him from the field, do you understand*?" The general then, a gratified man, galloped in the direction of his headquarters.

Then the work of the field went on. First, the prisoners were collected and sent to the rear. "There go the men," the Rebels were heard to say by some of our surgeons who were in Gettysburg at the time Pickett's division marched out to take position: "There go the men that will go through your d———d Yankee lines, for you." A good many of them did "*go through our lines, for us*," but in a very different way from the one they intended—not impetuous victors, sweeping away our thin line with ball and bayonet, but crestfallen captives, without arms, guarded by the true bayonets of the Union, with the cheers of their conquerors ringing in their ears. There was a grim truth, after all, in this Rebel remark. Collected, the prisoners began their dreary march—a miserable, melancholy stream of dirty gray to pour over the crest to our rear. Many of the officers were well-dressed, fine, proud gentlemen—such men as it would be a pleasure to meet when the war is over. I had no desire to exult over them, and pity and sympathy were the general feelings of us all upon the occasion. The cheering of our men, and the unceremonious handling of the captured flags were probably not gratifying to the prisoners; but not intended for taunt or insult to the men, they could take no exception to such practices.

When the prisoners were turned to the rear, and were crossing the crest, Lieutenant Colonel Morgan, General Hancock's chief of staff, was conducting a battery from the artillery reserve towards the Second Corps. As he saw the men in gray coming over the hill, he said to the officer in command of the battery: "See up there, the enemy has carried the crest. See them come pouring over. The Old Second Corps is gone; and you had better get your battery away from here as quickly as possible or it will be captured." The officer was actually giving the order to his men to move back, when closer observation discovered that the graybacks that were coming had no arms, and then the truth flashed upon the minds of the observers. The same mistake was made by others.

In view of results there that day—the success of the arms of the country—would not the people of the whole country, standing then upon the crest with General Meade, have said with him: "Thank God?"

I have no knowledge and little notion of how long a time elapsed from the moment the fire of the infantry commenced until the enemy was entirely repulsed, in this his grand assault. I judge from the amount of fighting and the changes of position that occurred that probably the fight was of nearly an hour duration—but I cannot tell, and I have seen none who knew. The time seemed but a very few minutes, when the battle was over.

When the prisoners were cleared away and order was again established upon our crest, where the conflict had impaired it, until between five and six o'clock, I remained upon the field directing some troops to their positions in conformity to the orders of General Meade. The enemy appeared no more in front of the Second Corps; but while I was engaged as I have mentioned, farther to our left some considerable force of the enemy moved out and made show of attack. Our artillery, now in good order again, in due time opened fire, and the shells scattered the *butternuts*, as clubs do the gray snowbirds of winter, before they came within range of our infantry. This, save unimportant outpost firing, was the last of the battle.

Of the pursuit of the enemy and the movements of the army subsequent to the battle until the crossing of the Potomac by Lee and the closing of the campaign, it is not my purpose to write. Suffice it, that on the night of the third of July the enemy withdrew his left, Ewell's corps, from our front, and on the morning of the fourth we again occupied the village of Gettysburg; and on that national day, victory was proclaimed to the country; that floods of rain on that day prevented army movements of any considerable magnitude, the day being passed by our army in position upon the field, in burying our dead and some of those of the enemy, and in making the movements already indicated; that on the fifth, the pursuit of the enemy was commenced, his dead were buried by us, and the corps of our army, upon various roads, moved from the battlefield.

With a statement of some of the results of the battle as to losses and captures, and of what I saw in riding over the field when the army was gone, my account is done.

Our own losses in "killed, wounded, and missing," I

estimate at *twenty-three thousand.* Of the "missing," the larger proportion were prisoners, lost on the first of July. Our loss in prisoners, not wounded, probably was *four thousand*. The losses were distributed among the different army corps about as follows: In the Second Corps, which sustained the heaviest loss of any corps, a little over *four thousand five hundred*, of whom the "missing" were a mere nominal number; in the First Corps, a little over *four thousand*, of whom a good many were "missing"; in the Third Corps, *four thousand*, of whom some were missing; in the Eleventh Corps, nearly *four thousand*, of whom the most were "missing"; and the rest of the loss, to make the aggregate mentioned, was shared by the Fifth, Sixth, and Twelfth corps, and the cavalry. Among these the "missing" were few; and the losses of the Sixth Corps and of the cavalry were light. I do not think the official reports will show my estimate of our losses to be far from correct, for I have taken great pains to question staff officers upon the subject and have learned approximate numbers from them. We lost no gun or flag that I have heard of in all the battle. Some small arms, I suppose, were lost on the first of July.

The enemy's loss in killed, wounded, and prisoners, I estimate, at *forty thousand*, and from the following *data* and for the following reasons: So far as I can learn we took *ten thousand* prisoners, who were not wounded; many more than these were captured, but several thousands of them were wounded. I have, so far as practicable, ascertained the number of dead the enemy left upon the field, approximately, by getting the reports of different burying parties; I think his dead upon the field were *five thousand*, almost all of whom, save those killed on the first of July, were buried by us, the enemy not having them in their possession. In looking at a great number of tables of killed and wounded in battles, I have found that the proportion of the killed to the wounded is as *one* to *five,* or more than five, rarely less than five. So with the killed at the number stated, *twenty-five thousand* would probably be wounded. Hence the aggregate that I have mentioned. I think *fourteen thousand* of the enemy, wounded, and unwounded, fell into our hands. Great numbers of his small arms, two or three guns, and forty or more—was there ever such bannered harvest?—of his regimental battle flags, were captured by us. Some day possibly we may learn the enemy's loss, but I doubt if he will ever tell truly how many flags he did not take home with him. I have great confidence, however, in my estimates, for they have been carefully made and after much inquiry and with no desire or motive to overestimate the enemy's loss.

The magnitude of the armies engaged, the number of the casualties, the object sought by the Rebel, the result, will all contribute to give Gettysburg a place among the great historic battles of the world. That General Meade's concentration was rapid (over thirty miles a day were marched by several of the corps), that his position was skillfully selected and his dispositions good, that he fought the battle hard and well, that his victory was brilliant and complete, I think all should admit. I cannot but regard it as highly fortunate to us, and commendable in General Meade, that the enemy was allowed the initiative, the offensive, in the main battle; that it was much better to allow the Rebel, for his own destruction, to come up and smash his lines and columns, upon the defensive solidity of our position, than it would have been to hunt him, for the same purpose, in the woods or to unearth him from his rifle pits. In this manner our losses were lighter, and his heavier, than if the case had been reversed. And whatever the books may say of troops fighting the better who make the attack, I am satisfied that in this war, Americans—the Rebels as well as ourselves—are best on the defensive. The proposition is deducible from the battles of the war, I think, and my observation confirms it.

But men there are who think that nothing was gained or done well in this battle because some other general did not have the command or because any portion of the army of the enemy was permitted to escape capture or destruction—as if one army of a hundred thousand men could encounter another of the same numbers, of as good troops, and annihilate it! Military men do not claim or expect this. But the McClellan destroyers do; the doughty knights of purchasable newspaper quills; the formidable warriors from the brothels of politics; men of much warlike experience against honesty and honor; of profound attainments in ignorance; who have the maxims of Napoleon, whose spirit they as little understand as they do most things, to quote, to prove all things, but who, unfortunately, have much influence in the country and with the government, and so over the army. It is very pleasant for these people, no doubt, at safe distances from guns, in the enjoyment of a lucrative office or of a fraudulently obtained government contract, surrounded by the luxuries of their own firesides—where mud, and flooding storms, and utter weariness never penetrate—to discourse of battles, and how campaigns should be conducted, and armies of the enemy destroyed. But it should be enough, perhaps, to say, that men, here or elsewhere, who have knowledge enough of military affairs to entitle them to express an opinion on such matters, and accurate information enough to realize the nature and the means of this desired destruction of Lee's army before it crossed the Potomac into Virginia, will be most likely to vindicate the Pennsylvania campaign of General Meade and to see that he accomplished all that could have been reasonably expected of any general, of any army. Complaint has been—and is—made specifically against Meade that he did not attack Lee near

Williamsport before he had time to withdraw across the river. These were the facts concerning the matter:

The thirteenth of July was the earliest day when such an attack, if practicable at all, could have been made. The time before this, since the battle, had been spent in moving the army from the vicinity of the field, finding something of the enemy, and concentrating before him. On that day the army was concentrated, and in order of battle, near the turnpike that leads from Sharpsburg to Hagerstown, Maryland, the right resting at or near the latter place, the left near Jones's Crossroads, some six miles in the direction of Sharpsburg, and in the following order from left to right: the Twelfth Corps, the Second, the Fifth, the Sixth, the First, the Eleventh—the Third being in reserve behind the Second. The mean distance to the Potomac was some six miles, and the enemy was between Meade and the river. The Potomac, swelled by the recent rain, was boiling and swift and deep, a magnificent place to have drowned all this Rebel crew. I have not the least doubt but that General Meade would have liked to drown them all if he could, but they were unwilling to be drowned and would fight first. To drive them into the river, then, they must first be routed.

General Meade, I believe, favored an attack upon the enemy at that time, and he summoned his corps commanders to a council upon the subject. The First Corps was represented by Wadsworth; the Second by William Hays; the Third by French; the Fifth by Sykes; the Sixth by Sedgwick; the Eleventh by Howard; the Twelfth by Slocum; and the cavalry by Pleasonton. Of the eight generals, three —Wadsworth, Howard, and Pleasonton—were in favor of immediate attack, and five—Hays, French, Sykes, Sedgwick, and Slocum—were not in favor of attack until better information was obtained of the positions and situation of the enemy. Of the *pros*, Wadsworth only temporarily represented the First Corps in the brief absence of Newton, who, had a battle occurred, would have commanded; Pleasonton, with his horses, would have been a spectator only; and Howard, with the *"brilliant Eleventh Corps,"* would have been trusted nowhere, but a safe distance from the enemy (not by General Howard's fault, however, for he is a good and brave man). Such was the position of those who felt sanguinarily inclined. Of the *cons* were all of the fighting generals of the fighting corps, save the First. This then was the feeling of these generals—all who would have had no responsibility or part, in all probability, *hankered* for a fight; those who would have had both part and responsibility did not. The attack was not made.

At daylight on the morning of the fourteenth, strong reconnaissances from the Twelfth, Second, and Fifth Corps were the means of discovering that between the enemy, except a thousand or fifteen hundred of his rear guard who fell into our hands, and the Army of the Potomac rolled the rapid unbridged river. The Rebel, General Pettigrew, was here killed. The enemy had constructed bridges, had crossed, during all the preceding night, but so close were our cavalry and infantry upon him in the morning that the bridges were destroyed before his rear guard had all crossed.

Among the considerations influencing these generals against the propriety of attack at that time were probably the following: The army was wearied and worn down by four weeks of constant forced marching or battle in the midst of heat, mud, and drenching showers, burdened with arms, accoutrements, blankets, sixty to a hundred cartridges, and five to eight days' rations. What such weariness means, few save soldiers know. Since the battle the army had been constantly diminished by sickness or prostration and by more straggling than I ever saw before. Poor fellows, they could not help it. The men were near the point when further efficient physical exertion was quite impossible. Even the sound of the skirmishing which was almost constant, and the excitement of impending battle, had no effect to arouse for an hour the exhibition of their wonted former vigor. The enemy's loss in battle, it is true, had been heavier than ours; but his army was less weary than ours, for in a given time since the first of the campaign, it had marched far less and with lighter loads. These Rebels are accustomed to hunger and nakedness, customs to which our men do not take readily. And the enemy had straggled less, for the men were going away from battle and towards home, and for them to straggle was to go into captivity, whose end they could not conjecture. The enemy was somewhere in position, in a ridgy, wooded country, abounding in strong defensive positions, his main bodies concealed, protected by rifle pits and epaulements, acting strictly on the defensive. His dispositions, his positions even, with any considerable degree of accuracy, were unknown; nor could they be known, except by reconnaissances in such force and carried to such extent as would have constituted their attacks, liable to bring on at any moment a general engagement, and at places where we were least prepared and least likely to be successful.

To have had a battle there, then, General Meade would have had to attack a cunning enemy in the dark, where surprises, undiscovered rifle pits and batteries, and unseen bodies of men might have met his forces at every point. With his not greatly superior numbers, under such circumstances, had General Meade attacked, would he have been victorious? The vote of those generals at the council shows their opinion—my own is that he would have been repulsed with heavy loss, with little damage to the enemy. Such a result might have satisfied the bloody politicians better than the end of the campaign as it was; but I think the country did not need that sacrifice of the Army of the Potomac at that time, that enough odor of sacrifice came up to its nostrils from the first Fredericksburg field to stop their snuffing for some time. I felt the probability of defeat strongly at the time, when we all supposed that a conflict would certainly ensue; for always before a battle—at least it so appears to me—some dim presentiment of results, some unaccountable foreshadowing, pervades the army. I never knew the result to prove it untrue, which rests with the weight of a conviction. Whether such shadows are cause or consequence, I shall not pretend to determine; but when, as they often are, they are general, I think they should not be wholly disregarded by the commander. I believe the Army of the Potomac is always willing, often eager, to fight the enemy whenever, as it thinks, there is a fair chance for victory, that it always will fight, let come victory or defeat, whenever it is ordered so to do. Of course, the army, both officers and men, had very great disappointment and very great sorrow that the Rebels *escaped* (so it was called) across the river; the disappointment was genuine, at least to the extent that disappointment is like surprise. But the sorrow—to judge by looks, tones, and actions rather than by words—was not of that deep, sable character, for which there is no balm.

Would it be an imputation upon the courage or patriotism of this army, if it was not rampant for fight at this particular time and under the existing circumstances? Had the enemy stayed upon the left bank of the Potomac twelve hours longer, there would have been a great battle there near Williamsport on the fourteenth of July.

After such digression, if such it is, I return to Gettysburg.

As good generalship is claimed for General Meade in this battle, so was the conduct of his subordinate commanders good. I know, and have heard, of no bad conduct or blundering on the part of any officer, save that of Sickles on the second of July—and that was so gross, and came so near being the cause of irreparable disaster, that I cannot discuss it with moderation. I hope this man may never return to the Army of the Potomac, or elsewhere to a position, where his incapacity—or something worse—may be the fruitless destruction to thousands again. The conduct of the officers and men was good. The Eleventh Corps behaved badly, but I have yet to learn the occasion when, in the opinion of any save their own officers and themselves, the men of this corps have behaved well on the march or before the enemy, either under Sigel or any other commander. With this exception, and some minor cases of very little consequence in the general result, our troops, whenever and wherever the enemy came, stood against their storms of impassable fire. Such was the infantry, such the artillery; the cavalry did less, but it did all that was required.

The enemy, too, showed a determination and valor worthy of a better cause; their conduct in this battle even makes me proud of them as Americans. They would have been victorious over any but the best of soldiers. Lee and his generals presumed too much upon some past successes and did not estimate how much they were due, on their part to position, as at Fredericksburg, or on our part to bad generalship, as at the Second Bull Run and Chancellorsville.

The fight of the first of July we do not, of course, claim as a victory; but even that probably would have resulted differently had Reynolds not been struck. The success of the enemy in the battle ended with the first of July. The Rebels were joyous and jubilant—so said our men in their hands and the citizens of Gettysburg—at their achievements on that day. Fredericksburg and Chancellorsville were remembered by them. They saw victory already won, or only to be snatched from the streaming coattails of the Eleventh Corps, or the *"raw Pennsylvania militia,"* as they thought they were when they saw them run; and already the spires of Baltimore and the dome of the national capitol were forecast upon their glad vision, only two or three days' march away through the beautiful valleys of Pennsylvania and *"my"* Maryland. Was there ever anything so fine before! How splendid it would be to enjoy the poultry and the fruit, the meats, the cakes, the beds, the clothing, the *whiskey*, without price, in this rich land of the Yankee! It would indeed! But on the second of July something of a change came over the spirit of these dreams. They were surprised at results and talked less, and thought more, as they prepared supper that night. After the fight of the third, they talked only of the means of their own safety from destruction. Pickett's splendid division had been almost annihilated, they said, and they talked not of how many were lost, but of who had escaped. They talked of those "Yanks" that had *clubs* on their flags and caps—the trefoils of the Second Corps that are like *clubs* in cards.

The battle of Gettysburg is distinguished in this war, not only as by far the greatest and severest conflict that has occurred, but for some other things that I may mention. The fight of the second of July on the left, which was almost a separate and complete battle, is, so far as I know, alone in the following particulars: the numbers of men actually engaged at one time, and the enormous losses that occurred in killed and wounded in the space of about two hours. If the truth could be obtained, it would probably show a much larger number of casualties in this than my estimate in a former part of these sheets. Few battles of the war that have had so many casualties altogether, as those of the two hours on the second of July.

The third of July is distinguished. Then occurred the "great cannonade" (so we call it, and so it would be called in any war and in almost any battle). And besides this, the main operations that followed have few parallels in history (none in this war) of the magnitude and magnificence of the assault, single and simultaneous, the disparity of the numbers engaged, and the brilliancy, completeness, and overwhelming character of the result, in favor of the side numerically the weakest.

I think I have not, in giving the results of this encounter, overestimated the numbers or the losses of the enemy. We learned on all hands, by prisoners and by their newspapers, that there were over two divisions that moved up to the assault, Pickett's and Pettigrew's, that this was the first engagement of Pickett's in the battle and the first of Pettigrew's, save a light participation on the first of July. The Rebel divisions usually number nine or ten thousand (or did at that time, as we understood). Then I have seen something of troops, and think I can estimate their number somewhat. The number of the Rebels killed here, I have estimated in this way: the second and third divisions of the Second Corps buried the Rebel dead in their own front and where they fought upon their own grounds; by count they buried over *one thousand eight hundred*. I think no more than about *two hundred* of these were killed on the second of July in front of the second division, and the rest must have fallen upon the third. My estimates that depend upon this contingency may be erroneous, but to no great extent. The rest of the particulars of this assault, our own losses, and our captures, I know are approximately accurate. Yet the whole sounds like romance, a grand stage piece of blood.

Of all the corps d'armée, for hard fighting, severe losses, and brilliant results, the palm should be, as by the army it is, awarded to the "*Old Second*." It did more fighting than any other corps, inflicted severer loss upon the enemy in killed and wounded (and sustained a heavier like loss), and captured more flags than all the rest of the army—and almost as many prisoners as the rest of the army. The loss of the Second Corps in killed and wounded in this battle—there is no other test of hard fighting—was almost as great as that of all General Grant's forces in the battles that preceded, and in, the siege of Vicksburg. Three-eighths of the whole corps were killed and wounded. Why does the western army suppose that the Army of the Potomac does not fight? Was ever a more absurd supposition! The Army of the Potomac is grand! Give it good leadership, let it alone, and it will not fail to accomplish all that reasonable men desire.

Of Gibbon's White Trefoil Division, if I am not cautious, I shall speak too enthusiastically. This division has been accustomed to distinguished leadership. Sumner, Sedgwick, and Howard have honored, and been honored by, its command. It was repulsed under Sedgwick at Antietam and under Howard at Fredericksburg; it was victorious under Gibbon at the Second Fredericksburg and at Gettysburg. At Gettysburg its loss in killed and wounded was over *one thousand seven hundred*, near one-half of all engaged; it captured *seventeen* battle flags and *two thousand three hundred prisoners.* Its bullets hailed on Pickett's division, and killed or mortally wounded four Rebel generals: *Barksdale* (on the second of July) with the three on the third (*Armistead*, *Garnett*, and *Kemper*). In losses, in killed and wounded, and in captures from the enemy of prisoners and flags, it stands preeminent among all the divisions at Gettysburg.

Under such generals as Hancock and Gibbon, brilliant results may be expected. Will the country remember them?

It is understood in the army that the president thanked the slayer of Barton Key for *saving the day* at Gettysburg. Does the country know any better than the president—that Meade, Hancock, and Gibbon were entitled to some little share of such credit?

At about six o'clock on the afternoon of the third of July,

my duties done upon the field, I quitted it to go to the general. My brave horse, *Dick* (poor creature, his good conduct in the battle that afternoon had been complemented by a brigadier), was a sight to see. He was literally covered with blood. Struck repeatedly, his right thigh had been ripped open in a ghastly manner by a piece of shell, and three bullets were lodged deep in his body; and from his wounds the blood oozed and ran down his sides and legs, and with the sweat formed a bloody foam. Dick's was no mean part in that battle. Good conduct in men, under such circumstances as he was placed, might result from a sense of duty; his was the result of his bravery. Most horses would have been unmanageable with the flash and roar of arms about, and the shouting; Dick was utterly cool and would have obeyed the rein had it been a straw. To Dick belongs the honor of first mounting that stormy crest before the enemy, not forty yards away, whose bullets smote him, and of being the only horse there during the heat of the battle. Even the enemy noticed Dick, and one of their reports of the battle mentions the "*solitary horseman*" who rallied our wavering line. He enabled me to do twelve times as much as I could have done on foot. It would not be dignified for an officer on foot to run; it is entirely so, mounted, to gallop. I do not approve of officers dismounting in battle, which is the time of all when they most need to be mounted, for thereby they have so much greater facilities for being everywhere present. Most officers, however, in close action, dismount. Dick deserves well of his country, and one day should have a horse monument. If there be "*ut sapientibus placet*," an equine Elysium, I will send to Charon the brass coin, the fee for Dick's passage over, and on the other side of the Styx, in those shadowy clover fields, he may nibble the blossoms forever.

I had been struck upon the thigh by a bullet, which I think must have glanced, and partially spent its force, upon my saddle. It had pierced the thick cloth of my trousers and two thicknesses of underclothing, but had not broken the skin, leaving me with an enormous bruise that for a time benumbed the entire leg. At the time of receiving it, I heard the thump and noticed it and the hole in the cloth, into which I thrust my finger; and I experienced a feeling of relief, I am sure, when I found that my leg was not pierced. I think, when I dismounted from my horse after that fight, that I was no very comely specimen of humanity. Drenched with sweat, the white of battle by the reaction now turned to burning red, I felt like a boiled man; and had it not been for the exhilaration at results, I should have been miserable. This kept me up, however, and having found a man to transfer the saddle from poor Dick, who was now disposed to lie down by loss of blood and exhaustion, to another horse, I hobbled on among the hospitals in search of General Gibbon.

The skulkers were about, and they were as loud as any in their rejoicings at the victory; and I took a malicious pleasure, as I went along and met them, in taunting the *sneaks* with their cowardice and telling them (it was not true) that General Meade had just given the order to the provost guards to arrest and shoot all men they could find away from their regiments who could not prove a good account of themselves. To find the general was no easy matter. I inquired for both Generals Hancock and Gibbon—I knew well enough that they would be together—and for the hospitals of the Second Corps. My search was attended with many incidents that were provokingly humorous. The stupidity of most men is amazing. I would ask of a man I met: "Do you know, sir, where the Second Corps hospitals are?" "The Twelfth Corps hospital is there!" Then I would ask sharply: "Did you understand me to ask for the Twelfth Corps hospital?" "No!" "Then why tell me what I do not ask or care to know." Then stupidity would stare or mutter about the ingratitude of some people for kindness. Did I ask for the generals I was looking for, they would announce the interesting fact, in reply, that they had seen some other generals. Some were sure that General Hancock, or Gibbon, was dead. They had seen his dead body. This was a falsehood, and they knew it. Then it was General Longstreet. This was also, as they knew, a falsehood.

Oh, sorrowful was the sight to see so many wounded! The whole neighborhood in rear of the field became one vast hospital of miles in extent. Some could walk to the hospitals; such as could not were taken upon stretchers from the places where they fell to selected points and thence the ambulances bore them, a miserable load, to their destination. Many were brought to the buildings along the Taneytown road and, too badly wounded to be carried further, died and were buried there, Union and Rebel soldiers together. At every house and barn and shed the wounded were; by many a cooling brook, or many a shady slope or grassy glade, the red flags beckoned them to their tented asylums; and there they gathered, in numbers a great army, a mutilated, bruised mass of humanity. Men with gray hair and furrowed cheeks, and soft-lipped, beardless boys were there; for those bullets have made no distinction between age and youth. Every conceivable wound that iron and lead can make, blunt or sharp, bullet, ball, and shell, piercing, bruising, tearing, was there—sometimes so light that a bandage and cold water would restore the soldier to the ranks again; sometimes so severe that the poor victim in his hopeless pain, remediless save by the only panacea for all mortal suffering, invoked that. The men are generally cheerful, and even those with frightful wounds often are talking with animated faces of nothing but the battle and the victory; but some are downcast, their faces distorted with pain. Some have undergone the surgeon's work; some, like men at a ticket office, await impatiently their turn, to have an arm or a leg cut off. Some walk about with an arm in a sling; some sit idly upon the ground; some at full length lie upon a little straw, or a blanket, with their brawny, now bloodstained, limbs bare, and you may see where the Minié bullet has struck or the shell has torn. From a small round hole upon many a manly breast, the red blood trickles; but the pallid cheek, the hard-drawn breath and dim-closed eyes, tell how near the source of life it has gone. The surgeons with coats off and sleeves rolled up, and the hospital attendants with green bands upon their caps, are about their work, and their faces and clothes are spattered with blood; and though they look weary and tired, their work goes systematically and steadily on—how much and how long they have worked the piles of legs, arms, feet, hands, fingers, about, partially tell. Such sounds are heard, sometimes (you would not have heard them upon the field) as convince that bodies, bones, sinews, and muscles are not made of insensible stone. Nearby appears a row of small fresh mounds placed side by side—they were not there day before yesterday; they will become more numerous every day.

Such things I saw as I rode along. At last I found the generals. General Gibbon was sitting in a chair that had been *borrowed* somewhere, with his wounded shoulder bare, and an attendant was bathing it with cold water. General Hancock was nearby in an ambulance. They were at the tents of the Second Corps hospitals, which were on Rock Run. As I approached General Gibbon, when he saw me he began to "hurrah" and wave his right hand—he had heard the result. I said: "O, General, long and *well* may you wave," and he shook me warmly by the hand. General Gibbon was struck by a bullet in the left shoulder which had passed from the front through the flesh and out behind, fracturing the shoulder blade and inflicting a severe, but not dangerous, wound. He thinks he was the mark of a sharpshooter of the enemy, hid in the bushes, near where he and I had sat so long during the cannonade; and he was wounded and taken off the field before the fire of the main lines of infantry had commenced—he being, at the time he was hit, near the left of his division. General Hancock was struck a little later, near the same part of the field, by a bullet piercing and almost going through his thigh, without touching the bone, however. His wound was severe also. He was carried back out of range, but before he would be carried off the field, he lay upon the ground in sight of the crest, where he could see something of the fight until he knew what would be the result.

And then at General Gibbon's request, I had to tell him—and a large voluntary crowd of the wounded who pressed around (now, for the wounds they showed, not rebuked for closing up to the generals)—the story of the fight. I was nothing loath; and I must say, though I used sometimes before the war to make speeches, that I never had so enthusiastic an audience before. Cries of "good," "glorious," frequently interrupted me; the storming of the wall was applauded by enthusiastic tears and the waving of battered, bloody hands.

By the custom of the service, the general had the right to have me along with him while away with his wound; but duty and inclination attracted me still to the field, and I obtained the general's consent to stay. Accompanying General Gibbon to Westminster, the nearest point to which railroad trains then ran, and seeing him transferred from an ambulance to the cars for Baltimore on the fourth, the next day I returned to the field to his division, since his wounding in the command of General Harrow.

On the sixth of July, while "my bullet bruise" was yet too inflamed and sensitive for me to be good for much in the way of duty, the division was then halted for the day some four miles from the field on the Baltimore Turnpike.

I could not repress the desire or omit the opportunity to see again where the battle had been. With the right stirrup-strap shortened in a manner to favor the bruised leg, I could ride my horse at a walk without serious discomfort. It seemed very strange, upon approaching the horseshoe crest again, not to see it covered with the thousands of troops, and the horses and guns, but they were all gone—the armies, to my seeming, had vanished—and on that lovely summer morning the stillness and silence of death pervaded the localities where so recently the shouts and the cannon had thundered. The recent rains had washed out many an unsightly spot and smoothed many a harrowed trace of the conflict; but one still needed no guide, save the eyes, to follow the track of that storm which the storms of heaven were powerless soon to entirely efface. The spade and shovel, so far as a little earth for the human bodies would render their task done, had completed their work—a great labor, that—but one still might see under some concealing bush or sheltering rock what once had been a man; and the thousands of stricken horses still lay scattered as they had died. The scattered small arms and the accoutrements had been collected and carried away, almost all that were of any value; but great numbers of bent and splintered muskets, rent knapsacks and haversacks, bruised canteens, shreds of caps, coats, trousers of blue or gray cloth, worthless belts and cartridge-boxes, torn blankets, ammunition boxes, broken wheels, smashed limbers, shattered gun carriages, parts of harness—of all that men or horses wear or use in battle were scattered broadcast over miles of the field. From these one could tell where the fight had been hottest. The rifle pits and epaulements, and the trampled grass, told where the lines had stood and the batteries—the former being thicker where the enemy had been than those of our own construction.

No soldier was to be seen; but numbers of civilians and

boys, and some girls even, were curiously loitering about the field, and their faces showed not sadness or horror but only staring wonder or smirking curiosity. They looked for mementoes of the battle to keep, they said; but their furtive attempts to conceal an uninjured musket or an untorn blanket—they had been told that all property left here belonged to the government—showed that the love of gain was an ingredient at least of their motive for coming here. Of course there was not the slightest objection to their taking anything they could find, now; but their manner of doing it was the objectionable thing. I could now understand why soldiers had been asked a dollar of a small strip of old linen to bind their own wound and not be compelled to go off to the hospitals.

Never elsewhere upon any field have I seen such abundant evidences of a terrific fire of cannon and musketry as upon this. Along the enemy's position, where our shells and shot had struck during the cannonade of the third, the trees had cast their trunks and branches as if they had been icicles shaken by a blast. And graves of the Rebels' making, and dead horses, and scattered accoutrements, showed that other things besides trees had been struck down by our projectiles. I must say that having seen the work of their guns upon the same occasion, I was gratified to see these things.

Along the slope of Culp's Hill, in front of the position of the Twelfth and the first division of the First Corps, the trees were almost literally peeled from the ground up some fifteen or twenty feet, so thick upon them were the scars the bullets had made. Upon a single tree, in several instances not over a foot-and-a-half in diameter, I actually counted as many as two hundred and fifty bullet marks. The ground was covered by the little twigs that had been cut off by the hailstorm of lead. Such were the evidences of the storm under which Ewell's bold Rebels assaulted our breastworks on the night of the second and the morning of the third of July. And those works looked formidable, zigzagging along those rocky crests even now, when not a musket was behind them. What madness on the part of the enemy to have attacked them! All along through these bullet-stormed woods were interspersed little patches of fresh earth, raised a foot or so above the surrounding grounds (some were very near the front of the works), and nearby upon a tree, whose bark had been smoothed by an ax, written in red chalk would be the words, not in fine handwriting: *"75 Rebils berid hear,"* "☞ *54* Rebs *there,"* and so on. Such was the burial, and such was the epitaph, of many of these famous men once led by the mighty Stonewall Jackson.

Oh, this damned rebellion will make brutes of us all, if it is not soon quelled! Our own men were buried in graves, not trenches; and upon a piece of board, or stave of a barrel, or bit of cracker-box placed at the head were neatly cut or pencilled the name and regiment of the one buried in each. This practice was general; but, of course, there must be some exceptions, for sometimes the cannon's load had not left enough of a man to recognize or name. The reasons here for the more careful interment of our own dead than such as was given to the dead of the enemy are obvious, and I think satisfactory: Our own dead were usually buried not long after they fell and without any general order to that effect. It was a work that the men's hearts were in, as soon as the fight was over and opportunity offered to hunt out their dead companions, to make them a grave in some convenient spot, and decently composed, with their blankets wrapt about them, to cover them tenderly with earth, and mark their resting place. Such burials were not without as scalding tears as ever fell upon the face of coffined mortality.

The dead of the enemy could not be buried until after

the close of the whole battle. The army was about to move—some of it was already upon the march—before such burial commenced. Tools, save those carried by the pioneers, were many miles away with trains, and the burying parties were required to make all haste in their work, in order to be ready to move with their regiments. To make long, shallow trenches; to collect the Rebel dead, often hundreds in one place; and to cover them hastily with a little earth, without name, number, or mark, save the shallow mound above them (their names, of course, they did not know), was the best that could be done. I should have been glad to have seen more formal burial even of these men of the rebellion, both because hostilities should cease with death, and of the respect I have for them as my brave, though deluded, countrymen. I found fault with such burial at the time, though I knew that the best was done that could be under the circumstances. But it may perhaps soften somewhat the rising feelings upon this subject of any who may be disposed to share mine, to remember that under similar circumstances—had the issue of the battle been reversed—our own dead would have had no burial at all at the hands of the enemy; but stripped of their clothing, their naked bodies would have been left to rot, and their bones to whiten, upon the top of the ground where they fell. Plenty of such examples of Rebel magnanimity are not wanting; and one occurred on this field, too. Our dead that fell into the hands of the enemy upon the first of July had been plundered of all their clothing, but they were left unburied until our own men buried them after the Rebels had retreated at the end of the battle.

All was bustle and noise in the little town of Gettysburg as I entered it on my tour of the field. From the afternoon of the first to the morning of the Fourth of July, the enemy was in possession. Very many of the inhabitants had, upon the first approach of the enemy or upon the retirement of our troops, fled their homes and the town not to return until after the battle. Now the town was a hospital, where gray and blue mingled in about equal proportions. The public buildings, the courthouse, the churches, and many private dwellings were full of wounded. There had been in some of the streets a good deal of fighting, and bullets had thickly spattered the fences and walls, and shells had riddled the houses from side to side. And the Rebels had done their work of pillage there, too. In spite of the smooth-sounding general order of the Rebel commander, enjoining a sacred regard for private property—the order was really good and would sound marvelously well abroad or in history—all stores of drugs and medicines, of clothing, tinware, and all groceries had been rifled and emptied without pay or offer of recompense. Libraries public and private had been entered and the books scattered about the yards or destroyed. Great numbers of private dwellings had been entered and occupied without ceremony, and whatever was liked had been appropriated or wantonly destroyed. Furniture had been smashed and beds ripped open, and apparently unlicensed pillage had reigned. Citizens and women who had remained had been kindly relieved of their money, their jewelry, and their watches—all this by the high-toned chivalry, the army of the magnanimous Lee! Put these things by the side of the acts of the "vandal Yankees" in Virginia and then let mad Rebeldom prate of honor!

But the people, the women and children, that had fled were returning, or had returned, to their homes—such homes—and amid the general havoc were restoring as they could order to the desecrated firesides. And the face of them all plainly told that with all they had lost, and bad as was the condition of all things they found, they were better pleased with such homes than with wandering houseless in the fields with the Rebels there. All had treasures of incidents of the battle and of the occupation of the enemy—wonderful sights, escapes, witnessed encounters, wounds, the marvelous passage of shells or bullets, which upon the asking, or even without, they were willing to share with the stranger. I heard of no more than one or two cases of any personal injury received by any of the inhabitants. One woman was said to have been killed, while at her washtub, sometime during the battle, but probably by a stray bullet coming a very long distance from our own men. For the next hundred years Gettysburg will be rich in legends and traditions of the battle.

I rode through the cemetery on "Cemetery Hill." How those quiet sleepers must have been astounded in their graves when the twenty-pound Parrott guns thundered above them and the solid shot crushed their grave stones! The flowers, roses, and creeping vines that pious hands had planted to bloom and shed their odors over the ashes of dear ones gone were trampled upon the ground and black with the cannon's soot. A dead horse lay by the marble shaft, and over it the marble finger pointed to the sky. The marble lamb that had slept its white sleep on the grave of a child now lies blackened upon a broken gun carriage. Such are the incongruities and jumblings of battle.

I looked away to *the group of trees*—the Rebel gunners know what ones I mean, and so do the survivors of Pickett's division—and a strange fascination led me thither. How thick are the marks of battle as I approach—the graves of the men of the third division of the Second Corps, the splintered oaks, the scattered horses (seventy-one dead horses were on a spot some fifty yards square, near the position of Woodruff's battery and where he fell).

I stood solitary upon the crest by "*the trees*," where less than three days ago I had stood before; but now how changed is all the eye beholds. Do these thick mounds cover the fiery hearts that in the battle rage swept the crest and stormed the wall? I read their names—them alas, I do not know—but I see the regiments marked on their frail monuments: "20th Mass. Vols.," "69th P.V.," "1st Minn. Vols.," and the rest; they are all represented and, as they fought, commingled here. So I am not alone—these my brethren of the fight are with me. Sleep, noble brave! The foe shall not desecrate your sleep. Yonder thick trenches will hold them. As long as patriotism is a virtue and treason a crime, your deeds have made this crest, your resting place, hallowed ground!

But I have seen and said enough of this battle. The unfortunate wounding of my general so early in the action of the third of July, leaving important duties which in the unreasoning excitement of the moment I in part assumed, enabled me to do for the successful issue something which, under other circumstances, would not have fallen to my rank or place. Deploring the occasion for taking away from the division in that moment of its need its soldierly, appropriate head, so cool, so clear, I am yet glad, as that was to be, that his example and his tuition have not been entirely in vain to me, and that my impulses then prompted me to do somewhat as he might have done had he been on the field. The encomiums of officers—so numerous and some of so high rank—generously accorded me for my conduct upon that occasion (I am not without vanity) were gratifying. My position as a staff officer gave me an opportunity to see much—perhaps as much as any one person—of that conflict. My observations were not so particular as if I had been attached to a smaller command, not so general as may have been those of a staff officer of the general commanding the army; but of such as they were, my heart was there, and I could do no less than to write something of them in the intervals between marches and during the subsequent repose of the army at the close of the campaign. I have put somewhat upon these pages. I make no apology for the egotism, if such there is, of this account; it is not designed to be a history, but simply *my account* of the battle. It should not be assumed, if I have told of some occurrences, that there were not other important ones. I would not have it supposed that I have attempted to do full justice to the good conduct of the fallen or the survivors of the First and Twelfth corps. Others must tell of them—I did not see their work.

A full account of *the battle as it was* will never, can never, be made. Who could sketch the changes, the constant shifting, of the bloody panorama! It is not possible. The official reports may give results as to losses, with statements of attacks and repulses; they may also note the means by which results were attained, which is a statement of the number and kind of the forces employed, but the connection between means and the mode, the battle proper, these reports touch lightly. Two prominent reasons at least exist which go far to account for the general inadequacy of these official reports, or to account for their giving no true idea of what they assume to describe: the literary infirmity of the reporters, and their not seeing themselves and their commands as others would have seen them.

And factions, and parties, and politics, the curses of this Republic, are already putting in their unreasonable demands for the foremost honors of this field. "General Hooker won Gettysburg." How? Not with the army in person or by infinitesimal influence—leaving it almost four days before the battle when both armies were scattered and fifty miles apart? Was ever claim so absurd? Hooker, and he alone, won the result at Chancellorsville. "General Howard won Gettysburg." "Sickles saved the day." Just heaven save the poor Army of the Potomac from its friends! It has more to dread and less to hope from them than from the red-bannered hosts of the rebellion. The states prefer each her claim for the sole brunt and winning of the fight. "Pennsylvania won it." "New York won it." Did not Old Greece or some tribe from about the sources of the Nile win it? For modern Greeks—from Cork—and African Hannibals were there. Those intermingled graves along the crest, bearing the names of every loyal state save one or two, should admonish these geese to cease their cackle. One of the armies of the country won the battle; and that army supposes that General Meade led it upon that occasion. If it be not one of the lessons that this war teaches that we have a country, paramount and supreme over faction and party and state, then was the blood of fifty thousand citizens shed on this field in vain?

For the reasons mentioned, of this battle greater than Waterloo, a history, just, comprehensive, complete, will never be written. By and by, out of the chaos of trash and falsehood that newspapers hold, out of the disjointed mass of reports, out of the traditions and tales that come down from the field, some eye that never saw the battle will select and some pen will write what will be named *the history*. With that the world will be—and if we are alive we must be—content.

Already as I rode down from the heights, nature's mysterious loom was at work, joining and weaving on her ceaseless web the shells had broken there! Another spring shall green these trampled slopes, and flowers planted by unseen hands shall bloom upon these graves; another autumn and the yellow harvest shall ripen there—all not in less, but higher, perfection for this poured-out blood. In another decade of years, in another century, or age, we hope that the Union, by the same means, may repose in a securer peace and bloom in a higher civilization. Then what matter if it lame Tradition glean on this field and hand down her garbled sheaf; if deft Story with furtive fingers plait her ballad wreaths, deeds of her heroes here; or if stately History fill as she list her arbitrary tablet, the sounding record of this fight: Tradition, Story, History—all will not efface the true grand epic of Gettysburg.

Haskell

ORDER OF BATTLE
ARMY OF THE POTOMAC
AND ARMY OF
NORTHERN VIRGINIA,
JULY 1863

Organization of the Army of the Potomac, Maj. Gen. George G. Meade, U.S. Army, commanding, at the battle of Gettysburg, July 1–3, 1863.

GENERAL HEADQUARTERS.

COMMAND OF THE PROVOST-MARSHAL-GENERAL.

Brig. Gen. MARSENA R. PATRICK.

93d New York, Col. John S. Crocker.
8th United States (eight companies), Capt. Edwin W. H. Read.
2d Pennsylvania Cavalry, Col. R. Butler Price.
6th Pennsylvania Cavalry, Companies E and I, Capt. James Starr.
Regular cavalry (detachments from 1st, 2d, 5th, and 6th Regiments).

SIGNAL CORPS.

Capt. LEMUEL B. NORTON.

GUARDS AND ORDERLIES.

Oneida (New York) Cavalry, Capt. Daniel P. Mann.

ARTILLERY.

Brig. Gen. HENRY J. HUNT.

ENGINEER BRIGADE.

Brig. Gen. HENRY W. BENHAM.

15th New York (three companies), Maj. Walter L. Cassin.
50th New York, Col. William H. Pettes.
United States Battalion, Capt. George H. Mendell.

FIRST ARMY CORPS.

Maj. Gen. ABNER DOUBLEDAY.
Maj. Gen. JOHN NEWTON.

GENERAL HEADQUARTERS.

1st Maine Cavalry, Company L, Capt. Constantine Taylor.

FIRST DIVISION.

Brig. Gen. JAMES S. WADSWORTH.

First Brigade.

Brig. Gen. SOLOMON MEREDITH.
Col. WILLIAM W. ROBINSON.

19th Indiana, Col. Samuel J. Williams.
24th Michigan:
Col. Henry A. Morrow.
Capt. Albert M. Edwards.
2d Wisconsin:
Col. Lucius Fairchild.
Maj. John Mansfield.
Capt. George H. Otis.
6th Wisconsin, Lieut. Col. Rufus R. Dawes.
7th Wisconsin:
Col. William W. Robinson.
Maj. Mark Finnicum.

Second Brigade.

Brig. Gen. LYSANDER CUTLER.

7th Indiana, Col. Ira G. Grover.
76th New York:
Maj. Andrew J. Grover.
Capt. John E. Cook.
84th New York (14th Militia), Col. Edward B. Fowler.
95th New York:
Col. George H. Biddle.
Maj. Edward Pye.
147th New York:
Lieut. Col. Francis C. Miller.
Maj. George Harney.
56th Pennsylvania (nine companies), Col. J. William Hofmann.

SECOND DIVISION.

Brig. Gen. JOHN C. ROBINSON.

First Brigade.

Brig. Gen. GABRIEL R. PAUL.
Col. SAMUEL H. LEONARD.
Col. ADRIAN R. ROOT.
Col. RICHARD COULTER.
Col. PETER LYLE.

16th Maine:
Col. Charles W. Tilden.
Maj. Archibald D. Leavitt.
13th Massachusetts:
Col. Samuel H. Leonard.
Lieut. Col. N. Walter Batchelder.
94th New York:
Col. Adrian R. Root.
Maj. Samuel A. Moffett.
104th New York, Col. Gilbert G. Prey.
107th Pennsylvania:
Lieut. Col. James MacThomson.
Capt. Emanuel D. Roath.

Second Brigade.

Brig. Gen. HENRY BAXTER.

12th Massachusetts:
Col. James L. Bates.
Lieut. Col. David Allen, jr.

83d New York (9th Militia), Lieut. Col. Joseph A. Moesch.
97th New York:
Col. Charles Wheelock.
Maj. Charles Northrup.
11th Pennsylvania:
Col. Richard Coulter.
Capt. Benjamin F. Haines.
Capt. John B. Overmyer.
88th Pennsylvania:
Maj. Benezet F. Foust.
Capt. Henry Whiteside.
90th Pennsylvania:
Col. Peter Lyle.
Maj. Alfred J. Sellers.

THIRD DIVISION.

Brig. Gen. THOMAS A. ROWLEY.
Maj. Gen. ABNER DOUBLEDAY.

First Brigade.

Col. CHAPMAN BIDDLE.
Brig. Gen. THOMAS A. ROWLEY.

80th New York (20th Militia), Col. Theodore B. Gates.
121st Pennsylvania:
Maj. Alexander Biddle.
Col. Chapman Biddle.
Maj. Alexander Biddle.
142d Pennsylvania:
Col. Robert P. Cummins.
Lieut. Col. A. B. McCalmont.
151st Pennsylvania:
Lieut. Col. George F. McFarland.
Capt. Walter L. Owens.
Col. Harrison Allen.

Second Brigade.

Col. ROY STONE.
Col. LANGHORNE WISTER.
Col. EDMUND L. DANA.

143d Pennsylvania:
Col. Edmund L. Dana.
Lieut. Col. John D. Musser.
149th Pennsylvania:
Lieut. Col. Walton Dwight.
Capt. James Glenn.
150th Pennsylvania:
Col. Langhorne Wister.
Lieut. Col. H. S. Huidekoper.
Capt. Cornelius C. Widdis.

Third Brigade.

Brig. Gen. GEORGE J. STANNARD.
Col. FRANCIS V. RANDALL.

12th Vermont, Col. Asa P. Blunt.
13th Vermont:
Col. Francis V. Randall,
Maj. Joseph J. Boynton.
Lieut. Col. William D. Munson.
14th Vermont, Col. William T. Nichols.
15th Vermont, Col. Redfield Proctor.
16th Vermont, Col. Wheelock G. Veazey.

ARTILLERY BRIGADE.

Col. CHARLES S. WAINWRIGHT.

Maine Light, 2d Battery (B), Capt. James A. Hall.
Maine Light, 5th Battery (E):
Capt. Greenleaf T. Stevens.
Lieut. Edward N. Whittier.
1st New York Light, Battery L:
Capt. Gilbert H. Reynolds.
Lieut. George Breck.
1st Pennsylvania Light, Battery B, Capt. James H. Cooper.
4th United States, Battery B, Lieut. James Stewart.

SECOND ARMY CORPS.

Maj. Gen. WINFIELD S. HANCOCK.
Brig. Gen. JOHN GIBBON.

GENERAL HEADQUARTERS.

6th New York Cavalry, Companies D and K, Capt. Riley Johnson.

FIRST DIVISION.

Brig. Gen. JOHN C. CALDWELL.

First Brigade.

Col. EDWARD E. CROSS.
Col. H. BOYD MCKEEN.

5th New Hampshire, Lieut. Col. Charles E. Hapgood.
61st New York, Lieut. Col. K. Oscar Broady.
81st Pennsylvania:
Col. H. Boyd McKeen.
Lieut. Col. Amos Stroh.
148th Pennsylvania, Lieut. Col. Robert McFarlane.

Second Brigade.

Col. PATRICK KELLY.

28th Massachusetts, Col. R. Byrnes.
63d New York (two companies):
Lieut. Col. Richard C. Bentley.
Capt. Thomas Touhy.
69th New York (two companies):
Capt. Richard Moroney.
Lieut. James J. Smith.
88th New York (two companies), Capt. Denis F. Burke.
116th Pennsylvania (four companies), Maj. St. Clair A. Mulholland.

Third Brigade.

Brig. Gen. Samuel K. Zook.
Lieut. Col. John Fraser.

52d New York:
Lieut. Col. C. G. Freudenberg.
Capt. William Scherrer.
57th New York, Lieut. Col. Alford B. Chapman.
66th New York:
Col. Orlando H. Morris.
Lieut. Col. John S. Hammell.
Maj. Peter Nelson.
140th Pennsylvania:
Col. Richard P. Roberts.
Lieut. Col. John Fraser.

Fourth Brigade.

Col. John R. Brooke.

27th Connecticut (two companies):
Lieut. Col. Henry C. Merwin.
Maj. James H. Coburn.
2d Delaware:
Col. William P. Baily.
Capt. Charles H. Christman.
64th New York:
Col. Daniel G. Bingham.
Maj. Leman W. Bradley.
53d Pennsylvania, Lieut. Col. Richards McMichael.
145th Pennsylvania (seven companies):
Col. Hiram L. Brown.
Capt. John W. Reynolds.
Capt. Moses W. Oliver.

SECOND DIVISION.

Brig. Gen. John Gibbon.
Brig. Gen. William Harrow.

First Brigade.

Brig. Gen. William Harrow.
Col. Francis E. Heath.

19th Maine:
Col. Francis E. Heath.
Lieut. Col. Henry W. Cunningham.
15th Massachusetts:
Col. George H. Ward.
Lieut. Col. George C. Joslin.
1st Minnesota:
Col. William Colvill, jr.
Capt. Nathan S. Messick.
Capt. Henry C. Coates.
82d New York (2d Militia):
Lieut. Col. James Huston.
Capt. John Darrow.

Second Brigade.

Brig. Gen. Alexander S. Webb.

69th Pennsylvania:
Col. Dennis O'Kane.
Capt. William Davis.
71st Pennsylvania, Col. Richard Penn Smith.
72d Pennsylvania:
Col. De Witt C. Baxter.
Lieut. Col. Theodore Hesser.

106th Pennsylvania, Lieut. Col. William L. Curry.

Third Brigade.

Col. Norman J. Hall.

19th Massachusetts, Col. Arthur F. Devereux.
20th Massachusetts:
Col. Paul J. Revere.
Lieut. Col. George N. Macy.
Capt. Henry L. Abbott.
7th Michigan:
Lieut. Col. Amos E. Steele, jr.
Maj. Sylvanus W. Curtis.
42d New York, Col. James E. Mallon.
59th New York (four companies):
Lieut. Col. Max A. Thoman.
Capt. William McFadden.

Unattached.

Massachusetts Sharpshooters, 1st Company:
Capt. William Plumer.
Lieut. Emerson L. Bicknell.

THIRD DIVISION.

Brig. Gen. Alexander Hays.

First Brigade.

Col. Samuel S. Carroll.

14th Indiana, Col. John Coons.
4th Ohio, Lieut. Col. Leonard W. Carpenter.
8th Ohio, Lieut. Col. Franklin Sawyer.
7th West Virginia, Lieut. Col. Jonathan H. Lockwood.

Second Brigade.

Col. Thomas A. Smyth.
Lieut. Col. Francis E. Pierce.

14th Connecticut, Maj. Theodore G. Ellis.
1st Delaware:
Lieut. Col. Edward P. Harris.
Capt. Thomas B. Hizar.
Lieut. William Smith.
Lieut. John T. Dent.
12th New Jersey, Maj. John T. Hill.
10th New York (battalion), Maj. George F. Hopper.
108th New York, Lieut. Col. Francis E. Pierce.

Third Brigade.

Col. George L. Willard.
Col. Eliakim Sherrill.
Lieut. Col. James M. Bull.

39th New York (four companies), Maj. Hugo Hildebrandt.
111th New York:
Col. Clinton D. MacDougall.
Lieut. Col. Isaac M. Lusk.
Capt. Aaron P. Seeley.
125th New York, Lieut. Col. Levin Crandell.
126th New York:
Col. Eliakim Sherrill.
Lieut. Col. James M. Bull.

ARTILLERY BRIGADE.

Capt. JOHN G. HAZARD.

1st New York Light, Battery B:
Lieut. Albert S. Sheldon.
Capt. James McKay Rorty.
Lieut. Robert E. Rogers.
1st Rhode Island Light, Battery A,
Capt. William A. Arnold.
1st Rhode Island Light, Battery B:
Lieut. T. Fred. Brown.
Lieut. Walter S. Perrin.
1st United States, Battery I:
Lieut. George A. Woodruff.
Lieut. Tully McCrea.
4th United States, Battery A:
Lieut. Alonzo H. Cushing.
Sergt. Frederick Fuger.

THIRD ARMY CORPS.

Maj. Gen. DANIEL E. SICKLES.
Maj. Gen. DAVID B. BIRNEY.

FIRST DIVISION.

Maj. Gen. DAVID B. BIRNEY.
Brig. Gen. J. H. HOBART WARD.

First Brigade.

Brig. Gen. CHARLES K. GRAHAM.
Col. ANDREW H. TIPPIN.

57th Pennsylvania (eight companies):
Col. Peter Sides.
Capt. Alanson H. Nelson.
63d Pennsylvania, Maj. John A. Danks.
68th Pennsylvania:
Col. Andrew H. Tippin.
Capt. Milton S. Davis.[?]
105th Pennsylvania, Col. Calvin A. Craig.
114th Pennsylvania:
Lieut. Col. Frederick F. Cavada.
Capt. Edward R. Bowen.
141st Pennsylvania, Col. Henry J. Madill.

Second Brigade.

Brig. Gen. J. H. HOBART WARD.
Col. HIRAM BERDAN.

20th Indiana:
Col. John Wheeler.
Lieut. Col. William C. L. Taylor.
3d Maine, Col. Moses B. Lakeman.
4th Maine:
Col. Elijah Walker.
Capt. Edwin Libby.
86th New York, Lieut. Col. Benjamin L. Higgins.
124th New York:
Col. A. Van Horne Ellis.
Lieut. Col. Francis M. Cummins.
99th Pennsylvania, Maj. John W. Moore.

1st United States Sharpshooters:
Col. Hiram Berdan.
Lieut. Col. Casper Trepp.
2d United States Sharpshooters (eight companies), Maj. Homer R. Stoughton.

Third Brigade.

Col. P. REGIS DE TROBRIAND.

17th Maine, Lieut. Col. Charles B. Merrill.
3d Michigan:
Col. Byron R. Pierce.
Lieut. Col. Edwin S. Pierce.
5th Michigan, Lieut. Col. John Pulford.
40th New York, Col. Thomas W. Egan.
110th Pennsylvania (six companies):
Lieut. Col. David M. Jones.
Maj. Isaac Rogers.

SECOND DIVISION.

Brig. Gen. ANDREW A. HUMPHREYS.

First Brigade.

Brig. Gen. JOSEPH B. CARR.

1st Massachusetts, Lieut. Col. Clark B. Baldwin.
11th Massachusetts, Lieut. Col. Porter D. Tripp.
16th Massachusetts:
Lieut. Col. Waldo Merriam.
Capt. Matthew Donovan.
12th New Hampshire, Capt. John F. Langley.
11th New Jersey:
Col. Robert McAllister.
Capt. Luther Martin.
Lieut. John Schoonover.
Capt. William H. Lloyd.
Capt. Samuel T. Sleeper.
26th Pennsylvania, Maj. Robert L. Bodine.
84th Pennsylvania, Lieut. Col. Milton Opp.

Second Brigade.

Col. WILLIAM R. BREWSTER.

70th New York, Col. J. Egbert Farnum.
71st New York, Col. Henry L. Potter.
72d New York:
Col. John S. Austin.
Lieut. Col. John Leonard.
73d New York, Maj. Michael W. Burns.
74th New York, Lieut. Col. Thomas Holt.
120th New York:
Lieut. Col. Cornelius D. Westbrook.
Maj. John R. Tappen.

Third Brigade.

Col. GEORGE C. BURLING.

2d New Hampshire, Col. Edward L. Bailey.

5th New Jersey:
Col. William J. Sewell.
Capt. Thomas C. Godfrey.
Capt. Henry H. Woolsey.
6th New Jersey, Lieut. Col. Stephen R. Gilkyson.
7th New Jersey:
Col. Louis R. Francine.
Maj. Frederick Cooper.
8th New Jersey:
Col. John Ramsey.
Capt. John G. Langston.
115th Pennsylvania, Maj. John P. Dunne.

ARTILLERY BRIGADE.

Capt. GEORGE E. RANDOLPH.
Capt. A. JUDSON CLARK.

New Jersey Light, 2d Battery:
Capt. A. Judson Clark.
Lieut. Robert Sims.
1st New York Light, Battery D, Capt. George B. Winslow.
New York Light, 4th Battery, Capt. James E. Smith.
1st Rhode Island Light, Battery E:
Lieut. John K. Bucklyn.
Lieut. Benjamin Freeborn.
4th United States, Battery K:
Lieut. Francis W. Seeley.
Lieut. Robert James.

FIFTH ARMY CORPS.

Maj. Gen. GEORGE SYKES.

GENERAL HEADQUARTERS.

12th New York Infantry, Companies D and E, Capt. Henry W. Rider.
17th Pennsylvania Cavalry, Companies D and H, Capt. William Thompson.

FIRST DIVISION.

Brig. Gen. JAMES BARNES.

First Brigade.

Col. WILLIAM S. TILTON.

18th Massachusetts, Col. Joseph Hayes.
22d Massachusetts, Lieut. Col. Thomas Sherwin, jr.
1st Michigan:
Col. Ira C. Abbott.
Lieut. Col. William A. Throop.
118th Pennsylvania, Lieut. Col. James Gwyn.

Second Brigade.

Col. JACOB B. SWEITZER.

9th Massachusetts, Col. Patrick R. Guiney.
32d Massachusetts, Col. G. L. Prescott.
4th Michigan:
Col. Harrison H. Jeffords.
Lieut. Col. George W. Lumbard.

62d Pennsylvania, Lieut. Col. James C. Hull.

Third Brigade.

Col. STRONG VINCENT.
Col. JAMES C. RICE.

20th Maine, Col. Joshua L. Chamberlain.
16th Michigan, Lieut. Col. Norval E. Welch.
44th New York:
Col. James C. Rice.
Lieut.Col.FreemanConner.8
3d Pennsylvania, Capt. Orpheus S. Woodward.

SECOND DIVISION.

Brig. Gen. ROMEYN B. AYRES.

First Brigade.

Col. HANNIBAL DAY.

3d United States (six companies):
Capt. Henry W. Freedley.
Capt. Richard G. Lay.
4th United States (four companies),
Capt. Julius W. Adams, jr.
6th United States (five companies),
Capt. Levi C. Bootes.
12th United States (eight companies),
Capt. Thomas S. Dunn.
14th United States (eight companies),
Maj. Grotius R. Giddings.

Second Brigade.

Col. SIDNEY BURBANK.

2d United States (six companies):
Maj. Arthur T. Lee.
Capt. Samuel A. McKee.
7th United States (four companies),
Capt. David P. Hancock.
10th United States (three companies),
Capt. William Clinton.
11th United States (six companies),
Maj. De Lancey Floyd-Jones.
17th United States (seven companies),
Lieut. Col. J. Durell Greene.

Third Brigade.

Brig. Gen. STEPHEN H. WEED.
Col. KENNER GARRARD.

140th New York:
Col. Patrick H. O'Rorke.
Lieut. Col. Louis Ernst.
146th New York:
Col. Kenner Garrard.
Lieut. Col. David T. Jenkins.
91st Pennsylvania, Lieut. Col. Joseph H. Sinex.
155th Pennsylvania, Lieut. Col. John H. Cain.

THIRD DIVISION.

Brig. Gen. SAMUEL W. CRAWFORD.

First Brigade.

Col. WILLIAM MCCANDLESS.

1st Pennsylvania Reserves (nine companies), Col. William C. Talley.
13th Pennsylvania Reserves:
Col. Charles F. Taylor.
Maj. William R. Hartshorne.

Third Brigade.

Col. JOSEPH W. FISHER.

5th Pennsylvania Reserves, Lieut. Col. George Dare.
2d Pennsylvania Reserves, Lieut. Col. George A. Woodward.
6th Pennsylvania Reserves, Lieut. Col. Wellington H. Ent.
9th Pennsylvania Reserves, Lieut. Col. James McK. Snodgrass.
10th Pennsylvania Reserves, Col. Adoniram J. Warner.
11th Pennsylvania Reserves, Col. Samuel M. Jackson.
12th Pennsylvania Reserves (nine companies), Col. Martin D. Hardin.

ARTILLERY BRIGADE.

Capt. AUGUSTUS P. MARTIN.

Massachusetts Light, 3d Battery (C), Lieut. Aaron F. Walcott.
1st New York Light, Battery C, Capt. Almont Barnes.
1st Ohio Light, Battery L, Capt. Frank C. Gibbs.
5th United States, Battery D:
Lieut. Charles E. Hazlett.
Lieut. Benjamin F. Rittenhouse.
5th United States, Battery I:
Lieut. Malbone F. Watson.
Lieut. Charles C. MacConnell.

SIXTH ARMY CORPS.

Maj. Gen. JOHN SEDGWICK.

GENERAL HEADQUARTERS.

1st New Jersey Cavalry, Company L,
1st Pennsylvania Cavalry, Company H, } Capt. William S. Craft.

FIRST DIVISION.

Brig. Gen. HORATIO G. WRIGHT.

Provost Guard.

4th New Jersey (three companies), Capt. William R. Maxwell.

First Brigade.

Brig. Gen. A. T. A. TORBERT.

1st New Jersey, Lieut. Col. William Henry, jr.
2d New Jersey, Lieut. Col. Charles Wiebecke.
3d New Jersey, Lieut. Col. Edward L. Campbell.
15th New Jersey, Col. William H. Penrose.

Second Brigade.

Brig. Gen. JOSEPH J. BARTLETT.

5th Maine, Col. Clark S. Edwards.
121st New York, Col. Emory Upton.
95th Pennsylvania, Lieut. Col. Edward Carroll.
96th Pennsylvania, Maj. William H. Lessig.

Third Brigade.

Brig. Gen. DAVID A. RUSSELL.

6th Maine, Col. Hiram Burnham.
49th Pennsylvania, (four companies), Lieut. Col. Thomas M. Hulings.
119th Pennsylvania, Col. Peter C. Ellmaker.
5th Wisconsin, Col. Thomas S. Allen.

SECOND DIVISION.

Brig. Gen. ALBION P. HOWE.

Second Brigade.

Col. LEWIS A. GRANT.

2d Vermont, Col. James H. Walbridge.
3d Vermont, Col. Thomas O. Seaver.
4th Vermont, Col. Charles B. Stoughton.
5th Vermont, Lieut. Col. John R. Lewis.
6th Vermont, Col. Elisha L. Barney.

Third Brigade.

Brig. Gen. THOMAS H. NEILL.

7th Maine (six companies), Lieut. Col. Selden Connor.
33d New York (detachment), Capt. Henry J. Gifford.
43d New York, Lieut. Col. John Wilson.
49th New York, Col. Daniel D. Bidwell.
77th New York, Lieut. Col. Winsor B. French.
61st Pennsylvania, Lieut. Col. George F. Smith.

THIRD DIVISION.

Maj. Gen. JOHN NEWTON.
Brig. Gen. FRANK WHEATON.

First Brigade.

Brig. Gen. ALEXANDER SHALER.

65th New York, Col. Joseph E. Hamblin.
67th New York, Col. Nelson Cross.
122d New York, Col. Silas Titus.
23d Pennsylvania, Lieut. Col. John F. Glenn.
82d Pennsylvania, Col. Isaac C. Bassett.

Second Brigade.

Col. HENRY L. EUSTIS.

7th Massachusetts, Lieut. Col. Franklin P. Harlow.
10th Massachusetts, Lieut. Col. Joseph B. Parsons.
37th Massachusetts, Col. Oliver Edwards.
2d Rhode Island, Col. Horatio Rogers, jr.

Third Brigade.

Brig. Gen. FRANK WHEATON.
Col. DAVID J. NEVIN.

62d New York:
Col. David J. Nevin.
Lieut. Col. Theodore B. Hamilton.
93d Pennsylvania, Maj. John I. Nevin.
98th Pennsylvania, Maj. John B. Kohler.
102d Pennsylvania, Col. John W. Patterson.
139th Pennsylvania:
Col. Frederick H. Collier.
Lieut. Col. William H. Moody.

ARTILLERY BRIGADE.

Col. CHARLES H. TOMPKINS.

Massachusetts Light, 1st Battery (A), Capt. William H. McCartney.
New York Light, 1st Battery, Capt. Andrew Cowan.
New York Light, 3d Battery, Capt. William A. Harn.
1st Rhode Island Light, Battery C, Capt. Richard Waterman.
1st Rhode Island Light, Battery G, Capt. George W. Adams.
2d United States, Battery D, Lieut. Edward B. Williston.
2d United States, Battery G, Lieut. John H. Butler.
5th United States, Battery F, Lieut. Leonard Martin.

ELEVENTH ARMY CORPS.

Maj. Gen. Oliver O. Howard.

GENERAL HEADQUARTERS.

1st Indiana Cavalry, Companies I and K, Capt. Abram Sharra.
8th New York Infantry (one company), Lieut. Hermann Foerster.

FIRST DIVISION.

Brig. Gen. Francis C. Barlow.
Brig. Gen. Adelbert Ames.

First Brigade.

Col. Leopold von Gilsa.

41st New York (nine companies), Lieut. Col. Detleo von Einsiedel.
54th New York:
Maj. Stephen Kovacs.
Lieut. Ernst Both [?].
68th New York, Col. Gotthilf Bourry.
153d Pennsylvania, Maj. John F. Frueauff.

Second Brigade.

Brig. Gen. Adelbert Ames.
Col. Andrew L. Harris.

17th Connecticut:
Lieut. Col. Douglas Fowler.
Maj. Allen G. Brady.
25th Ohio:
Lieut. Col. Jeremiah Williams.
Capt. Nathaniel J. Manning.
Lieut. William Maloney.
Lieut. Israel White.
75th Ohio:
Col. Andrew L. Harris.
Capt. George B. Fox.
107th Ohio:
Col. Seraphim Meyer.
Capt. John M. Lutz.

SECOND DIVISION.

Brig. Gen. Adolph von Steinwehr.

First Brigade.

Col. Charles R. Coster.

134th New York, Lieut. Col. Allan H. Jackson.
154th New York, Lieut. Col. D. B. Allen.
27th Pennsylvania, Lieut. Col. Lorenz Cantador.
73d Pennsylvania, Capt. D. F. Kelley.

Second Brigade.

Col. Orland Smith.

33d Massachusetts, Col. Adin B. Underwood.
136th New York, Col. James Wood, jr.
55th Ohio, Col. Charles B. Gambee.
73d Ohio, Lieut. Col. Richard Long.

THIRD DIVISION.

Maj. Gen. CARL SCHURZ.

First Brigade.

Brig. Gen. ALEX. SCHIMMELFENNIG.
Col. GEORGE VON AMSBERG.

82d Illinois, Lieut. Col. Edward S. Salomon.
45th New York:
Col. George von Amsberg.
Lieut. Col. Adolphus Dobke.
157th New York, Col. Philip P. Brown, jr.
61st Ohio, Col. Stephen J. McGroarty.
74th Pennsylvania:
Col. Adolph von Hartung.
Lieut. Col. Alexander von Mitzel.
Capt. Gustav Schleiter.
Capt. Henry Krauseneck.

Second Brigade.

Col. W. KRZYZANOWSKI.

58th New York:
Lieut. Col. August Otto.
Capt. Emil Koenig.
119th New York:
Col. John T. Lockman.
Lieut. Col. Edward F. Lloyd.
82d Ohio:
Col. James S. Robinson.
Lieut. Col. David Thomson.
75th Pennsylvania:
Col. Francis Mahler.
Maj. August Ledig.
26th Wisconsin:
Lieut. Col. Hans Boebel.
Capt. John W. Fuchs.

ARTILLERY BRIGADE.

Maj. THOMAS W. OSBORN.

1st New York Light, Battery I, Capt. Michael Wiedrich.
New York Light, 13th Battery, Lieut. William Wheeler.
1st Ohio Light, Battery I, Capt. Hubert Dilger.
1st Ohio Light, Battery K, Capt. Lewis Heckman.
4th United States, Battery G:
Lieut. Bayard Wilkeson.
Lieut. Eugene A. Bancroft.

TWELFTH ARMY CORPS.

Maj. Gen. HENRY W. SLOCUM.
Brig. Gen. ALPHEUS S. WILLIAMS.

PROVOST GUARD.

10th Maine (four companies), Capt. John D. Beardsley.

FIRST DIVISION.

Brig. Gen. ALPHEUS S. WILLIAMS.
Brig. Gen. THOMAS H. RUGER.

First Brigade.

Col. ARCHIBALD L. MCDOUGALL.

5th Connecticut, Col. W. W. Packer.
20th Connecticut, Lieut. Col. William B. Wooster.
3d Maryland, Col. Jos. M. Sudsburg.
123d New York:
Lieut. Col. James C. Rogers.
Capt. Adolphus H. Tanner.
145th New York, Col. E. L. Price.
46th Pennsylvania, Col. James L. Selfridge.

Second Brigade.

Brig. Gen. HENRY H. LOCKWOOD.

1st Maryland, Potomac Home Brigade, Col. William P. Maulsby.
1st Maryland, Eastern Shore, Col. James Wallace.
150th New York, Col. John H. Ketcham.

Third Brigade.

Brig. Gen. THOMAS H. RUGER.
Col. SILAS COLGROVE.

27th Indiana:
Col. Silas Colgrove.
Lieut. Col. John R. Fesler.
2d Massachusetts:
Lieut. Col. Charles R. Mudge.
Maj. Charles F. Morse.
13th New Jersey, Col. Ezra A. Carman.
107th New York, Col. Nirom M. Crane.
3d Wisconsin, Col. William Hawley.

SECOND DIVISION.

Brig. Gen. JOHN W. GEARY.

First Brigade.

Col. CHARLES CANDY.

5th Ohio, Col. John H. Patrick.
7th Ohio, Col. William R. Creighton.
29th Ohio:
Capt. Wilbur F. Stevens.
Capt. Edward Hayes.
66th Ohio, Lieut. Col. Eugene Powell.
28th Pennsylvania, Capt. John Flynn.
147th Pennsylvania (eight companies), Lieut. Col. Ario Pardee, jr.

Second Brigade.

Col. GEORGE A. COBHAM, Jr.
Brig. GEN. THOMAS L. KANE.
Col. GEORGE A. COBHAM, Jr.

29th Pennsylvania, Col. William Rickards, jr.
109th Pennsylvania, Capt. F. L. Gimber.
111th Pennsylvania:
Lieut. Col. Thomas M. Walker.
Col. George A. Cobham, jr.
Lieut. Col. Thomas M. Walker.

Third Brigade.

Brig. Gen. GEORGE S. GREENE.

60th New York, Col. Abel Godard.
78th New York, Lieut. Col. Herbert von Hammerstein.
102d New York:
Col. James C. Lane.
Capt. Lewis R. Stegman.
137th New York, Col. David Ireland.
149th New York:
Col. Henry A. Barnum.
Lieut. Col. Charles B. Randall.

ARTILLERY BRIGADE.

Lieut. EDWARD D. MUHLENBERG.

1st New York Light, Battery M, Lieut. Charles E. Winegar.
Pennsylvania Light, Battery E, Lieut. Charles A. Atwell.
4th United States, Battery F, Lieut. Sylvanus T. Rugg.
5th United States, Battery K, Lieut. David H. Kinzie.

CAVALRY CORPS.

Maj. Gen. ALFRED PLEASONTON.

FIRST DIVISION.

Brig. Gen. JOHN BUFORD.

First Brigade.

Col. WILLIAM GAMBLE.

8th Illinois, Maj. John L. Beveridge.
12th Illinois (four cos.), } Col. George H. Chapman.
3d Indiana (six cos.), }
8th New York, Lieut. Col. William L. Markell.
3d West Virginia (two companies), Capt. Seymour B. Conger.

Second Brigade.

Col. THOMAS C. DEVIN.

6th New York, Maj. Wm. E. Beardsley.
9th New York, Col. William Sackett.
17th Pennsylvania, Col. J. H. Kellogg.

Reserve Brigade.

Brig. Gen. WESLEY MERRITT.

6th Pennsylvania, Maj. James H. Haseltine.
1st United States, Capt. Richard S. C. Lord.
2d United States, Capt. T. F. Rodenbough.
5th United States, Capt. Julius W. Mason.
6th United States:
Maj. Samuel H. Starr.
Lieut. Louis H. Carpenter.
Lieut. Nicholas Nolan.
Capt. Ira W. Claflin.

SECOND DIVISION.

Brig. Gen. DAVID McM. GREGG.

Headquarters Guard.

1st Ohio, Company A, Capt. Noah Jones.

First Brigade.

Col. JOHN B. McINTOSH.

1st Maryland (eleven companies), Lieut. Col. James M. Deems.
Purnell (Maryland) Legion, Company A, Capt. Robert E. Duvall.
1st Massachusetts, Lieut. Col. Greely S. Curtis.
1st New Jersey, Maj. M. H. Beaumont.
1st Pennsylvania, Col. John P. Taylor.
3d Pennsylvania, Lieut. Col. E. S. Jones.
3d Pennsylvania Heavy Artillery, Section Battery H, Capt. W. D. Rank.

Second Brigade.

Col. PENNOCK HUEY.

2d New York, Lieut. Col. Otto Harhaus.
4th New York, Lieut. Col. Augustus Pruyn.
6th Ohio (ten companies), Maj. William Stedman.
8th Pennsylvania, Capt. William A. Corrie.

Third Brigade.

Col. J. IRVIN GREGG.

1st Maine (ten companies), Lieut. Col. Charles H. Smith.
10th New York, Maj. M. Henry Avery.
4th Pennsylvania, Lieut. Col. William E. Doster.
16th Pennsylvania, Lieut. Col. John K. Robison.

THIRD DIVISION.

Brig. Gen. JUDSON KILPATRICK.

Headquarters Guard.

1st Ohio, Company C, Capt. Samuel N. Stanford.

First Brigade.

Brig. Gen. ELON J. FARNSWORTH.
Col. NATHANIEL P. RICHMOND.

5th New York, Maj. John Hammond.
18th Pennsylvania, Lieut. Col. William P. Brinton.
1st Vermont, Lieut. Col. Addison W. Preston.
1st West Virginia (ten companies):
Col. Nathaniel P. Richmond.
Maj. Charles E. Capehart.

Second Brigade.

Brig. Gen. GEORGE A. CUSTER.

1st Michigan, Col. Charles H. Town.
5th Michigan, Col. Russell A. Alger.
6th Michigan, Col. George Gray.
7th Michigan (ten companies), Col. William D. Mann.

HORSE ARTILLERY.

First Brigade.

Capt. JAMES M. ROBERTSON.

9th Michigan Battery, Capt. Jabez J. Daniels.
6th New York Battery, Capt. Joseph W. Martin.
2d United States, Batteries B and L,
Lieut. Edward Heaton.
2d United States, Battery M, Lieut. A. C. M. Pennington, jr.
4th United States, Battery E, Lieut. Samuel S. Elder.

Second Brigade.

Capt. JOHN C. TIDBALL.

1st United States, Batteries E and G,
Capt. Alanson M. Randol.
1st United States, Battery K, Capt. William M. Graham.
2d United States, Battery A, Lieut. John H. Calef.
3d United States, Battery C, Lieut. William D. Fuller.

ARTILLERY RESERVE.

Brig. Gen. ROBERT O. TYLER.
Capt. JAMES M. ROBERTSON.

Headquarters Guard.

32d Massachusetts Infantry, Company C, Capt. Josiah C. Fuller.

First Regular Brigade.

Capt. DUNBAR R. RANSOM.

1st United States, Battery H:
Lieut. Chandler P. Eakin.
Lieut. Philip D. Mason.
3d United States, Batteries F and K, Lieut. John G. Turnbull.
4th United States, Battery C, Lieut. Evan Thomas.
5th United States, Battery C, Lieut. Gulian V. Weir.

First Volunteer Brigade.

Lieut. Col. FREEMAN MCGILVERY.

Massachusetts Light, 5th Battery (E), Capt. Charles A. Phillips.
Massachusetts Light, 9th Battery:
Capt. John Bigelow.
Lieut. Richard S. Milton.
New York Light, 15th Battery, Capt. Patrick Hart.
Pennsylvania Light, Batteries C and F, Capt. James Thompson.

Second Volunteer Brigade.

Capt. ELIJAH D. TAFT.

1st Connecticut Heavy, Battery B, Capt. Albert F. Brooker.
1st Connecticut Heavy, Battery M, Capt. Franklin A. Pratt.

Connecticut Light, 2d Battery, Capt. John W. Sterling.
New York Light, 5th Battery, Capt. Elijah D. Taft.

Third Volunteer Brigade.

Capt. JAMES F. HUNTINGTON.

New Hampshire Light, 1st Battery, Capt. Frederick M. Edgell.
1st Ohio Light, Battery H, Lieut. George W. Norton.
1st Pennsylvania Light, Batteries F and G, Capt. R. Bruce Ricketts.
West Virginia Light, Battery C, Capt. Wallace Hill.

Fourth Volunteer Brigade.

Capt. ROBERT H. FITZHUGH.

Maine Light, 6th Battery (F), Lieut. Edwin B. Dow.
Maryland Light, Battery A, Capt. James H. Rigby.
New Jersey Light, 1st Battery, Lieut. Augustin N. Parsons.
1st New York Light, Battery G, Capt. Nelson Ames.
1st New York Light, Battery K, Capt. Robert H. Fitzhugh.

Train Guard.

4th New Jersey Infantry (seven companies), Maj. Charles Ewing.

Organization of the Army of Northern Virginia, Gen. Robert E. Lee, C.S. Army, Commanding at the battle of Gettysburg, July 1–3.

FIRST ARMY CORPS.

Lieut. Gen. JAMES LONGSTREET.

M'LAWS'S DIVISION.

Maj. Gen. LAFAYETTE MCLAWS.

Kershaw's Brigade.

Brig. Gen. J. B. KERSHAW.

2d South Carolina:
Col. J. D. Kennedy.
Lieut. Col. F. Gaillard.
3d South Carolina:
Maj. R. C. Maffett.
Col. J. D. Nance.
7th South Carolina, Col. D. Wyatt Aiken.
8th South Carolina, Col. J. W. Henagan.
15th South Carolina:
Col. W. D. De Saussure.
Maj. William M. Gist.
3d South Carolina Battalion, Lieut. Col. W. G. Rice.

Barksdale's Brigade.

Brig. Gen. WILLIAM BARKSDALE.
Col. B. G. HUMPHREYS.

13th Mississippi, Col. J. W. Carter.
17th Mississippi:
Col. W. D. Holder.
Lieut. Col. John C. Fiser.
18th Mississippi:
Col. T. M. Griffin.
Lieut. Col. W. H. Luse.
21st Mississippi, Col. B. G. Humphreys.

Semmes' Brigade.

Brig. Gen. P. J. SEMMES.
Col. GOODE BRYAN.

10th Georgia, Col. John B. Weems.
50th Georgia, Col. W. R. Manning.
51st Georgia, Col. E. Ball.
53d Georgia, Col. James P. Simms.

Wofford's Brigade.

Brig. Gen. W. T. WOFFORD.

16th Georgia, Col. Goode Bryan.
18th Georgia, Lieut. Col. S. Z. Ruff.
24th Georgia, Col. Robert McMillan.
Cobb's (Georgia) Legion, Lieut. Col. Luther J. Glenn.
Phillips (Georgia) Legion, Lieut. Col. E. S. Barclay.

Artillery.

Col. H. G. Cabell.

1st North Carolina Artillery, Battery A, Capt. B. C. Manly.
Pulaski (Georgia) Artillery:
Capt. J. C. Fraser.
Lieut. W. J. Furlong.
1st Richmond Howitzers, Capt. E. S. McCarthy.
Troup (Georgia) Artillery:
Capt. H. H. Carlton.
Lieut. C. W. Motes.

PICKETT'S DIVISION.

Maj. Gen. George E. Pickett.

Garnett's Brigade.

Brig. Gen. R. B. Garnett.
Maj. C. S. Peyton.

8th Virginia, Col. Eppa Hunton.
18th Virginia, Lieut. Col. H. A. Carrington.
19th Virginia:
Col. Henry Gantt.
Lieut. Col. John T. Ellis.
28th Virginia:
Col. R. C. Allen.
Lieut. Col. William Watts.
56th Virginia:
Col. W. D. Stuart.
Lieut. Col. P. P. Slaughter.

Kemper's Brigade.

Brig. Gen. J. L. Kemper.
Col. Joseph Mayo, Jr.

1st Virginia:
Col. Lewis B. Williams.
Lieut. Col. F. G. Skinner.
3d Virginia:
Col. Joseph Mayo, jr.
Lieut. Col. A. D. Callcote.
7th Virginia:
Col. W. T. Patton.
Lieut. Col. C. C. Flowerree.
11th Virginia, Maj. Kirkwood Otey.
24th Virginia, Col. William R. Terry.

Armistead's Brigade.

Brig. Gen. L. A. Armistead.
Col. W. R. Aylett.

9th Virginia, Maj. John C. Owens.
14th Virginia:
Col. James G. Hodges.
Lieut. Col. William White.
38th Virginia:
Col. E. C. Edmonds.
Lieut. Col. P. B. Whittle.
53d Virginia, Col. W. R. Aylett.
57th Virginia, Col. John Bowie Magruder.

Artillery.

Maj. JAMES DEARING.

Fauquier (Virginia) Artillery, Capt. R. M. Stribling.
Hampden (Virginia) Artillery, Capt. W. H. Caskie.
Richmond Fayette Artillery, Capt. M. C. Macon.
Virginia Battery, Capt. Joseph G. Blount.

HOOD'S DIVISION.

Maj. Gen. JOHN B. HOOD.
Brig. Gen. E. M. LAW.

Law's Brigade.

Brig. Gen E. M. LAW.
Col. JAMES L. SHEFFIELD.

4th Alabama, Lieut. Col. L. H. Scruggs.
15th Alabama:
Col. William C. Oates.
Capt. B. A. Hill.
44th Alabama, Col. William F. Perry.
47th Alabama:
Col. James W. Jackson.
Lieut. Col. M. J. Bulger.
Maj. J. M. Campbell.
48th Alabama:
Col. James L. Sheffield.
Capt. T. J. Eubanks.

Robertson's Brigade.

Brig. Gen. J. B. ROBERTSON.

3d Arkansas:
Col. Van H. Manning.
Lieut. Col. R. S. Taylor.
1st Texas, Lieut. Col. P. A. Work.
4th Texas:
Col. J. C. G. Key.
Maj. J. P. Bane.
5th Texas:
Col. R. M. Powell.
Lieut. Col. K. Bryan.
Maj. J. C. Rogers.

Anderson's Brigade.

Brig. Gen. GEORGE T. ANDERSON.
Lieut. Col. WILLIAM LUFFMAN.

7th Georgia, Col. W. W. White.
8th Georgia, Col. John R. Towers.
9th Georgia:
Lieut. Col. John C. Mounger.
Maj. W. M. Jones.
Capt. George Hillyer.
11th Georgia:
Col. F. H. Little.
Lieut. Col. William Luffman.
Maj. Henry D. McDaniel.
Capt. William H. Mitchell.
59th Georgia:
Col. Jack Brown.
Capt. M. G. Bass.

Benning's Brigade.

Brig. Gen. HENRY L. BENNING.

2d Georgia:
Lieut. Col. William T. Harris.
Maj. W. S. Shepherd.
15th Georgia, Col. D. M. DuBose.
17th Georgia, Col. W. C. Hodges,
20th Georgia:
Col. John A. Jones.
Lieut. Col. J. D. Waddell.

Artillery.

Maj. M. W. HENRY.

Branch (North Carolina) Artillery, Capt. A. C. Latham.
German (South Carolina) Artillery, Capt. William K. Bachman.
Palmetto (South Carolina) Light Artillery, Capt. Hugh R. Garden.
Rowan (North Carolina) Artillery, Capt. James Reilly.

ARTILLERY RESERVE.

Col. J. B. WALTON.

Alexander's Battalion.

Col. E. P. ALEXANDER.

Ashland (Virginia) Artillery:
Capt. P. Woolfolk, jr.
Lieut. James Woolfolk.
Bedford (Virginia) Artillery, Capt. T. C. Jordan.
Brooks (South Carolina) Artillery, Lieut. S. C. Gilbert.
Madison (Louisiana) Light Artillery, Capt. George V. Moody.
Virginia Battery, Capt. W. W. Parker.
Virginia Battery, Capt. O. B. Taylor.

Washington (Louisiana) Artillery.

Maj. B. F. ESHLEMAN.

First Company, Capt. C. W. Squires.
Second Company, Capt. J. B. Richardson.
Third Company, Capt. M. B. Miller.
Fourth Company:
Capt. Joe Norcom.
Lieut. H. A. Battles.

SECOND ARMY CORPS.

Lieut. Gen. RICHARD S. EWELL.

Escort.

Randolph's Company Virginia Cavalry, Capt. William F. Randolph.

EARLY'S DIVISION.

Maj. Gen. JUBAL A. EARLY.

Hays' Brigade.

Brig. Gen. HARRY T. HAYS.

5th Louisiana:
Maj. Alexander Hart.
Capt. T. H. Biscoe.
6th Louisiana, Lieut. Col. Joseph Hanlon.
7th Louisiana, Col. D. B. Penn.
8th Louisiana:
Col. T. D. Lewis.
Lieut. Col. A. de Blanc.
Maj. G. A. Lester.
9th Louisiana, Col. Leroy A. Stafford.

Smith's Brigade.

Brig. Gen. WILLIAM SMITH.

31st Virginia, Col. John S. Hoffman.
49th Virginia, Lieut. Col. J. Catlett Gibson.
52d Virginia, Lieut. Col. James H. Skinner.

Hoke's Brigade.

Col. ISAAC E. AVERY.
Col. A. C. GODWIN.

6th North Carolina, Maj. S. McD. Tate.
21st North Carolina, Col. W. W. Kirkland.
57th North Carolina, Col. A. C. Godwin.

Gordon's Brigade.

Brig. Gen. J. B. GORDON.

13th Georgia, Col. James M. Smith.
26th Georgia, Col. E. N. Atkinson.
31st Georgia, Col. Clement A. Evans.
38th Georgia, Capt. William L. McLeod.
60th Georgia, Capt. W. B. Jones.
61st Georgia, Col. John H. Lamar.

Artillery.

Lieut. Col. H. P. JONES.

Charlottesville (Virginia) Artillery, Capt. James McD. Carrington.
Courtney (Virginia) Artillery, Capt. W. A. Tanner.
Louisiana Guard Artillery, Capt. C. A. Green.
Staunton (Virginia) Artillery, Capt. A. W. Garber.

JOHNSON'S DIVISION.

Maj. Gen. EDWARD JOHNSON.

Steuart's Brigade.

Brig. Gen. GEORGE H. STEUART.

1st Maryland Battalion Infantry:
Lieut. Col. J. R. Herbert.
Maj. W. W. Goldsborough.
Capt. J. P. Crane.
1st North Carolina, Lieut. Col. H. A. Brown.
3d North Carolina, Maj. W. M. Parsley.
10th Virginia, Col. E. T. H. Warren.
23d Virginia, Lieut. Col. S. T. Walton.
37th Virginia, Maj. H. C. Wood.

Stonewall Brigade.

Brig. Gen. JAMES A. WALKER.

2d Virginia, Col. J. Q. A. Nadenbousch.
4th Virginia, Maj. William Terry.
5th Virginia, Col. J. H. S. Funk.
27th Virginia, Lieut. Col. D. M. Shriver.
33d Virginia, Capt. J. B. Golladay.

Nicholls' Brigade.

Col. J. M. WILLIAMS.

1st Louisiana, Capt. E. D. Willett.
2d Louisiana, Lieut. Col. R. E. Burke.
10th Louisiana, Maj. T. N. Powell.
14th Louisiana, Lieut. Col. David Zable.
15th Louisiana, Maj. Andrew Brady.

Jones's Brigade.

Brig. Gen. JOHN M. JONES.
Lieut. Col. R. H. DUNGAN.

21st Virginia, Capt. W. P. Moseley.
25th Virginia:
Col. J. C. Higginbotham.
Lieut. Col. J. A. Robinson.
42d Virginia:
Lieut. Col. R. W. Withers.
Capt. S. H. Saunders.
44th Virginia:
Maj. N. Cobb.
Capt. T. R. Buckner.
48th Virginia:
Lieut. Col. R. H. Dungan.
Maj. Oscar White.
50th Virginia, Lieut. Col. L. H. N. Salyer.

Artillery.

Maj. J. W. LATIMER.
Capt. C. I. RAINE.

1st Maryland Battery, Capt. William F. Dement.
Alleghany (Virginia) Artillery, Capt. J. C. Carpenter.
Chesapeake (Maryland) Artillery, Capt. William D. Brown.
Lee (Virginia) Battery:
Capt. C. I. Raine.
Lieut. William W. Hardwicke.

RODES' DIVISION.

Maj. Gen. R. E. RODES.

Daniel's Brigade.

Brig. Gen. JUNIUS DANIEL.

32d North Carolina, Col. E. C. Brabble.
43d North Carolina:
Col. T. S. Kenan.
Lieut. Col. W. G. Lewis.
45th North Carolina:
Lieut. Col. S. H. Boyd.
Maj. John R. Winston.
Capt. A. H. Gallaway.
Capt. J. A. Hopkins.
53d North Carolina, Col. W. A. Owens.
2d North Carolina Battalion:
Lieut. Col. H. L. Andrews.
Capt. Van Brown.

Doles's Brigade.

Brig. Gen. GEORGE DOLES.

4th Georgia:
Lieut. Col. D. R. E. Winn.
Maj. W. H. Willis.
12th Georgia, Col. Edward Willis.
21st Georgia, Col. John T. Mercer.
44th Georgia:
Col. S. P. Lumpkin.
Maj. W. H. Peebles.

Iverson's Brigade.

Brig. Gen. ALFRED IVERSON.

5th North Carolina:
Capt. Speight B. West.
Capt. Benjamin Robinson.
12th North Carolina, Lieut. Col. W. S. Davis.
20th North Carolina:
Lieut. Col. Nelson Slough.
Capt. Lewis T. Hicks.
23d North Carolina:
Col. D. H. Christie.
Capt. William H. Johnston.

Ramseur's Brigade.

Brig. Gen. S. D. RAMSEUR.

2d North Carolina:
Maj. D. W. Hurtt.
Capt. James T. Scales.
4th North Carolina, Col. Bryan Grimes.
14th North Carolina:
Col. R. Tyler Bennett.
Maj. Joseph H. Lambeth.
30th North Carolina:
Col. Francis M. Parker.
Maj. W. W. Sillers.

O'Neal's Brigade.

Col. E. A. O'NEAL.

3d Alabama, Col. C. A. Battle.
5th Alabama, Col. J. M. Hall.
6th Alabama:
Col. J. N. Lightfoot.
Capt. M. L. Bowie.
12th Alabama, Col. S. B. Pickens.
26th Alabama, Lieut. Col. John C. Goodgame.

Artillery.

Lieut. Col. THOMAS H. CARTER.

Jeff. Davis (Alabama) Artillery, Capt. W. J. Reese.
King William (Virginia) Artillery, Capt. W. P. Carter.
Morris (Virginia) Artillery, Capt. R. C. M. Page.
Orange (Virginia) Artillery, Capt. C. W. Fry.

ARTILLERY RESERVE.

Col. J. THOMPSON BROWN.

First Virginia Artillery.

Capt. WILLIS J. DANCE.

2d Richmond (Virginia) Howitzers, Capt. David Watson.
3d Richmond (Virginia) Howitzers, Capt. B. H. Smith, jr.
Powhatan (Virginia) Artillery, Lieut. John M. Cunningham.
Rockbridge (Virginia) Artillery, Capt. A. Graham.
Salem (Virginia) Artillery, Lieut. C. B. Griffin.

Nelson's Battalion.

Lieut. Col. WILLIAM NELSON.

Amherst (Virginia) Artillery, Capt. T. J. Kirkpatrick.
Fluvanna (Virginia) Artillery, Capt. J. L. Massie.
Georgia Battery, Capt. John Milledge, jr.

THIRD ARMY CORPS.

Lieut. Gen. AMBROSE P. HILL.

ANDERSON'S DIVISION.

Maj. Gen. R. H. ANDERSON.

Wilcox's Brigade.

Brig. Gen. CADMUS M. WILCOX.

8th Alabama, Lieut. Col. Hilary A. Herbert.
9th Alabama, Capt. J. H. King.
10th Alabama:
Col. William H. Forney.
Lieut. Col. James E. Shelley.
11th Alabama:
Col. J. C. C. Sanders.
Lieut. Col. George E. Tayloe.
14th Alabama:
Col. L. Pinckard.
Lieut. Col. James A. Broome.

Mahone's Brigade.

Brig. Gen. WILLIAM MAHONE.

6th Virginia, Col. George T. Rogers.
12th Virginia, Col. D. A. Weisiger.
16th Virginia, Col. Joseph H. Ham.
41st Virginia, Col. William A. Parham.
61st Virginia, Col. V. D. Groner.

Wright's Brigade.

Brig. Gen. A. R. WRIGHT.
Col. WILLIAM GIBSON.

3d Georgia, Col. E. J. Walker.
22d Georgia:
Col. Joseph Wasden.
Capt. B. C. McCurry.
48th Georgia:
Col. William Gibson.
Capt. M. R. Hall.
2d Georgia Battalion:
Maj. George W. Ross.
Capt. Charles J. Moffett.

Perry's Brigade.

Col. DAVID LANG.

2d Florida, Maj. W. R. Moore.
5th Florida, Capt. R. N. Gardner.
8th Florida, Col. David Lang.

Posey's Brigade.

Brig. Gen. CARNOT POSEY.

12th Mississippi, Col. W. H. Taylor.
16th Mississippi, Col. Samuel E. Baker.
19th Mississippi, Col. N. H. Harris.
48th Mississippi, Col. Joseph M. Jayne.

Artillery (Sumter Battalion).

Maj. JOHN LANE.

Company A, Capt. Hugh M. Ross.
Company B, Capt. George M. Patterson.
Company C, Capt. John T. Wingfield.

HETH'S DIVISION.

Maj. Gen. HENRY HETH.
Brig. Gen. J. J. PETTIGREW.

First Brigade.

Brig. Gen. J. J. PETTIGREW.
Col. J. K. MARSHALL.

11th North Carolina, Col. Collett Leventhorpe.
26th North Carolina:
Col. Henry K. Burgwyn, jr.
Capt. H. C. Albright.
47th North Carolina, Col. G. H. Faribault.
52d North Carolina:
Col. J. K. Marshall.
Lieut. Col. Marcus A. Parks.

Second Brigade.

Col. J. M. Brockenbrough.

40th Virginia:
Capt. T. E. Betts.
Capt. R. B. Davis.
47th Virginia, Col. Robert M. Mayo.
55th Virginia, Col. W. S. Christian.
22d Virginia Battalion, Maj. John S. Bowles.

Third Brigade.

Brig. Gen. James J. Archer.
Col. B. D. Fry.
Lieut. Col. S. G. Shepard.

13th Alabama, Col. B. D. Fry.
5th Alabama Battalion, Maj. A. S. Van de Graaff.
1st Tennessee (Provisional Army), Maj. Felix G. Buchanan.
7th Tennessee, Lieut. Col. S. G. Shepard.
14th Tennessee, Capt. B. L. Phillips.

Fourth Brigade.

Brig. Gen. Joseph R. Davis.

2d Mississippi, Col. J. M. Stone.
11th Mississippi, Col. F. M. Green.
42d Mississippi, Col. H. R. Miller.
55th North Carolina, Col. J. K. Connally.

Artillery.

Lieut. Col. John J. Garnett.

Donaldsonville (Louisiana) Artillery, Capt. V. Maurin.
Huger (Virginia) Artillery, Capt. Joseph D. Moore.
Lewis (Virginia) Artillery, Capt. John W. Lewis.
Norfolk Light Artillery Blues, Capt. C. R. Grandy.

PENDER'S DIVISION.

Maj. Gen. William D. Pender.
Brig. Gen. James H. Lane.
Maj. Gen. I. R. Trimble.

First Brigade.

Col. Abner Perrin.

1st South Carolina (Provisional Army), Maj. C. W. McCreary.
1st South Carolina Rifles, Capt. William M. Hadden.
12th South Carolina, Col. John L. Miller.
13th South Carolina, Lieut. Col. B. T. Brockman.
14th South Carolina, Lieut. Col. Joseph N. Brown.

Second Brigade.

Brig. Gen. James H. Lane.
Col. C. M. Avery.

7th North Carolina:
Capt. J. McLeod Turner.
Capt. James G. Harris.
18th North Carolina, Col. John D. Barry.
28th North Carolina:
Col. S. D. Lowe.
Lieut. Col. W. H. A. Speer.
33d North Carolina, Col. C. M. Avery.
37th North Carolina, Col. W. M. Barbour.

Third Brigade.

Brig. Gen. EDWARD L. THOMAS.

14th Georgia.
35th Georgia.
45th Georgia.
49th Georgia, Col. S. T. Player.

Fourth Brigade.

Brig. Gen. A. M. SCALES.
Lieut. Col. G. T. GORDON.
Col. W. LEE J. LOWRANCE.

13th North Carolina:
Col. J. H. Hyman.
Lieut. Col. H. A. Rogers.
16th North Carolina, Capt. L. W. Stowe.
22d North Carolina, Col. James Conner.
34th North Carolina:
Col. William Lee J. Lowrance.
Lieut. Col. G. T. Gordon.
38th North Carolina:
Col. W. J. Hoke.
Lieut. Col. John Ashford.

Artillery.

Maj. WILLIAM T. POAGUE.

Albemarle (Virginia) Artillery, Capt. James W. Wyatt.
Charlotte (North Carolina) Artillery, Capt. Joseph Graham.
Madison (Mississippi) Light Artillery, Capt. George Ward.
Virginia Battery, Capt. J. V. Brooke.

ARTILLERY RESERVE.

Col. R. LINDSAY WALKER.

McIntosh's Battalion.

Maj. D. G. MCINTOSH.

Danville (Virginia) Artillery, Capt. R. S. Rice.
Hardaway (Alabama) Artillery, Capt. W. B. Hurt.
2d Rockbridge (Virginia) Artillery, Lieut. Samuel Wallace.
Virginia Battery, Capt. M. Johnson.

Pegram's Battalion.

Maj. W. J. PEGRAM.
Capt. E. B. BRUNSON.

Crenshaw (Virginia) Battery.
Fredericksburg (Virginia) Artillery, Capt. E. A. Marye.
Letcher (Virginia) Artillery, Capt. T. A. Brander.
Pee Dee (South Carolina) Artillery, Lieut. William E. Zimmerman.
Purcell (Virginia) Artillery, Capt. Joseph McGraw.

CAVALRY.

STUART'S DIVISION.

Maj. Gen. J. E. B. STUART.

Hampton's Brigade.

Brig. Gen. WADE HAMPTON.
Col. L. S. BAKER.

1st North Carolina, Col. L. S. Baker.
1st South Carolina.
2d South Carolina.
Cobb's (Georgia) Legion.
Jeff. Davis Legion.
Phillips (Georgia) Legion.

Robertson's Brigade.

Brig. Gen. BEVERLY H. ROBERTSON.

4th North Carolina, Col. D. D. Ferebee.
5th North Carolina.

Fitz. Lee's Brigade.

Brig. Gen. FITZ. LEE.

1st Maryland Battalion:
Maj. Harry Gilmor.
Maj. Ridgely Brown.
1st Virginia, Col. James H. Drake.
2d Virginia, Col. T. T. Munford.
3d Virginia, Col. Thomas H. Owen.
4th Virginia, Col. Williams C. Wickham.
5th Virginia, Col. T. L. Rosser.

Jenkins's Brigade.

Brig. Gen. A. G. JENKINS.
Col. M. J. FERGUSON.

14th Virginia.
16th Virginia.
17th Virginia.
34th Virginia Battalion, Lieut. Col. V. A. Witcher.
36th Virginia Battalion.
Jackson's (Virginia) Battery, Capt. Thomas E. Jackson.

Jones's Brigade.

Brig. Gen. WILLIAM E. JONES.

6th Virginia, Maj. C. E. Flournoy.
7th Virginia, Lieut. Col. Thomas Marshall.
11th Virginia, Col. L. L. Lomax.

W. H. F. Lee's Brigade.

Col. J. R. CHAMBLISS, Jr.

2d North Carolina.
9th Virginia, Col. R. L. T. Beale.
10th Virginia, Col. J. Lucius Davis.
13th Virginia.

Stuart Horse Artillery.

Maj. R. F. BECKMAN.

Breathed's (Virginia) Battery, Capt. James Breathed.
Chew's (Virginia) Battery, Capt. R. P. Chew.

Griffin's (Maryland) Battery, Capt. W. H. Griffin.
Hart's (South Carolina) Battery, Capt. J. F. Hart.
McGregor's (Virginia) Battery, Capt. W. M. McGregor.
Moorman's (Virginia) Battery, Capt. M. N. Moorman.

IMBODEN'S COMMAND.

Brig. Gen. J. D. IMBODEN.

18th Virginia Cavalry, Col. George W. Imboden.
62d Virginia Infantry, Col. George H. Smith.
Virginia Partisan Rangers, Capt. John H. McNeill.
Virginia Battery, Capt. J. H. McClanahan.

ARTILLERY.

Brig. Gen. W. N. PENDLETON.

FUTURE YEARS will never know the seething hell and the black infernal background of countless minor scenes and interiors (not the official surface-courteousness of the Generals, not the few great battles) of the Secession war," wrote Walt Whitman, "and it is best that they should not—the real war will never get in the books." Perhaps not. How could the pen ever hope to recreate fittingly the pathos and the romance, the sheer horror and the soaring heroism, the folly and the gallantry of that titanic struggle that recreated the United States and gave, as Lincoln so perfectly put it, "a new birth of freedom?"

Grim statistics give one facet of Whitman's "real war." For the North, just short of 360,000 died while another 275,000 were wounded. For the South, at least 260,000 perished with another 194,000 maimed. [Well over 620,000 of the nearly three million Americans who fought the Civil War were consumed by it.] (Union casualties alone exceed American losses in World War II, while deaths

North and South are more than the losses in all of America's other wars combined.) While this was but two percent of a rapidly growing population, the numbers belie an even greater social impact. The scars of war reached beyond the half million maimed to touch countless others who carried hidden wounds that would never heal. Millions more mourned fathers, brothers, and sons who never returned—futures unrealized, dreams aborted, songs unsung. What might have been is a part of Whitman's real war that writers can only hint at.

Whitman's admonition notwithstanding, it is not for want of effort that the real war remains elusive. Countless works of fiction and history, poetry and painting, film, stage, and television drama have addressed the great conflict. Civil War statuary, and even one carved mountain, can be found throughout the nation. Clearly the Civil War is America's *Iliad,* yet no Homer has emerged as its chronicler. The most sublime literary works inspired by the war came from the pen of Abraham Lincoln while the conflict still raged.

Most of our greatest fiction writers have ignored the war, or dealt with it only tangentially. Whitman's poetry is magnificent, but narrowly focused. Herman Melville, despite critical interpretations of *Moby Dick* as a metaphor for the coming war, dealt with the real conflict only in passing. The same can be said of that wise deserter Mark Twain. F. Scott Fitzgerald, William Faulkner, and Robert Penn Warren all wrote on the war, but only in relatively minor works. Ambrose Bierce produced a classic short story, Stephen Crane a classic novel, and Stephen Vincent Benét a classic poem, but all fell short of becoming America's Tolstoy.

Popular writers have always found a ready audience for Civil War fiction, but their work has generally been far from epic. Winston Churchill's fine *The Crisis*, John Fox's sentimental *The Little Shepherd of Kingdom Come,* and Thomas Dixon's vicious *The Clansman* were early popular triumphs, but all paled in comparison with the wild success of Margaret Mitchell's lost-cause homily, *Gone With the Wind*. While later novelists never came close to the commercial triumph of Mitchell's novel (twenty eight million copies sold to date), they nevertheless came far nearer to an approximation of the real war; MacKinlay Kantor's grim *Andersonville,* Shelby Foote's gritty *Shiloh,* Richard Slotkin's remarkable *The Crater,* and Michael Shaara's magnificent *The Killer Angels* ranking as the most notable.

Despite this prodigious output, the fact remains that this central moment of American history has inspired but a handful of literary works of a truly high order. Harvard professor Daniel Aaron titled his 1973 book on American writers and the Civil War *The Unwritten War*. Novelist and historian Shelby Foote, in his 1957 literary anthology *The Night Before Chancellorsville,* bluntly stated: "In this country, historical fiction in general has been left to second raters and hired brains, and this is particularly true of those who have chosen the Civil War as a subject. With the exception of Stephen Crane, our best writers have given it either mere incidental attention or none at all."

In this century the new medium of motion pictures has paralleled high literature in its hesitancy to deal with the Civil War. While hundreds of historical films have dealt with westward expansion or World War II, there has been no similar output on the Civil War. While nearly fifty films have dealt with General George A. Custer's last stand at the Little Big Horn, only two have concerned his important role in the Civil War (and both of those were westerns with Civil War components). Lincoln has proven a popular figure with Hollywood, but only one film, D. W. Griffith's *Abraham Lincoln* in 1930, dealt with the Great Emancipator's entire life. The two best Lincoln films, *Young Mr.*

Lincoln in 1939 and *Abe Lincoln in Illinois* the following year, covered Lincoln's career before his election as president. Usually Lincoln appeared as a cameo (often played by stage actor Frank McGlynn, Sr.) in films as diverse as *The Littlest Rebel* with Shirley Temple, John Ford's *The Prisoner of Shark Island* with Warner Baxter as the unfortunate Dr. Samuel Mudd (who set John Wilkes Booth's broken leg, was imprisoned for it, and thus gave to the American language the phrase "your name is mud"), and Cecil B. DeMille's overblown western epic *The Plainsman.* Yet, to put this into perspective, it should be noted that Lincoln has been portrayed in far fewer films than has the young outlaw Billy the Kid. Nor have any films of a truly remarkable artistic order, with the notable exception of D. W. Griffith's 1915 *The Birth of a Nation,* dealt with the Civil War. The Griffith film's unrelenting racism, however, has lost it a modern audience beyond students of the cinema.

As with literature, some fine Civil War films have been made—Buster Keaton's *The General,* John Huston's *The Red Badge of Courage,* William Wyler's *Friendly Persuasion,* John Ford's *The Horse Soldiers,* and Edward Zwick's *Glory*. And, of course, as with popular literature, one of Hollywood's greatest commercial triumphs was David Selznick's adaptation of Mitchell's *Gone With the Wind* (which, despite the fact that its racial sensibilities are only slightly advanced beyond *The Birth of a Nation,* still remains an immensely popular film). Despite the box-office success and enduring appeal of *Gone With the Wind,* Hollywood has generally found Civil War films to be poor commercial performers. It is, after all, a rather dangerous topic, replete with opportunities to offend some major regional or racial segment of American society. For the same reasons television, despite the spectacular but isolated triumphs of the miniseries "Roots" and the more recent multipart documentary on PBS, has only hesitatingly treated the war. It has remained, then, for historians to be the major interpreters of the Civil War. They are the keepers of the flame.

No other topic of American history has proven more popular, or more controversial, than the Civil War. It has attracted some of the best minds and most skilled pens of all American historiography. The turn-of-the-century multivolume history by James Ford Rhodes and the eight post–World War II volumes by Allan Nevins on the war era still stand as unrivaled examples of the historian's art. Similarly, the 1988 one-volume synthesis by James M. McPherson, *Battle Cry of Freedom,* has been rightly acclaimed as a masterpiece.

Much of the best scholarship has focused on the institution of slavery and its central role in bringing on the war. From the valuable if dated *American Negro Slavery* by U. B. Phillips, through the powerful revisionist works of Kenneth Stampp, Stanley Elkins, Eugene Genovese, Willie Lee Rose, Herbert Gutman, and John Blassingame, the "peculiar institution" has emerged as perhaps the most lively, challenging, and compelling historical topic of this century. In the last two decades a new historical consensus has formed, harkening back to the words of James Ford Rhodes at the turn of the century that "of the American Civil War it may safely be asserted there was a single cause, slavery." Even those who remain troubled by "mono-causation" in history agree that without slavery there would have been no war.

Of course, other divisions mixed into the witch's brew of mutual misunderstanding and shared contempt that drove North and South apart. Constitutional differences, economic differences, moral differences, class differences, and social differences all contributed to a breakdown of the political process. Historians have argued incessantly over these differences—Charles Beard seeing a primacy in economic conflict, Frank Owsley romanticizing the South as the defenders of an agrarian ideal against a vicious industrial onslaught, and Avery Craven emphasizing the merging of moral with political issues. James G. Randall felt all wars, and the Civil War in particular, to be irrational acts and laid the blame on fanaticism both North and South. Arthur M. Schlesinger, Jr., and Oscar Handlin were the two most noted historians who were puzzled by Randall's logic, or lack there of, and generally disdainful of those who would downplay the intensity of morality in bringing on the war. "There is surely a difference," Handlin dryly noted, "between being a fanatic for freedom and being a fanatic for slavery."

Several fine historians have dealt with the rise of the moral ideology of the 1850s and of the resultant breakdown of the political process. The works of David M. Potter, and most notably his 1976 *The Impending Crisis,* are crucial to an understanding of the sectional crisis. Eric Foner's *Free Soil, Free Labor, Free Men* remains indispensable to comprehending the rise of the Republican party, while Robert Johannsen's biography of Stephen Douglas details the fatal flaws of the Democratic party.

While academic historians have focused on causation and consequence, other historical writers have dealt with campaigns, battles, and personalities. The fruit of their labor ranks among some of the finest narrative history ever produced. Of course, not all academics have disdained military history or grand narrative, as the writings of James McPherson, T. Harry Williams, and Frank Vandiver prove, but most of our epic narratives on the war come from those outside the academy. It is from the incredibly talented pens of the likes of Bruce Catton and Shelby Foote that Whitman's "real war" comes closest to realization.

The careers of Civil War officers have provided a rich

field for biographers. Douglas Southall Freeman's multi-volume work on Lee remains a classic, although his effusiveness has been tempered by the more recent works of Thomas L. Connelly and Alan Nolan. Stonewall Jackson has been treated kindly in two classic biographies by British soldier G. F. R. Henderson and American historian Frank Vandiver. J. E. B. Stuart is a natural subject for colorful biography and has received his fair due in books by both Emory Thomas and Burke Davis. James I. Robertson's recent biography of that solid war-horse A. P. Hill was instantly recognized as a standard. Falling into the same category of modern classics are biographies of P. G. T. Beauregard by T. Harry Williams and John S. Mosby by Virgil Carrington Jones.

Bruce Catton's two volumes on Grant at war have never been equaled, despite William S. McFeely's more critical 1981 biography. Those with a taste for soaring prose will enjoy Lloyd Lewis on Sherman, while others more interested in keen analysis will discover rewards in B. H. Liddell Hart's *Sherman.* Stephen Sears's recent biography of George McClellan has garnered great acclaim, while older works by Freeman Cleaves on Generals Meade and Thomas and Jay Monaghan on Custer remain modest standards.

Two classic collective biographies have fleshed out the varied problems of high command both North and South: T. Harry Williams's *Lincoln and His Generals* and Douglas Southall Freeman's *Lee's Lieutenants.* Readers in search of careers of lesser-known officers can find brief biographies of all Civil War generals in Ezra Warner's two valuable guides, *Generals in Blue* and *Generals in Gray.* Nor have the lives of the men in the ranks been ignored, thanks to the exceptional volumes *The Life of Johnny Reb* and *The Life of Billy Yank* by Bell Irvin Wiley.

To do full justice to the rich and varied historiography of the Civil War era requires far more space than is available here. Detailed accounts of nearly every campaign and battle of the war are available, as are biographies of all the major, and many of the minor, military and political leaders of the conflict. Library shelves are bowed with the weight of generations of remarkable productivity in this field, with no end in sight.

Yet for all the magnificent narratives, keen analyses, and illuminating biographies that fill our libraries, those in search of Whitman's "real war" will find it best represented in the memoirs and autobiographies of the participants themselves. No conflict in our history has produced such a remarkable body of autobiographical writing. The remarkably literate generation that fought the Civil War grasped the importance of the conflict, and many wished to record their role in the republic's greatest drama. Some were talented with the pen, others not so, but all had a story to tell. Some of their narratives, especially those of the generals, are defensive in tone; there were actions to justify, scores to settle, places in history to secure. Other narratives are remarkably myopic, cloyingly nostalgic, or frustratingly wrongheaded. The years often clouded memories, and sometimes the haze of battle obscured events for even the most truthful observer.

Still, it is from these eyewitnesses to the Civil War that the most dramatic, personal, and telling accounts of that great struggle emerge. They bring the real war vividly to life, recording flashes of personal history more incredible than any fiction: Phil Sheridan, cursing and cajoling his stricken army to turn around and fight on to victory at Cedar Creek; George Custer, a freshly minted brigadier at twenty-three, leading his wolverines in charge after charge to block Stuart at Gettysburg; Luis Emilio, junior captain of the 54th Massachusetts Volunteer Infantry, assuming command of his shattered regiment after all officers senior to him fall dead or wounded in the assault on Fort Wagner;

John Mosby boldly penetrating a Union camp to take General Edwin Stoughton prisoner; John Worsham stunned as four men beside him are mowed down by a single cannonball at Second Manassas; Stonewall Jackson sternly admonishing General Dick Taylor for cursing in the heat of battle at Bowers Hill; Colonel Joshua Chamberlain ordering the 20th Maine, its ammunition expended, to fix bayonets and charge down Little Round Top; Frank Haskell standing transfixed in awe as Pickett's gray host, red flags fluttering above a forest of gleaming steel, advances in the climactic hour of Gettysburg; Horace Porter recording the quiet dignity of Lee and Grant at Appomattox as a nation is reborn.

These proud warriors of the North and South express surprisingly little bitterness. They had played their part as best they could and now looked back without rancor to do honor to themselves and to those they had served with. Most could clearly see that out of the turmoil, chaos, and sacrifice of war something grand had emerged: a better, stronger, more just nation.

Now they spoke no longer of the United States as a plural, but rather as a singular. The great evil and singular hypocrisy of slavery was no more. Four million Americans, and their descendants, were forever free. The Thirteenth, Fourteenth, and Fifteenth Amendments to the U.S. Constitution wrought a radical legal transformation that generations yet unborn would seize upon to ensure a truer equality between the races.

The South found comfort in the myth of the lost cause. So compelling was that story that soon all Americans, North and South, came to embrace Confederate soldiers like Lee, Jackson, and Stuart as preeminent national heroes. Within a decade home rule was established throughout the South, with black rights sacrificed on the altar of regional reconciliation and economic development. Some complained that the South had lost the war but won the peace, but that was hardly true. The war had not only swept away slavery, but also the class-based, agricultural, and rural society that it supported. The United States now turned from that past to heartily embrace a new national vision.

Mark Twain tagged it the Gilded Age. With the triumph of free-labor industrial capitalism in the war came an orgy of speculation, growth, and greed undreamed of before 1861. Technology thrived in this atmosphere, making astonishing leaps forward. Northern industry, fueled by the sweat of millions of new immigrants from Europe and Asia, expanded beyond the wildest expectations. The cities swelled. Railroads spanned the continent. The West was conquered. Fabulous fortunes were made, some of them even by the new immigrants or their children, but mostly the rich got richer and the poor poorer.

Finally the children of the veterans of the Civil War wrought their own social and political revolution, bringing order out of chaotic growth and establishing a semblance of fair play and genuine opportunity to a previously unbridled capitalism. Then they turned their eyes to new opportunities abroad. Before the last veterans of the Civil War passed from the scene, the nation they had witnessed torn asunder by the Civil War stood as the world's preeminent economic and military power, and as a beacon of freedom to a troubled world. National greatness, those grizzled veterans surely could see, had come out of the terrible travail of Civil War.

The cost had been high. Many questioned if the results were worth the price. Others said the war had been avoidable. Others claimed that the same results could have been achieved without bloodshed. Others cast blame. But Lincoln, martyred before he could taste the sweet fruits of his labors, saw the causes and consequences of the Civil War with a clarity of vision lost on many of his own generation and those that followed. His words, spoken at the second inauguration, reach down to us through the ages:

> The Almighty has his own purposes. "Woe unto the world because of offenses! for it must needs be that offenses come; but woe to that man by whom the offense cometh." If we shall suppose that American slavery is one of those offenses which, in the providence of God, must needs come, but which having continued through his appointed time, he now wills to remove, and that he gives to both the North and South this terrible war, as the woe due to those by whom the offense came, shall we discern therein any departure from those divine attributes which the believers in a living God always ascribe to him? Fondly do we hope—fervently do we pray—that this mighty scourge of war may speedily pass away. Yet if God wills that it continue until all the wealth piled by the bondsman's two hundred and fifty years of unrequited toil shall be sunk, and until every drop of blood drawn with the lash shall be paid by another drawn with the sword, as was said, "The judgements of the Lord are true and righteous altogether."
>
> With malice toward none; with charity for all; with firmness in the right, as God gives us to see the right, let us strive on to finish the work we are in; to bind up the nation's wounds; to care for him who shall have borne the battle, and for his widow, and his orphan—to do all which may achieve and cherish a just and lasting peace among ourselves, and with all nations.

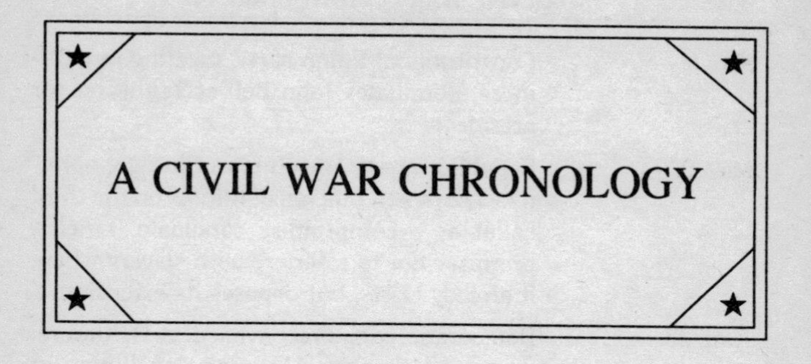

A CIVIL WAR CHRONOLOGY

1859

October 16 — John Brown, with sixteen whites and five blacks, captures the arsenal at Harpers Ferry in anticipation of fomenting a slave rebellion in Virginia. U.S. troops led by Lt. Col. Robert E. Lee storm the arsenal and capture Brown, on the morning of October 18th.

December 2 — John Brown is hanged for treason. Among his final words: "I, John Brown, am now quite certain that the crimes of this guilty land will never be purged away but with blood."

1860

May 3 — Democratic party, meeting in Charleston, South Carolina, adjourns unable to agree upon a candidate following the withdrawal of delegates from eight southern states.

May 9 — Constitutional Union party, meeting in Baltimore, nominates John Bell of Tennessee for president.

May 16 — Republican party, meeting in Chicago, nominates Abraham Lincoln of Illinois on the third ballot as a compromise candidate. Lincoln promises not to interfere with slavery where it already exists, but opposes its extension.

June 23 — Democratic party, reconvened in Baltimore, nominates Stephen A. Douglas of Illinois on a popular-sovereignty platform regarding slavery (each territory to decide for itself). Outraged southern Democrats walk out and later nominate John C. Breckinridge of Kentucky.

November 6 — Lincoln wins the election. Though he has but 40 percent of the popular vote, his Electoral College count is 180, versus 72 for Breckinridge, 39 for Bell, and 12 for Douglas.

November 9 — The state of South Carolina calls a secession convention.

December 20 — South Carolina secedes from the Union.

December 26 — Major Robert Anderson withdraws federal forces in Charleston to Fort Sumter. He has but eighty men.

1861

January 9 — South Carolina shore batteries open fire on the *Star of the West,* carrying supplies and reinforcements to Fort Sumter. The ship is forced out of Charleston Harbor. On the same day Mississippi secedes from the Union.

January 10 — Florida secedes from the Union.

January 11 —	Alabama secedes from the Union.
January 19 —	Georgia secedes from the Union.
January 26 —	Louisiana secedes from the Union.
February 1 —	Texas secedes from the Union. Governor Sam Houston is removed from office for opposing secession.
February 4 —	A convention meets in Montgomery, Alabama to create a new government for the seceded states. It passes a constitution on the eighth and elects Jefferson Davis of Mississippi provisional president and Alexander Stephens of Georgia provisional vice-president on the ninth.
February 11 —	Lincoln departs from Springfield for Washington. "I now leave, not knowing when, or whether ever, I may return, with a task before me greater than that which rested upon Washington," he tells his friends and neighbors.
February 18 —	Davis is inaugurated at Montgomery, declaring that obstacles "can not long prevent the progress of a movement sanctified by its justice and sustained by a virtuous people."
February 23 —	Lincoln reaches Washington, entering the city secretly for fear of assassins.
March 4 —	Lincoln is inaugurated, declaring that "In your hands, my dissatisfied countrymen, and not in mine is the momentous issue of Civil War."
March 6 —	The Confederate States of America calls for 100,000 volunteers for its army.
April 4 —	Lincoln orders an expedition to relieve besieged Fort Sumter, and it departs from New York four days later.

April 12 —	At 4:30 A.M. General P.G.T. Beauregard orders his men to open fire on Fort Sumter. The commander of the fort had been his artillery instructor at West Point.
April 13 —	Major Anderson surrenders after 34 hours of bombardment.
April 15 —	Lincoln calls upon the states for 75,000 militia to suppress the insurrection in South Carolina.
April 17 —	Virginia secedes from the Union.
April 19 —	Lincoln orders a blockade of Confederate ports.
April 20 —	Col. Robert E. Lee resigns from the U.S. Army. "Whatever may be the result of the contest," he writes a friend, "I foresee that the country will have to pass through a terrible ordeal, a necessary expiation for our national sins."
May 6 —	Arkansas secedes from the Union.
May 6 —	Tennessee secedes from the Union.
May 13 —	Great Britain declares neutrality, in effect recognizing the Confederacy as a belligerent.
May 20 —	North Carolina secedes from the Union.
May 21 —	The Confederacy decides to move its capital to Richmond, Virginia.
May 23 —	Virginia voters endorse secession.
June 3 —	Union troops under Gen. George B. McClellan defeat Confederates at Philippi in western Virginia.

June 10 —	France declares neutrality.
June 11 —	Pro-Union counties in western Virginia disavow secession and are recognized by Lincoln as the loyal Virginia government. This soon evolves into the new state of West Virginia.
July 16 —	Gen. Irvin McDowell, with 30,000 Union troops, advances toward Manassas Junction, Virginia.
July 21 —	Battle of Bull Run ends in the defeat of Union forces, although the Rebels are too disorganized to follow up their victory. A strong stand by Thomas J. Jackson's Virginia brigade earns him the nickname "Stonewall." Each side suffers about 625 killed.
July 27 —	McDowell is replaced by McClellan as commander of the troops around Washington.
August 6 —	A Confiscation Act is passed which allows the seizure of all property used for insurrectionary purposes. This includes slaves.
August 10 —	Confederates under Sterling Price and Ben McCulloch defeat a Union force under Gen. Nathaniel Lyon at Wilson's Creek, Missouri. Lyon is killed in action, and each side suffers about 1,300 casualties.
August 30 —	Gen. John C. Fremont, in command of Union forces in the West, orders the confiscation of all property, including slaves, belonging to Missouri Confederates.

September 10 — Gen. Albert Sidney Johnston of Texas assumes command of Confederate forces in the West.

November 1 — McClellan replaces Gen. Winfield Scott as Union general in chief.

November 2 — Fremont is relieved of his command in the West, and is soon replaced by Gen. Henry W. Halleck.

November 8 — Capt. Charles Wilkes of the U.S. Navy stops the British mail steamer *Trent* and arrests Confederate envoys James Mason and John Slidell, setting off an international incident. They will be released on December 27 after British saber rattling.

1862

January 19 — Union Gen. George Thomas, a Virginian loyal to the Old Flag, defeats Rebel forces at Mill Springs, Kentucky, securing federal control of the eastern section of that state.

February 6 — Gen. Ulysses S. Grant, with 15,000 troops and several naval gunboats under Flag Officer Andrew Foote, attacks Fort Henry on the Tennessee River. The fort quickly falls to Foote's naval forces, but most of its defenders escape to Fort Donelson, a dozen miles away on the Cumberland River.

February 7 — Gen. Johnston orders his forces to retreat from southwestern Kentucky.

February 13 — Grant, with 40,000 troops, attacks Fort Donelson, defended by 18,000 Confederates.

February 16 — Gen. Simon Bolivar Buckner surrenders Fort

Donelson. Grant's terms, unconditional surrender, win him a nickname.

February 21 — Confederate troops under Gen. Henry H. Sibley defeat Union forces under Gen. Edward Canby and Col. Kit Carson at Valverde, New Mexico. Sibley is then able to occupy Albuquerque and Santa Fe.

February 25 — The Confederates are forced to abandon Nashville.

March 3 — Andrew Johnson is named military governor of Tennessee by Lincoln.

March 8 — Gen. Samuel Curtis defeats Gen. Earl Van Dorn at Pea Ridge and Union control of Missouri is secured.

March 8 — The *Virginia,* a Rebel ironclad converted from the captured Union warship the *Merrimac,* destroys the Union wooden warships the *Congress* and the *Cumberland* and drives the *Minnesota* aground at Hampton Roads, Virginia.

March 9 — The *Monitor,* a Union iron-plated raft with a revolving gun turret built by John Ericsson, engages the *Virginia* (*Merrimac*) at Hampton Roads. They battle inconclusively all morning, but the *Virginia* withdraws and does not again threaten the Union blockade. A revolution in naval warfare has been wrought. The *Virginia* is burned to prevent its capture a month later. The *Monitor* sinks in a storm off Cape Hatteras on December 31, 1862.

March 11 —	Lincoln reorganizes the Union high command: Halleck takes charge of all troops west of the Appalachians while McClellan is reduced from general in chief to commander of the Army of the Potomac.
March 17 —	McClellan begins moving his forces by sea to Fort Monroe in anticipation of the Peninsular Campaign against Richmond.
March 23 —	Stonewall Jackson is defeated at Kernstown, Virginia, by a much stronger Union force. The battle raises fears in Washington of a Confederate attack, and troops are withheld from McClellan to defend the capital.
March 28 —	Union forces defeat the Confederate invaders at Glorieta Pass, New Mexico.
April 4 —	McClellan's forces on the peninsula advance toward Richmond.
April 6 —	Grant's 37,000 men at Shiloh Church and Pittsburg Landing, Tennessee, are surprised by A. S. Johnston's 42,000 Confederates and almost defeated. Johnston is killed and Beauregard assumes command.
April 7 —	Grant, reinforced by 25,000 fresh troops under Don Carlos Buell and Lew Wallace, attacks at Shiloh, recapturing all lost ground. Each side suffers 10,000 casualties. Beauregard retreats to Corinth, Mississippi.
April 8 —	Gen. John Pope captures Island No. 10 in the Mississippi River, taking 5,000 Confederate prisoners.
April 12 —	James J. Andrews leads fifteen men on a bold

raid to seize a Western and Atlantic Railroad locomotive at Big Shanty, Georgia, and then race north in it burning all bridges on the line between Atlanta and Chattanooga. The raid fails after a wild eight-hour railway chase, and Andrews and seven of his men are eventually hanged.

April 16 — The Confederate Congress passes a conscription bill.

April 16 — Slavery is abolished in the District of Columbia.

April 25 — New Orleans is captured by Union naval forces under Flag Officer David C. Farragut.

May 1 — Union troops under Gen. Benjamin Butler begin the occupation of New Orleans.

May 3 — McClellan's army forces Gen. Joseph E. Johnston to retreat from Yorktown, Virginia.

May 8 — Stonewall Jackson's 10,000 men in the Shenandoah Valley defeat attacking federals under Gen. Robert Schenk at McDowell, Virginia.

May 9 — Gen. David Hunter at Hilton Head, South Carolina, declares slaves in South Carolina, Georgia, and Florida to be free. His act is later repudiated by Lincoln.

May 9 — Confederate forces retreat from Norfolk.

May 10 — Union forces occupy Pensacola, Florida.

May 12 — Baton Rouge, Louisiana, is occupied by Union forces.

May 25 — Jackson crushes Gen. Nathaniel Banks's 8,000-man force at Winchester, Virginia.

June 1 —	Robert E. Lee assumes command of Confederate forces defending Richmond after Joseph E. Johnston is wounded at the Battle of Fair Oaks.
June 8 —	At the Battle of Cross Keys, Virginia, Union forces under Gen. John C. Frémont are defeated by Jackson's men.
June 9 —	Jackson again defeats Union forces under Frémont and Gen. James Shields at Port Royal.
June 12 —	Gen. James E. "Jeb" Stuart leads his Rebel cavalrymen on a bold four-day reconnaissance completely around McClellan's forces on the peninsula.
June 17 —	Jackson's victorious army departs the Shenandoah to reinforce Lee.
June 19 —	Slavery is abolished in all federal territories.
June 25 —	The Seven Days' Battles begin as the forces of McClellan and Lee contend inconclusively.
July 1 —	Lee's forces are defeated in their assault on the Army of the Potomac at Malvern Hill. He has lost 20,000 men. Nevertheless, the Seven Days' Battles conclude with the nervous McClellan retreating and Richmond secure.
July 4 —	Confederate Col. John Hunt Morgan begins a daring raid into Kentucky.
July 11 —	Halleck is named general in chief of Union forces.
July 17 —	A second Confiscation Act is passed by Congress, freeing the slaves of those who are in rebellion against the government.

July 29 — The Rebel cruiser *Alabama* departs Liverpool, England, under the command of Captain Raphael Semmes. In the next two years it will capture or destroy sixty four merchant ships.

August 9 — Jackson defeats Union forces under Banks at Cedar Mountain, Virginia.

August 16 — McClellan moves north to unite with the Northern Army of Virginia under Gen. John Pope at Alexandria.

August 26 — Jackson captures the railroad line at Manassas Junction.

August 28 — Gen. Braxton Bragg leads his Rebel forces from Chattanooga to unite with Gen. Kirby Smith in Kentucky.

August 29 — The Second Battle of Bull Run begins as Pope attacks Jackson. The overly confident Pope sends a victory telegram to Washington.

August 30 — Confederate reinforcements under Gen. James Longstreet turn the tide at Second Bull Run and Pope's army is routed.

September 2 — McClellan is given command of Pope's army and the forces defending Washington.

September 5 — Lee leads 55,000 men into Maryland.

September 9 — Lee sends Jackson to capture the 12,000 Union troops at Harpers Ferry. Jackson is then to rejoin Lee for a movement against Harrisburg, Pennsylvania.

September 13 — Near Frederick, Maryland, two Union soldiers discover a copy of Lee's plans wrapped around three cigars lost by a Confederate officer.

September 14 — McClellan, who has 80,000 men and his opponent's plans, still waits eighteen hours before moving. This delay proves crucial in allowing Lee to regroup his army.

September 15 — Jackson captures Harpers Ferry.

September 16 — Jackson hurriedly rejoins Lee at Sharpsburg, Maryland. McClellan masses his forces a mile east across Antietam Creek.

September 17 — The Battle of Antietam becomes the single bloodiest day of the war as the two sides fight to a grisly standstill. 6,000 are killed and 17,000 are wounded.

September 18 — Lee escapes into Virginia.

September 22 — Lincoln decides to issue the Emancipation Proclamation freeing all slaves in states in rebellion as of January 1.

October 8 — Don Carlos Buell's Union forces defeat Gen. Bragg's Confederates at Perryville, Kentucky, repelling the Rebel invasion of Kentucky.

October 30 — Gen. William Rosecrans replaces Buell in command of the redesignated Army of the Cumberland.

November 2 — Grant moves against Vicksburg, Mississippi.

November 7 — McClellan is replaced as commander of the Army of the Potomac by Gen. Ambrose Burnside.

December 13 — Burnside is defeated by Lee at Fredericksburg, Virginia.

December 15 — The Army of the Potomac retreats.

December 31 — Bragg attacks Rosecrans at Stones River near Murfreesboro, Tennessee.

1863

January 1 — Lincoln signs the Emancipation Proclamation.

January 2 — Rosecrans wins the second day of heavy fighting at Stones River. Bragg retreats on January 3.

January 26 — Gen. Joseph Hooker replaces Burnside as commander of the Army of the Potomac.

March 3 — The U.S. Congress passes a conscription act that provides for a draft of all men between twenty and forty-five.

March 9 — Confederate partisan ranger John S. Mosby makes a daring raid behind Union lines and captures Brig. Gen. Edwin H. Stoughton. Lincoln, upon being informed that Mosby has taken Stoughton, thirty-two soldiers, and fifty-eight horses, responds: "Well, I'm sorry for that. I can make new brigadier generals, but I can't make horses."

April 16 — Admiral David Porter's Union gunboats make a daring run past the shore batteries at Vicksburg.

April 17 — Col. Benjamin Grierson leads 1,700 cavalrymen out of La Grange, Tennessee, and heads south. His goal is to disrupt Confederate communications and divert attention from Vicksburg.

April 30 — The Army of the Potomac, 115,000 strong,

begins to concentrate at Chancellorsville. Lee faces them with but 60,000 men.

May 1 — Gen. Hooker's 70,000 infantry inconclusively engage Gen. Lee's forces at Chancellorsville. Hooker inexplicably pulls back after fighting in a forest called the Wilderness. That night Lee and Jackson plan a daring flanking attack on Hooker.

May 2 — Lee faces Hooker with but 15,000 men while Jackson leads 30,000 infantry on a flank march across the Union front. Jackson attacks at 5:15 P.M. and rolls up the Union right, but is mistakenly wounded by his own pickets that night while scouting.

May 2 — Grierson's cavalry reach Union lines at Baton Rouge after a daring 600-mile raid.

May 3 — Gen. Stuart assumes command of Jackson's corps at Chancellorsville and continues to pound the faltering Federals.

May 4 — Gen. John Sedgwick has no success against Lee's rear and retires to Fredericksburg.

May 6 — Hooker retreats, and Lee achieves his greatest victory. Confederate forces suffer 13,000 casualties while Union losses are over 17,000.

May 10 — Stonewall Jackson dies at Guiney's Station. "Let us cross over the river and rest under the shade of the trees," are his last words.

May 16 — Grant, advancing on Vicksburg, defeats Gen. John C. Pemberton's forces at Champion's Hill.

May 18 — Pemberton pulls his forces into the Vicksburg defenses.

May 19 — Governor John Andrew of Massachusetts presents four flags to Col. Robert Gould Shaw and the 54th Massachusetts Regiment, the first black regiment raised in the Northeast. The regiment is ordered to join Gen. David Hunter at Hilton Head, South Carolina. Already with Hunter is Col. Thomas Wentworth Higginson's First Regiment of South Carolina Volunteers, made up of contrabands (liberated slaves).

May 19 — Grant's forces assault Vicksburg but fail to breach the defenses.

May 22 — Grant's second assault on Vicksburg is repulsed with heavy losses. He begins a siege.

May 27 — Gen. Banks fails in his assaults on Port Hudson, Louisiana, and lays siege.

June 3 — Lee departs Fredericksburg for a second invasion of the North. He has three infantry corps and six cavalry brigades—75,000 men.

June 9 — Gen. Alfred Pleasonton's 11,000 Union cavalry surprise Stuart's 10,000 horsemen at Brandy Station, and the greatest cavalry engagement of the war follows. Stuart holds his ground but Lee's advance is revealed.

June 15 — Gen. Richard S. Ewell captures Winchester in the Shenandoah.

June 20 — West Virginia is admitted to the Union.

June 25 — Stuart leads three cavalry brigades on a ride

around Hooker's army. The raid causes great alarm in Washington, but Stuart's separation from the Army of Northern Virginia will prove costly.

June 28 — Gen. Jubal Early captures York, Pennsylvania.

June 28 — Gen. George Gordon Meade assumes command of the Army of the Potomac, replacing Hooker.

June 29 — Lee orders his forces to reunite near Gettysburg, Pennsylvania.

July 1 — Gen. A. P. Hill's infantry, in search of shoes in Gettysburg, clash with two brigades of Union cavalry under Gen. John Buford. Soldiers from both armies rush to the sound of the guns, and the Rebels soon sweep the Yankees in disorder through the town. Union forces dig in on Cemetery Ridge while the Confederates take up positions on Seminary Ridge.

July 2 — Lee sends Gen. James Longstreet against the Union left while Gen. Richard Ewell assaults the Union right. Both assaults fail. Stuart finally rejoins the army.

July 3 — After a terrific artillery barrage, Lee sends 14,000 men against the Union center in Pickett's Charge. Scarcely half return.

July 4 — Gen. Pemberton surrenders his 30,000 men, and Vicksburg, to Grant.

July 8 — Gen. John Hunt Morgan leads 2,500 men across the Ohio River into Indiana and toward Ohio.

July 9 — Port Hudson surrenders to Gen. Banks. The Mississippi is again a Union river and the Confederacy is split.

July 13 — Four days of antidraft rioting begins in New York City. Much of the violence is directed at blacks before troops suppress a mob estimated at 50,000.

July 18 — Battery Wagner, defending the entrance to Charleston harbor, is assaulted by Union troops. Spearheading the attack are 600 men of the 54th Massachusetts. The position is impregnable, although the black soldiers of the 54th gain Wagner's parapets and hold them for an hour before falling back. Col. Robert Shaw is killed and the regiment suffers casualties of over 40 percent.

July 19 — Over 800 of Morgan's raiders are killed or captured at Buffington, Ohio.

July 26 — Gen. Morgan is captured at New Lisbon, Ohio.

August 21 — Col. William Clarke Quantrill's Confederate guerrillas sack Lawrence, Kansas.

September 9 — Gen. Rosecrans's Federal troops enter Chattanooga as Gen. Bragg's forces retire into northern Georgia.

September 19 — Gen. Bragg, reinforced by Longstreet's corps, attacks Gen. George Thomas's corps on the left of Rosecrans's army at Chickamauga Creek, Georgia.

September 20 — Longstreet routs the Union right, and the army is only saved by Thomas's bold stand;

Thomas earns the nickname of "Rock of Chickamauga." Rosecrans's army retreats to Chattanooga, where it is besieged. Bragg occupies high ground at Lookout Mountain, south of the city, and along Missionary Ridge to the east. In the fighting each side has suffered 28-percent casualties.

October 15 — The Confederate submarine *Hunley* sinks during a practice run in Charleston harbor, drowning its inventor and seven crewmen.

October 17 — Grant is named commander of all Union forces west of the Appalachians.

October 19 — Thomas replaces Rosecrans as commander of the 35,000-man Army of the Cumberland in Chattanooga.

October 23 — Grant arrives in Chattanooga.

November 4 — Bragg sends Longstreet and 15,000 men to attack Knoxville, thus weakening his forces at Chattanooga.

November 19 — Lincoln, at Gettysburg, gives an immortal speech.

November 20 — Gen. William T. Sherman reaches Chattanooga with 17,000 men from the Army of the Tennessee. Hooker has already arrived on September 24 with 20,000 reinforcements from the Army of the Potomac. Bragg faces them with just over 64,000 troops.

November 24 — Hooker's men take Lookout Mountain at Chattanooga.

November 25 — Sherman's attacks on Bragg's right fail, but Thomas's Army of the Cumberland makes an incredible charge up Missionary Ridge and defeats the Confederates. Bragg, barely escaping capture, retreats into Georgia.

November 27 — Gen. Morgan escapes from the Ohio State Penitentiary.

November 29 — Longstreet's attack on Knoxville fails, and he soon retreats toward Virginia.

December 16 — Gen. Joseph E. Johnston takes command of the Army of Tennessee. Bragg is named an adviser to President Davis.

1864

February 9 — Col. Thomas Rose leads 109 Union prisoners in a daring escape from Libby Prison in Richmond. Rose and forty-seven others are recaptured.

February 14 — Gen. Sherman occupies Meridian, Mississippi, and his troops begin to dismantle the city.

February 17 — The Confederate submarine *Hunley* sinks the *Housatonic* in Charleston harbor, but goes down with the Union sloop.

February 22 — Gen. Nathan Bedford Forrest's cavalry defeat Union cavalry under Gen. William Sooy Smith at Okolona, Mississippi.

March 3 — Gen. Judson Kilpatrick's cavalry raid on Richmond ends in disaster with Col. Ulrich Dahlgren killed. Papers are found on Dahlgren's body insinuating that his mission was to kill Jefferson Davis.

March 17 — Grant is named general in chief and promoted to lieutenant general.

March 18 — Sherman is named commander of Union forces in the West.

April 8 — Gen. Richard Taylor's Confederates stop Gen. Banks's advance on Shreveport at Sabine Crossroads to end the Union's Red River campaign.

April 12 — Gen. Forrest captures Fort Pillow, Tennessee, where surrendering black soldiers are murdered by his troops.

April 17 — Grant halts the practice of exchanging prisoners.

May 4 — Grant advances across the Rapidan with 122,000 men. Lee faces him with under 70,000. Grant also orders troops under Gen. Benjamin Butler to move up the James River against Richmond. In Chattanooga, Sherman prepares to move south against Atlanta.

May 6 — Longstreet reinforces Lee, and Grant is defeated in the Wilderness. Longstreet is seriously wounded.

May 9 — Lee's forces entrench at Spotsylvania and repel Union assaults. Union Gen. John Sedgwick is killed.

May 9 — Grant sends Gen. Phil Sheridan's 10,000 cavalrymen on a raid against Richmond.

May 11 — Sheridan's cavalry defeat Stuart's horsemen at Yellow Tavern. Stuart, mortally wounded, dies the next day.

May 12 — Bitter fighting at the "Bloody Angle" at Spotsylvania does not break Lee's lines.

May 15 — In the Shenandoah, Gen. John Breckinridge's 5,000-man force, including V.M.I. cadets, defeats Gen. Franz Sigel's 6,500-man Union force at New Market.

May 16 — Gen. Butler is defeated at Drewry's Bluff, eight miles south of Richmond, by Gen. Beauregard.

May 20 — Grant abandons his Spotsylvania positions in an attempt to flank Lee.

May 24 — Lee takes up new positions on the North Anna River.

May 24 — Sheridan's victorious cavalrymen rejoin Grant.

May 25 — The Battle of New Hope Church, Georgia, begins between the forces of Sherman and Johnston.

May 31 — Sheridan's cavalry battles Rebel horsemen under Gen. Fitzhugh Lee and seizes the junction at Cold Harbor.

June 1 — Union forces, 109,000 strong, and Confederate forces, numbering 59,000, entrench for seven miles around Cold Harbor. In four weeks of constant fighting, the Federals have suffered 44,000 casualties and the Confederates 25,000.

June 3 — Grant launches futile frontal assaults against Lee's lines at Cold Harbor at a cost of 7,000 more casualties.

June 8 — Abraham Lincoln and Andrew Johnson are nominated for president and vice-president by the Republican (National Union) Convention in Baltimore.

June 12 — Wade Hampton's Rebel cavalry blocks Sheridan's cavalry at Trevilian Station from raiding westward to unite with Gen. David Hunter's forces in the Shenandoah. Both sides suffer 20-percent casualties in the bloodiest cavalry battle of the war.

June 14 — Grant begins to move his army across the James River to attack Petersburg.

June 18 — Grant's assaults on Petersburg fail and he begins a siege.

June 18 — Gen. Jubal Early defeats Gen. Hunter at Lynchburg. Hunter retreats into West Virginia, leaving the Shenandoah to Early.

June 19 — The *Kearsage* sinks the Rebel cruiser *Alabama* in a duel off Cherbourg, France.

June 27 — Johnston repulses Sherman's attacks at Kennesaw Mountain, Georgia.

July 6 — Early invades Maryland.

July 11 — Having swept aside Federal defenders at Monocacy River, Early reaches the defenses of Washington. The Sixth Corps, detached from Grant's forces, arrives on the same day.

July 12 — Early pulls back from Washington, heading for the Shenandoah.

July 17 — Gen. John Bell Hood replaces Johnston as commander of the Army of Tennessee.

July 20 — Hood attacks Thomas's forces at Peachtree Creek, Georgia, and is defeated.

July 22 — Hood attacks Gen. James B. McPherson's Army of the Tennessee and is again defeated. McPherson is killed in action.

July 28 — Hood again attacks the Army of the Tennessee, now commanded by Gen. Oliver Otis Howard, at Ezra Church and is again defeated.

July 30 — A 511-foot tunnel has been dug beneath the Rebel lines at Petersburg and four tons of gunpowder placed at the end. The explosion creates a 170-foot-long, 30-foot-deep crater, but the Federal assault that follows is disorganized and halfhearted. 4,000 casualties and a big hole in the ground is all Grant has by nightfall.

July 31 — Gen. George Stoneman, raiding south from Sherman's army to liberate the prisoners at Andersonville, is captured along with 500 of his men.

August 1 — Sheridan is given command of Union forces in the Shenandoah.

August 5 — Admiral Farragut defeats the defending Confederate ships in Mobile Bay. "Damn the torpedoes, full speed ahead," Farragut reportedly exclaims during the action.

August 22 — Gen. Judson Kilpatrick's cavalry raid against Hood's Atlanta supply lines fails.

August 23 — Fort Morgan, in Mobile Bay, falls to Union forces.

August 29 —	George B. McClellan is nominated for president by the Democrats.
August 31 —	Howard defeats Hood at Jonesboro while Gen. John Schofield's forces cut the last railroad line into Atlanta.
September 1 —	Hood evacuates Atlanta.
September 2 —	Sherman enters Atlanta.
September 4 —	John Hunt Morgan is killed at Greeneville, Tennessee.
September 17 —	John C. Frémont, nominated for president by Radical Republicans unhappy with Lincoln, announces that he will withdraw from the race for fear of splitting the Republican vote.
September 19 —	Sheridan defeats Early at Winchester.
September 22 —	Sheridan crushes Early's army at Fisher's Hill.
September 27 —	Confederate guerrillas under Bloody Bill Anderson loot Centralia, Missouri, and murder twenty-two captured Union soldiers. They then slaughter over 100 pursuing Federals under Maj. A.V.E. Johnston. Young Jesse James kills Maj. Johnston.
September 28 —	Sherman orders Gen. Thomas to Nashville to defend that city from Hood's army.
September 29 —	In the fighting around Petersburg, Grant takes Fort Harrison but is repulsed from Fort Gilmore.
October 2 —	A Federal raid into southwest Virginia is defeated near Saltville, and over 100 Union pris-

oners, mostly black soldiers, are murdered by their captors.

October 6 — Sheridan begins the systematic destruction of the Shenandoah Valley.

October 13 — Confederate partisans under Mosby capture a train near Kearneyville and escape with nearly $2 million from Union paymasters on board.

October 16 — Sheridan leaves his army for a meeting with Stanton and Halleck on the Valley Campaign.

October 19 — Lt. Bennett Young leads Rebel raiders across the Canadian border to St. Albans, Vermont. They rob three banks and escape back over the border.

October 19 — Sheridan's army is taken by surprise when Early's army strikes at dawn. The left flank of the Union army, under Gen. George Crook, is routed, but the sudden arrival of Sheridan on the field (he gallops in from Winchester) rallies the men. The Union counterattack destroys the Confederate army. The Battle of Cedar Creek ends the Rebel threat in the Shenandoah. The North is captivated by "Sheridan's Ride," soon immortalized in a popular poem.

October 23 — Gen. Curtis defeats Gen. Sterling Price at the Battle of Westport, ending the Confederate threat to Missouri.

October 26 — Bloody Bill Anderson is killed in a Union ambush near Richmond, Missouri.

October 27 — Lt. William P. Cushing destroys the Confederate ram *Albemarle* in the Roanoke River, North Carolina.

October 30 — Sherman sends Schofield to reinforce Thomas at Nashville.

November 8 — Lincoln is reelected.

November 16 — Sherman's army, 62,000 strong, departs Atlanta to begin the March to the Sea to Savannah. Atlanta burns behind the Federals as they advance.

November 25 — Confederate raiders fail in their attempt to burn New York City.

November 30 — Schofield repulses Hood's assaults at Franklin and retreats under cover of darkness toward Nashville.

December 1 — Schofield unites with Thomas at Nashville.

December 13 — Fort McAllister, guarding Savannah, is captured by Sherman's troops.

December 15 — Thomas attacks Hood before Nashville.

December 16 — Hood's army is routed at Nashville.

December 21 — Sherman's army enters Savannah.

1865

January 7 — Gen. Benjamin Butler is relieved as commander of the Army of the James.

January 15 — Gen. Alfred H. Terry captures Fort Fisher, closing the last major Confederate port at Wilmington, North Carolina.

January 23 — Gen. Richard Taylor is given command of what is left of the Army of Tennessee.

January 31 — The Thirteenth Amendment to the Constitution, abolishing slavery, is passed by the House of Representatives and sent to the states for ratification.

February 6 — Lee is named commander of all Confederate forces.

February 17 — Sherman occupies the South Carolina capital, and that night the city burns. Sherman blames fleeing Rebels, but on the eighteenth his troops begin the destruction of what is left of Columbia.

February 17 — The Confederates abandon Charleston, and Fort Sumter again comes under Union control.

February 18 — Lee speaks out in favor of arming blacks for service in the Confederate army in exchange for their freedom.

February 22 — Schofield's Union troops occupy Wilmington.

March 2 — Sheridan's cavalry, under Gen. George A. Custer, destroys the last remnant of Early's army at the Battle of Waynesboro.

March 4 — Lincoln's second inaugural address calls for reconciliation: "With malice toward none; with charity for all; with firmness in the right as God gives us to see the right, let us strive on to finish the work we are in; to bind up the nation's wounds; to care for him who shall have borne the battle and for his widow, and his orphan—to do all which May achieve and cherish a just and lasting peace among ourselves, and with all nations."

March 13 — President Davis signs a bill, narrowly passed by the Confederate Congress after heated debate, that calls for the use of black slaves as soldiers. The question of emancipation in exchange for service is left to the individual states.

March 17 — Gen. Edward Canby opens the assault on Mobile, Alabama.

March 22 — Gen. James Wilson begins a cavalry raid through Alabama to capture Selma.

March 26 — Sheridan rejoins Grant before Petersburg.

April 1 — Sheridan defeats Gen. George Pickett at Five Forks, capturing that vital crossroads and large numbers of Rebel prisoners.

April 2 — Grant assaults Lee's weakened lines at Petersburg with great success. Gen A. P. Hill is killed in action. Lee retreats toward Amelia Courthouse.

April 3 — Petersburg is occupied. Richmond surrenders. Jefferson Davis and his cabinet flee to Danville, Virginia.

April 4 — President Lincoln tours Richmond.

April 5 — Sheridan blocks Lee's route southward, forcing the Confederates westward.

April 6 — 6,000 Confederates are captured at Sayler's Creek, including Gen. Richard Ewell, as Lee's retreat continues.

April 8 — Custer blocks Lee's retreat route at Appomattox Station.

April 9 — Lee surrenders the Army of Northern Virginia

to Grant in the home of Wilmer McLean at Appomattox Courthouse.

April 12 — Wilson captures Montgomery, Alabama. Federal troops occupy Mobile.

April 12 — Grant accords to Gen. Joshua Chamberlain of Maine the honor of accepting the formal surrender of the flags and arms of the Army of Northern Virginia.

April 14 — John Wilkes Booth mortally wounds President Lincoln at Ford's Theater in Washington.

April 15 — President Lincoln dies and Andrew Johnson becomes president.

April 21 — Mosby disbands his rangers.

April 26 — Gen. Johnston surrenders his nearly 30,000 men to Gen. Sherman.

April 26 — Booth is trapped by troops and killed.

May 4 — Gen. Taylor surrenders to Gen. Canby in Alabama.

May 10 — Confederate guerrilla chief William Quantrill is mortally wounded near Taylorsville, Kentucky.

May 10 — Union cavalrymen capture Jefferson Davis and his party in Georgia.

May 22 — Davis is imprisoned at Fort Monroe, Virginia. He will be released in May 1867.

May 23 — Nearly 200,000 Union soldiers begin a two-day grand review up Pennsylvania Avenue in Washington, D.C.—once more the capital of a united nation.

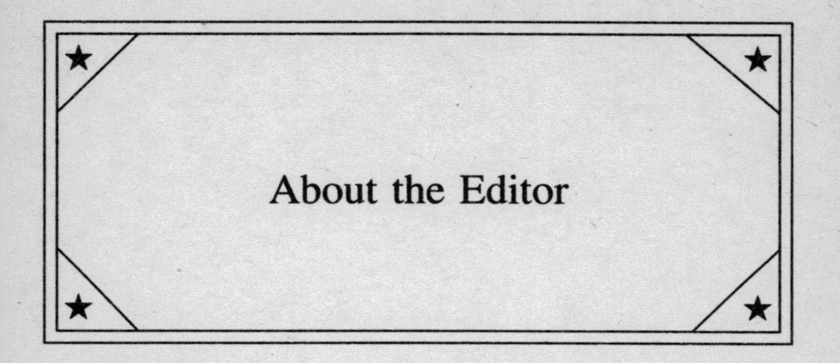

About the Editor

GLENN LAFANTASIE IS Deputy Historian of the United States Department of State and General Editor of *The Foreign Relations of the United States.* He formerly served as the Director of Publications at the Woodrow Wilson International Center for Scholars, Editor/Director of The Papers of Albert Gallatin, and Editor of Publications at the Rhode Island Historical Society. His writings cover the breadth of American history from the Puritans to the twentieth century, and include *The Correspondence of Roger Williams* (2 vols., 1988), as well as numerous articles and reviews in scholarly and popular journals. He is currently writing a biography of William C. Oates.

The fascinating true stories behind these extraordinary public figures

IT DOESN'T TAKE A HERO: *The Autobiography*

by General H. Norman Schwarzkopf with Peter Petre

Rarely does a figure appear of such compelling leadership and personal charisma as to capture the imagination of an entire nation. Now, in this candid, outspoken, and eagerly awaited autobiography, General Schwarzkopf reveals the full story of his remarkable life and a career spanning nearly four decades. ____56338-6 $6.99/$7.99 in Canada

I COULD NEVER BE SO LUCKY AGAIN

by General James H. "Jimmy" Doolittle with Carroll V. Glines

Confidant and adviser to presidents and winner of virtually every medal his country had to offer, Doolittle's life is a story of the successes and adventures, the triumphs and tragedies of a true American hero whose courage, devotion, and daring continue to make their influence felt to this day. ____29725-2 $6.99/$8.50

YEAGER: *An Autobiography*

by Chuck Yeager with Leo Janos

From his humble West Virginia roots to his role as the test pilot who first broke the sound barrier, this is the story of the man who rose to lead America into space. ____25674-2 $6.99/$8.99

MARINE! *The Life of Chesty Puller*

by Burke Davis

This is the explosive true story of the most courageous and controversial commander of them all--the only marine in history to win five Navy crosses. Here is the fabulous tale of a real-life hero. ____27182-2 $6.50/$8.99

Ask for these books at your local bookstore or use this page to order.

Please send me the books I have checked above. I am enclosing $____ (add $2.50 to cover postage and handling). Send check or money order, no cash or C.O.D.'s, please.

Name ________________________________

Address ________________________________

City/State/Zip ________________________________

Send order to: Bantam Books, Dept. HF 14, 2451 S. Wolf Rd., Des Plaines, IL 60018
Allow four to six weeks for delivery.
Prices and availability subject to change without notice. WW 9 3/96

Vivid, compelling narrative histories of some of America's most memorable decades

VOICES OF FREEDOM

An Oral History of the Civil Rights Movement from the 1950s through the 1980s

by Henry Hampton and Steve Fayer

Martin Luther King Jr. and Malcolm X, JFK and LBJ. From the bus boycott in Montgomery to busing in Boston, from the marches on Selma to the riots in Miami, *Voices of Freedom* illuminates the long, impassioned, sometimes painful, sometimes joyful struggle for a truly democratic society that continues today.

____35232-6 $18.95/$26.95 in Canada

"Utterly fascinating. *Voices of Freedom* tells the greatest American story ever told. These voices are extraordinary. So is the book."
—Pat Conroy, author of *The Prince of Tides*

THE GLORY AND THE DREAM

A Narrative History of America, 1932–1972

by William Manchester

A narrative history that spans four unforgettable decades.

____34589-3 $27.95/$38.95

"A fascinating work of history . . . Solidly researched, bold and imaginative in its conception, it is written with a fine sensitivity to the nuances of the American experience in the 40 years before, during and after the Second World War." —William L. Shirer

Ask for these books at your local bookstore or use this page to order.

Please send me the books I have checked above. I am enclosing $____ (add $2.50 to cover postage and handling). Send check or money order, no cash or C.O.D.'s, please.

Name ______________________________

Address ______________________________

City/State/Zip ______________________________

Send order to: Bantam Books, Dept. NFB36, 2451 S. Wolf Rd., Des Plaines, IL 60018
Allow four to six weeks for delivery.
Prices and availability subject to change without notice. NFB 36 5/96